ANCIENT SKY WATCHERS & MYTHIC THEMES

A SKY LORE ANTHOLOGY: VOLUME ONE

JULIE LOAR

Capella Press

17 Lofty Court, Pagosa Springs, CO 81147

www.JulieLoar.com

Cover Design: Sue Andra Lion

ISBN 9781792335143

Manufactured in the United States of America

10 9 8 7 6 5 4 3 2 1

❄ Created with Vellum

For Ted

Being deeply loved by someone gives you strength.
Loving someone deeply gives you courage.

Lao Tzu

CONTENTS

WHAT OTHERS ARE SAYING ABOUT ANCIENT SKY WATCHERS

Ancient Sky Watchers is the first in a two-volume series from *Atlantis Rising's* award-winning astrology columnist. For many years, Julie's column was the clearest, most reliable, and most readable source of ancient sky lore to be found in print or on the web. Her thoughtful presentation of historical and mythical detail, informed by extensive in-depth personal research into classic astrology, made her an authority not only to the astrologically minded, but to anyone interested in the forgotten riches of our ancient, and little understood, past. Volume Two: As Above, So Below will be available soon.

Doug Kenyon, Publisher, *Atlantis Rising*

"There is no one who writes about astrology, symbols, mythology, and lore like Julie Loar. No one! She is like a *Joseph Campbell* in her ability to make real for the modern mind all of the intrigue, romance, and inner knowing that was once so much a part of everyone's life. Astrologers in days of yore were every bit a seer in their ability to understand the rhythms of the Great Breath, the universe in all its glory. Our Julie is one of them. A typical "reading" for her is a glimpse at balance and rhythm, that which connects, explores, and unveils at the same time. I consider it an honor to speak up for her, and let everyone know, here is a special genius who can see beyond sight. Consider yourself lucky to have any of her work, her articles, her books."

P. M. H. Atwater, L.H.D., one of the original researchers in the field of near-death studies and author of 18 books, her latest *The Forever Angels: Near-Death Experiences in Childhood and Their Lifelong Impact*.

"*Ancient Sky Watchers and Mythic Themes* is a treasure chest of knowledge that is critical to our time, even as it was to those who walked our Earth long ago. Julie is a wise keeper of the ancient wisdom, which she so generously and lovingly shares with us all. It is a joy to lose myself in the depth of her writings, magnetized by the infinite layers of meaning beneath the words. This is a book I will return to again and again."

Catherine Grace Landry, author of *The Way of the Simple Soul, The Way of the Lightkeeper*.

"Julie Loar has an uncanny ability to discuss ancient phenomena and relate it to modern times in an articulate and approachable way. Her thorough understanding of astrology, the patterns of the sun, moon, and stars, and her depth of knowledge of ancient cultures makes this a fascinating dive into the pool of venerable sky watchers. Now there is an e-book that I can take with me when I travel - what could be better."

Susan Andra Lion, Author and Illustrator of *Night Threads, A Weaving of Soul Stories from the Dreamtime* and *How the Trees Got Their Voices*.

"Well Julie, it looks like you have another award-winning book on your hands . . . it's a polished and many-faceted jewel."

Ted Denmark PhD, Astrologer and award-winning author of *Winged Messengers*.

"The amassing of Julie Loar's encyclopedic knowledge of her subject is astonishing, as is her master of her ability to share it. The depth of the respect accorded her by her peers is not less impressive. Many kudos to this complex intelligence and talent"

Donald Norsic, author of *Nicholas and Alexandra: The Truth*

INTRODUCTION

The forty articles contained in this volume, and the forty in the second volume to follow, originally appeared in issues of *Atlantis Rising* magazine from 2001 until 2019. They are reproduced here with full permission from J. Douglas Kenyon, Publisher of *Atlantis Rising*. Although the printed version of the magazine was suspended in 2019, a new form of *Atlantis Rising,* with access to legacy content and new information, has been reborn and is now online at https://atlantisrising.com

The articles in this two-volume anthology are arranged by category, or topic, and not chronologically as they first appeared in *Atlantis Rising* over two decades. The only changes made were small syntax items like commas, spaces, or other minor items missed at the time of original publication. I also added a few parenthetical remarks where a new discovery or development might have altered my opinion from the original writing. Otherwise, the content of the articles has not been changed, and I hope you will agree that the material has stood the test of time.

Images are author's, Wikipedia's Creative Commons, public domain, or http://www.Snappygoat.com with much gratitude.

Julie Loar http://www.JulieLoar.com

PREFACE

This two-volume Anthology contains a collection of my articles on astrology, astronomy, and mythology that were published in *Atlantis Rising* magazine, spanning two decades of contributions. Edited and published by J. Douglas Kenyon *Atlantis Rising* was described by many as the best "hardcopy" magazine dealing with ancient mysteries, unexplained anomalies, and future science. I was always proud to be associated with Doug and the magazine.

I became a charter subscriber after I acquired my copy of the first issue, which I still have. I submitted my first piece titled *The Lore of a Shaman* after returning from an amazing journey to South Africa in the late 90s where I had two audiences with renowned Zulu shaman Credo Mutwa, author of *Song of the Stars*. The article appeared in Issue 23 (Chapter 11 in this volume) and examined his star knowledge and my visit to the amazing site of the Timbavati game preserve inside Krueger National Park. Subsequently, Doug Kenyon invited me to contribute a regular astrology feature to the magazine. I readily agreed, and that began a long relationship. What followed were regular feature articles in every issue from February 2001 until Doug stopped printing in spring of 2019 and decided the time had come to turn his attention to other efforts and a new online incarnation of *Atlantis Rising*. http://www.AtlantisRising.com

Family, friends, and clients have urged me for some time to examine the decades of writing these articles represent and to compile the "best of the best." Since I feel a measure of pride in this long-term accomplishment I agreed. It feels like a worthy and empowering endeavor to bring a measure of immortality to a body of one's work.

My articles ranged from traditional astrological reports to a broader range of astronomy and myth. I appreciated the scope I was able to explore and the challenges some topics offered in terms of research and synthesis. Doug gave me incredible freedom under the wide umbrella of astrology, and I explored topics that fascinated me. I wrote about blue moons, Pluto's moons, moon phases, dwarf planets, Egyptian astronomy, and ancient astronomer priests to name a few. One article on the *Bible & Astrology* was featured on the cover and another article titled *Nemesis & Tyche: Does Our Sun Have a Sister?* in issue #90 won first place in a prestigious national writing contest. Ironically, my Saturn-Pluto conjunction article that was slated to appear in Issue #136, and which counseled letting go of forms whose time has come, presaged the suspension of the printed magazine.

While considering which topics to include in this compilation I counted the articles I'd written over two decades. I discovered there were 108 and was astonished by the power of the symbolism. 108 is considered a sacred number in Hinduism, Buddhism, and yogic tradition that symbolizes spiritual completion. 108 is the number of beads on a *mala*, "garland" in Sanskrit, which is a string of beads used in prayer and meditation and is like a rosary. There are also 108 letters in the Sanskrit alphabet. Vedic mathematicians calculate the Sun's diameter to be 108 times larger than the diameter of the Earth, and measure the distance between the Sun and Earth to be 108 times the Sun's diameter. It feels like a significant confirmation of this effort, especially since the articles themselves form a garland. Seen in this way, it is a thrill to envision each article as a pearl on a strand that forms a sacred circle.

80 of these articles appear in two volumes. Volume I -- *Ancient Sky Watchers & Mythic Themes* contains forty articles covering the topics of ancient astronomy, mythology, prophecy, zodiacs of antiquity, and

closes with recent discoveries in astrophysics. Volume II – *As Above, So Below: Sun, Moon, and Stars* has forty articles that span the topics of stars, planets, dwarf planets. Book Two also explores other fascinating objects in our Solar System and their possible symbolic significance.

I hope this compilation will reconnect with the audience who enjoyed these articles the first time and that a new group of readers interested in these topics will be drawn to these books. My deep respect and gratitude go to Doug Kenyon for years of holding the torch of wisdom high and bright so others might awaken to the truth in its light. Doug gave me a voice to express the timeless wisdom of astrology and myth and to spread the wings of my writing. I also owe a special debt to *Atlantis Rising* since my now husband Ted Denmark, a long-time subscriber, fellow astrologer and writer, reached out to me a decade ago after having read my articles for years. And thanks to everyone whose encouragement prompted me to compile this collection of articles. It's been a labor of love, pride, and humility to see these pieces come together in this way.

Julie Loar www.JulieLoar.com

Pagosa Springs, Colorado

Spring 2020

PART I
ANCIENT SKY WATCHERS

CHAPTER 1

KEEPING TIME: CYCLES OF
SUN, MOON & EARTH

"The only reason for time is so everything doesn't happen at once."

Albert Einstein

Vintage Antique Clock

Before clocks and calendars the turning of Earth and cycles of the Sun, Moon, and stars were how humans tracked time. A day is one rotation of Earth, and one cycle of the phases of the Moon gave us the month, while Earth's circuit around the Sun is the year. Tracking days, months, and larger divisions of time has ancient roots as the human need to move with cycles of time is universal. Time relates to everything from cooking and gardening to music and medicine.

Archeologists have reconstructed methods of keeping time that reach back to prehistoric periods. Researchers have deduced from excavated tally sticks that people counted days in relation to the Moon's phases as early as the Upper Paleolithic, Stone Age, 50,000 years ago. Ancient cultures such as the Inca, Maya, and Hopi, and other American Indian tribes, as well as Babylonians, Buddhists, and Hindus perceive time like a wheel. Time is experienced as cyclical, not linear, consisting of repeating cycles that happen in measured ages and states of development from the birth of the Universe until its end. According to the large cycle of precession, Hindu cosmology has a wheel of ages called *yugas* that range from light to dark. The Greek and Roman system perceived ages that ranged from an idyllic golden age to the current iron age that is filled with conflict and pain.

In the ancient Greek view, time was seen in two ways--*Chronos* and *Kairos*. The first referred to numeric or chronological time since the god Chronus was the personification of time. Kairos conveyed the idea of "the right moment" and is related to "divine timing." Kairos is qualitative while Chronos is quantitative, and casting and interpreting an astrology chart requires both. According to the Hebrew Qabalah, time is a paradox and an illusion as both past and future are perceived as simultaneously present. In the Old Testament book of Ecclesiastes, traditionally attributed to Solomon, time has often been translated from Hebrew as "age," and seen as the unfolding of prophecies or predestined events. The Islamic and Judeo-Christian worldview tends to regard time as linear and directional, beginning with a divine act of creation. Time will end at some point *teleologically*, an ending understood to be intrinsic to the order of things.

Ancient calendars were usually lunisolar and were based on observation, requiring an intercalary month to bring the solar and lunar years into alignment. The Moon's motion is complex because the Sun, Earth, and planets all exert gravity. The Moon rotates on its axis every 27.5 days, the same time it takes to circle Earth. This is called the sidereal period as the Moon returns to the same place relative to the stars. This dual motion is why the same side of the Moon is always visible to Earth. However, the far side is not always dark since the Moon's rotation exposes the whole surface to sunlight. Even though we don't ever see the "dark side" from Earth, it is fully illuminated at the New Moon.

The synodic month is the most familiar and is defined as the interval between two consecutive lunar phases, as seen by an observer on

Earth. The mean synodic length (rounded) is 29.5 days. The distinction between sidereal and synodic cycles was recognized in historical times in Babylonian lunar astronomy. The synodic period is longer because while the Moon is orbiting Earth we travel about thirty degrees of arc each month in our annual trek around the Sun. The Moon has to compensate since the Earth-Moon system is orbiting the Sun in the same direction as the Moon is orbiting the Earth, so it takes about 2.2 days longer for the Moon to return to the same apparent position with respect to the Sun. Dividing the number days of the year by the 29.5 days of the synodic lunar cycle yields about 12.37 New Moons or Full Moons each year, which are called lunations. Numerous cultures have wrestled with the problem of solar-lunar cycles, and many cultures used multiple calendars to distinguish sacred, secular, and agricultural domains.

Regardless of how time is understood philosophically, clocks mark the passage of time and calendars organize segments of time. Water clocks are some of the oldest time-measuring instruments. Where and when they were first invented is unknown given their great antiquity. The simple bowl-shaped outflow water clock existed in Babylon and Egypt around the 16th century BCE (Before Current Era). India and China also have early evidence of water clocks. Some authors claim that water clocks appeared in China as early as 4000 BCE. The hourglass, or sand clock, ancestor of the modern kitchen timer, is thought to have developed from the water clock in ancient India. The sand flows down from the upper bowl, which is seen as the past, through the narrow neck that represents the present moment, and into the lower bowl that is seen as the future.

A sundial tells the time of day by the shadow cast by the apparent movement of the Sun. As the Sun moves across the sky, the shadow aligns with different hour lines that are marked on the dial to indicate the time of day. The earliest sundials known from archaeological finds are shadow clocks used in Babylonian astronomy 3,500 years ago. An ancient sundial from Egypt, in the Valley of the Kings, dates to 2,500 years ago.

Calendars are explicit schemes for keeping time and organizing dates for social, religious, commercial, or administrative purposes. Calendars give names to periods of time such as days, weeks, months, and years. The word calendar comes from *calends*, the term for the first day of the month in the Roman calendar. It's related to the verb *calare*, "to call out," referring to the announcement that the first sliver of new moon had been seen, beginning the month. Latin *calendarium* meant "account book," or "register," as accounts were settled and debts were collected on the *calends* of each month.

Historically, the first formalized calendars date to the Bronze Age around 5,000 years ago and were dependent on the development of writing in the Ancient Near East. The Sumerian calendar is the earliest known, followed by the Egyptian, Assyrian, and Elamite calendars. A larger number of calendar systems of the Ancient Near East appear in the Iron Age archeological record, based on the Assyrian and Babylonian calendars. A 1079 calendar reform in Persia, led by Khayyam, measured the length of the year as 365.24219858156 days. Since the length of the year changes in the sixth decimal place over a lifetime, this was remarkably accurate. The length of the year at the end of the 19th century was 365.242196 days, while today it is 365.242190 days.

The Roman calendar contained ancient remnants of a pre-Etruscan ten-month solar year but was reformed by Julius Caesar and implemented by edict in 45 BCE. The Julian calendar no longer depended on observation of the New Moon but followed an algorithm of introducing a leap day every four years. However, this created a still ongoing dissociation of the calendar month from the lunation. The Gregorian calendar was introduced as a refinement to the Julian calendar in 1582 CE and is still the main calendar in worldwide use today.

The Gregorian calendar has twelve fixed months of differing lengths, so as the cycles change, the shorter lunar cycle (29.5 days) can fall twice in a calendar month. This creates an artifact in our modern calendar that is called a "blue moon." This is not because the Moon appears blue, but because two Full Moons fall in one calendar month.

There is also a "dark moon," two New Moons in a calendar month. A blue moon month typically occurs once in 2.7 years. However, 2018 will have two blue moon months, one in January and one in March, causing February of 2018 to be a month without a Full Moon. The last time this occurred was in 1999 when the blue moons also occurred in January and March. This cyclical recurrence is because of the nineteen year Metonic cycle of lunar phases.

The discovery of this cycle is credited to Meton (432 BCE) an Athenian astronomer. Mathematically, nineteen tropical years have 6,939.60 days, while 235 synodic months have 6,939.69 days. After nineteen years, the phases of the Moon occur on the same dates of the year, after which the Moon's phases recur on the same days of the solar year, or year of the seasons. There are 235 lunar months and 236 Full Moons during one Metonic cycle. There are also 228 calendar months, so at least eight of those months will have two Full Moons.

Since this is almost equal to twenty eclipse years (6,932.4) it is also possible for a series of four or five eclipses to occur on the same dates nineteen years apart. Edmund Halley, of comet fame, mistakenly linked the naming of the cycle of 223 synodic months with Suidas, a tenth century Greek, who had actually called the Metonic cycle "Saros." Halley wrongly named the eclipse cycle Saros, and the name stuck.

Astrologically, the Moon moves thirteen degrees a day through an astrological sign and makes thirteen orbits of Earth in a year. Usually, there is one New Moon and one Full Moon in each of the twelve zodiac signs. Symbolically, the cycles and phases of the Moon's light offer periodic illumination into our individual and collective natures. Just as space travel has given us a glimpse of the Moon's hidden side, the relationship between Earth and Moon is a journey of ever-changing, but ever-increasing, light and consciousness.

The Moon represents our instincts, memories, habitual behaviors, and the general inheritance of the past. The Moon is seen symbolically as our lost psyche, partly hidden in shadow, and separated from our waking consciousness as we journey through time. The Moon reflects our evolving personalities. The hidden side conceals our habitual selves and holds unconscious patterns that need to be healed or reclaimed. The dark side is the realm of depth psychology analysis and astrological insight that can reveal what's in the shadow and work to bring these issues into the light of conscious awareness. Astronomy is science, based on observation and measurement. Astrology is an interpretative discipline that applies meaning and correspondences to what has been observed over thousands of years. Not so long ago they were the same. I believe we've lost a great deal as a result of the radical severance of these disciplines. When we separate meaning from measurement, we cleave the mind and heart.

Increasingly, our personal electronic devices display both calendars and clocks simultaneously, further separating us from the cycles and rhythms that inform both. Clocks and calendars are useful devices, but they make it easy to lose touch with the real rhythms to which we are attuned, both biologically and spiritually. Artificial light disconnects us from the night, sweeping lunatics and werewolves under the carpet, and denying our instinctual response to deep impulses that dwell in the darkness. Technology is a fact of modern life and has given rise to many timesaving inventions. However, lest we lose touch with nature, we should pay attention to the recurring cycles that keep our hearts, our personal ticking clocks, in rhythm and harmony with the natural world.

Atlantis Rising #127 December 2017

CHAPTER 2

PERSIA'S ROYAL STARS: ARE THE ANCIENT GUARDIANS OF THE FOUR CORNERS OF HEAVEN ABOUT TO RETURN?

"One good deed is worth a thousand prayers."

Zoroaster

Aldebaron (SnappyGoat.com)

Zoroaster (Zarathustra) was a legendary Persian prophet; Persia is modern Iran. Historians say his followers honored the agricultural cycles of the year as a religious doctrine. Some scholars place his lifetime as early as 1,500 BCE while others believe he lived around 500 CE. His Greek name Zoroaster means "star worshiper." It is safe to say that Zarathustra watched the skies and the cyclical patterns that unfolded there. Although these Persian gods were probably legacies of an earlier time, the stories of Zarathustra's Persian pantheon seem to tell the tales of what we now call the four Royal Stars of Persia.

Because we have four clearly defined seasonal events, two equinoxes and two solstices, the year is automatically divided into four. Likewise our twenty-four hour day has four quarters of sunrise, noon, sunset and midnight. This quartering of the circle is an ancient and worldwide practice. The fourfold division of time seems to lead naturally to a fourfold division of space, and the custom over ages has been to denote sunrise and spring to the east where day begins. West is sunset and autumn. North, which most cultures think of as "above" is therefore noon and summer, and south, is "below" the place of midnight and winter.

The Royal Stars of Persia are so named because roughly five thousand years ago, during the fabled pyramid age of Egypt, these luminaries held tremendous influence. Endowed with almost archangelic power, these legendary stars of antiquity are Aldebaron, alpha Taurus, Regulus, alpha Leo, Antares, alpha Scorpio, and Fomalhaut, which is alpha Pisces Austrinus as Aquarius (same longitude) has no bright star. In the epoch of 5,000 years ago they were considered to be guardians of the four corners of heaven and watchers of the directions, forming a heavenly cross near the ecliptic.

In this capacity these bright stars marked the seasonal signposts of the year, the equinoxes and the solstices. Regulus watched the north, Fomalhaut presided over the south, while Antares guarded the west, and Aldebaron the east. Each Royal Star also correlates with the "fixed" signs of astrology: Taurus, Leo, Scorpio, and Aquarius. The first three correlate with the fixed signs, but Aquarius is missing from the quartet. Fomalhaut is a bright star, shining alone in the fourth arm of the zodiacal fixed cross, and sharing the same celestial longitude, (similar to terrestrial longitude), with Sadalmelik, the alpha star of Aquarius, which is not as major a luminary.

The fixed signs play a powerful role in the theme of precession. Although these Royal Stars once marked the seasons, the cardinal points of the sky, due to the slow backward march of precession, their seasonal anchoring waxes and wanes. But at certain points in the Grand Year, (a full cycle of precession, lasting roughly 26,000 years), they move to hold the corners again. We are now approaching another of these junctures as Fomalhaut, holding the space for Aquarius, advances to the eastern, or spring, arm of this great cross. A brief review of celestial mechanics might be helpful.

Earth wobbles as she spins and is also inclined 23 degrees on her axis of rotation. This tilt creates the seasons, and the wobble creates the phenomenon astronomers and astrologers alike call precession. Like a slowly spinning top, earth's wobble causes the axis to trace an imaginary circle in the heavens. This imaginary stylus moves at the rate of roughly one degree of arc in seventy-two years. An additional byproduct of this wobble causes the spring equinox sun (northern hemisphere) to rise due east against a backdrop of stars that slowly shifts. Because this occurs on the ecliptic, (the apparent path of the sun through the year), the stellar backdrop is formed by the slowly moving starry curtain of the twelve zodiacal constellations.

The zodiacal constellations are divisions of space which contain stars and deep sky objects within borders outlined by astronomers. Zodiacal constellations are twelve of eighty-eight divisions of space recognized by astronomers since 1930. The zodiacal "signs" on the other hand are divisions of time, beginning with the spring equinox. The astrological sign of Aries is the symbolic birth of the new year. In the northern hemisphere spring, and zero degrees Aries, begins at the vernal equinox when the balance of light and dark achieves momentary equilibrium, before tilting toward increasing light. Down under the seasons march in the opposite ratio of light and dark.

For roughly two thousand years, spring equinox sunrise has occurred against the stars of Pisces, the Fishes. Soon, as the backward march of the ages shifts, the "dawning of the Age of Aquarius" will be heralded as this constellation moves to center stage and defines the new world age. About 3,000 years ago the stars of Aries provided the backdrop for spring equinox sunrise. Before that the stars of Taurus held the distinction, and it was at that time, roughly 5,000 years ago, that the Royal Stars watched the directions and guarded the destinies of kings. As the ages changed sacrifices of bulls shifted when Moses chose the ram as the sacrificial animal of the new age. In our time Jesus was both Lamb of God and Fisher of Men as the sacrificial symbol for the age of Pisces, the Fishes.

5,000 years ago Aquarius held the winter position in the seasons of the Grand Year while the influence of these Royal Stars held maximum sway. Now, due to the gradual movement of precession, Aquarius has advanced to the springtime place in the northern hemisphere. As these famous stars once again move to positions of prominence, their ancient lore may come to the forefront.

Fomalhaut, The Solitary One - Fomalhaut held the southern seasonal anchor in antiquity and is now advancing toward spring equinox. The constellation of Piscis Austrinus, The Southern Fish, is home to this star. This constellation is most often shown as a fish, seeming to swim upstream in the waters of Aquarius. Sometimes called the "Solitary One" Fomalhaut stands like a brilliant but solitary beacon in an otherwise undistinguished region of the sky. This bright star, whose name derives from the Arabic for "mouth of the fish," is depicted on old star charts as drinking the water which flows from the Water Bearer's urn.

The eighteenth brightest, Fomalhaut is a blue white star that culminates at midnight in late August, and has traditionally been a star of navigation. Fomalhaut is in the watery portion of the celestial ocean. Occupants of this area include the Water Bearer, the Sea Goat, the Crane, the Whale, the River, and the Fishes.

One source traces Piscis Austrinus back to Egyptian mythology as the infamous Nile fish who swallowed the phallus of Osiris. Some scholars view this constellation as the parent fish of Pisces, The Fishes. As such, swallowing Osiris's creative appendage may well be a precessional symbol of the shift from the age of Aries to the age of Pisces. Fomalhaut was equated with the Persian god Zal, and is said to bestow charisma and to engender the test of remaining true to our ideals.

Antares, Rival of Mars - Antares was the ancient watcher of the west and is now shifting to the southern corner. Inhabiting the heart of Scorpius, the name Antares is almost universal for this star and is believed to derive from the Greek, meaning anti Ares, or "rival of Mars." Antares is a red supergiant, four hundred times larger than our sun, culminating in June. According to R. H. Allen in *Egyptian Astronomy* Antares represented the goddess Selkit, the Scorpion goddess, heralding sunrise at her temples at the autumn equinox about 3,700 BC and was also the symbol of Isis in the pyramid ceremonials.

Bernadette Brady says as a star of an equinox, Antares was considered one of four gateways to the otherworld, a bringer of darkness, for as the Sun entered this constellation, it moved into the southern hemisphere and the dark part of the year. Antares was equated with the Persian god of the dead, Yima, and is believed to convey passion and the test of addiction to intensity.

Aldebaron, The Follower - Aldebaron was the ancient watcher of the east, now moving to summer. A pale rose beauty, Aldebaron is the "Follower" of the Pleiades because this star rises and sets just after these asterisms, (star groupings within constellations). Aldebaron is a member of the Hyades cluster, marking the red eye of the bull and is probably linked with the term, "hitting the bull's eye." Allen says the name was originally given to the entire group of the Hyades asterism and the Vedic lunar mansion which, as *Na'ir al Dabaran*, the Bright One of the Follower, our modern star Aldebaron marked. In all astrology Aldebaron has been thought to be eminently fortunate, portending riches and honor.

The Apis bull of ancient Egypt was an actual creature chosen to serve as the earthly vessel of the spirit of Osiris. The Serapeum at Memphis is believed to have once housed mummies of sacred bulls although only one burial has been found. Aldebaron culminates at midnight in early December. Aldebaron was equated with the Persian god of light, Ahura Mazda, and is said to endow integrity and to engender the test of honor.

Regulus, Heart of the Lion - Ancient watcher of the north, now shifting to autumn, Regulus means "little king." This blue white star is the faintest of the first magnitude stars. Regulus forms the Lion's Heart, and culminates in mid-April. The Lion's head and mane are formed by an asterism which is known as the Sickle. Regulus lies on the ecliptic, and according to G. Cornelius, was the leader of the four royal Stars since the Egyptians connected Leo with the heliacal rising of Sirius and the beginning of their new year.

The stars we call Leo were recognized as a lion by the Sumerians, Syrians, Greeks and Romans. The Chinese zodiac saw these stars as a horse, and some scholars believe the Incas saw a springing puma. One theory of how the shape of a lion was seen was because lions cooled themselves on the banks of the Nile during the hottest days of the year. Sky watchers connected them with the constellation through which the sun passed at that time. Regulus was equated with the mythical Persian king, Feridun, and is said to bestow success, power of position and the test of withholding revenge

As the march of ages measures its slow movement, the four Royal Stars will once again advance to positions aligned with the seasonal quarters. Based on Fomalhaut's celestial longitude, and the projected rate of precession, the perfect equinox alignment won't occur for nearly another millennium, and maybe coinciding with the stellar beginning of the Age of Aquarius. Perhaps by then humanity will have learned our lessons, be able to live in peace, and another golden age might dawn.

But what might be the role of these stars in an individual life? Astrologer and author Bernadette Brady assures us that the four Royal Stars of Persia are powerful stars, and each one offers the possibility of glory, success, or happiness, but only if a particular nemesis can be overcome. An accurate astrological birth chart is necessary to determine if your life is linked to a royal star. The rising, culminating and setting positions of these stars are compared with planets or "angles" in your horoscope. If a connection is found, Fate may have something special in store for you.

Atlantis Rising #27 February 2001

CHAPTER 3

LASCAUX CAVES: A
PALEOLITHIC PLANETARIUM

D*o these famous paintings depict an ancient zodiac?*

"The stars we are given; the constellations we make. The stars exist in
the cosmos, but constellations are the imaginary lines we draw
between them, the reading we give the sky, the stories we tell."

Rebecca Solnit

Lascaux Cave - public domain

Lascaux Cave, *Grotte de Lascaux*, is in the Vezere river valley in the
Dordogne region of southwestern France. The cave is situated in an
area rich in earlier Prehistoric sites—caves, rock shelters, and
settlements. The discovery of the cave paintings at Lascaux was first
made public in 1880 and led to bitter controversy between experts,
which continued into the early 20th century. Many "experts" did not
believe that prehistoric humans had the intellectual capacity to
produce this kind of artistic expression, let alone create the magnificent
art on the cave walls. Acknowledgment of the authenticity of the
paintings finally came in 1902 and changed forever the perception of
prehistoric humans. The Lascaux paintings are dated to 17,000 years
ago and have been called the Sistine Chapel of Paleolithic Art.

There are more than 350 cave art sites in France and Spain alone that
were occupied at various times over the 25,000 years preceding the end
of the last ice age, about 12,000 years ago. Lascaux in France and
Altamira in Spain are the most famous. Until recently, the earliest
European Paleolithic cave art dated from around 32,000 years ago, at
Chauvet in France. However, new research published in June 2012 in

Science, reveals that hand stencils and disks, made by blowing paint onto the wall in El Castillo cave in Northern Spain, have been dated to at least 40,800 years ago, making them the oldest known cave art in Europe. A large club-shaped symbol in the famous polychrome chamber at Altamira was found to be at least 35,600 years old, indicating that painting started there 10,000 years earlier than previously thought, and that the cave was revisited and painted a number of times over a period spanning more than 20,000 years.

Four young boys exploring Lascaux Hill found the Lascaux Caves in 1940. The cave walls are decorated with more than 1,500 stunning images, spanning a distance of 850 feet (250 meters). Lascaux has long been closed to the public in order to protect the priceless prehistoric artwork, but December of 2016 marked the unveiling of a $94 million full-scale replica. Called Lascaux 4, the project has completely reconstructed one of the most significant archaeological discoveries of the 20th century. Simon Coencas, now 89, is the last surviving member of the original explorers. He was a special guest at the unveiling of the new replica.

Lascaux has three long and narrow subterranean galleries in the form of a letter 'K', including what have become known as the Axial Gallery, the Hall of the Bulls, the Chamber of Felines, the Nave, the Apse, and the Shaft. Numerous monochrome and polychrome paintings and engravings cover most parts of the cave. Images include horses, aurochs (ancestors of modern cattle), bison, oxen, stags, ibex, felines, woolly rhinoceros, birds, bears, an anthropoid, and a chimera. There are some possible abstract representations of plants, symbols, geometric figures, series and sets of dots. Carbon-14 dates from charcoal used sparingly for painting, pollen analysis, and stylistic evaluations suggest that the majority of the rock pictures are associated with what is called the Lower Magdalenian culture from 17,000 –15,000 BP (Before Present). Magdalenians are considered Cro-Magnon and were known as reindeer hunters.

Some researchers have suggested that the Lascaux paintings are sympathetic magic, relating only to the hunt. Copying the animals onto the cave walls created a place to prepare, understand, and follow the animals during their seasonal migration. However, the idea that paintings at Lascaux represent stars or constellations is not new. In the 1990s Frank Edge, who taught mathematics and cosmology at Mitchell Community College in North Carolina, saw the Hall of the Bulls as a map of the summer sky. He explored his ideas in a research paper titled *Aurochs in the Sky*. The key to his vision were seven dots painted above the shoulder of one of the bulls. Edge saw this as the Pleiades star cluster above Taurus, the Bull. The Pleiades, because of their position on the ecliptic, have drawn the attention of many cultures. The aurochs is the ancestor of modern cattle, suggesting that this animal was an earlier depiction of what is now the constellation Taurus, the Bull. If true, this places the origin and identity of Taurus at least 10,000 years earlier than is currently believed.

French researcher Dr. Chantal Jegues-Wolkiewiez has been working on this for a decade. She affirms that there was a long tradition of skywatching among the Cro-Magnon people of Europe during the period from 30,000 -10,000 BCE. Dr. Jegues-Wolkiewiez visited 130 caves in France over a seven-year period to identify solar alignments. She found orientations to sunset during solstices in 122 of the sites. She believes the famous paintings in the caves at Lascaux record the constellations of a prehistoric zodiac, which includes major stars as well as solstice points. She examined alignments using modern astronomy software. Models were made of the western map of each constellation and then the orientation of the paintings was measured according to an astronomical compass. She was able to determine that summer solstice sunsets penetrated the caves and illuminated certain paintings. Her work is based on identification of dots and tracings superimposed on the paintings of bulls, horses, and aurochs on the cave walls. These appear to correspond to the constellation of Taurus, the asterism of the Pleiades, and the stars Aldebaran and Antares.

Dr. Michael Rappenglueck, from the University of Munich, has arrived at similar conclusions. He believes the paintings of Lascaux represent not only constellations but also the cosmology of Paleolithic shamans. He suggests that an enigmatic painting of a male figure, a bull, and a bird on a pole represent the stars Vega, Deneb, and Altair, which supports the earlier work of Frank Edge. These bright stars form what is now called the Summer Triangle. Rappenglueck says these three stars would have been prominent in early spring skies 17,000 years ago.

Rappenglueck also identified what might be the earliest known depiction of Orion that was carved into the tusk of a mammoth and has been dated to 32,000 years ago. He also identified what could be the oldest lunar calendar on the walls of Lascaux, showing symbolic paintings, dating back 15,000 years. The German researcher says groups of dots and squares painted among representations of bulls, antelopes, and horses depict the 29-day cycle of the Moon.

A number of Lascaux pictures have possible astronomical significance. These include the 'Chinese horse' and 'fronting ibex' in the Axial Gallery and the 'crossed bison' in the Chamber of Felines; the stag-and-horse motif and related dots in the Axial Gallery and the five 'swimming stags' in the Nave; the aurochs in the Hall of the Bulls with its clusters of dots; and two pictograph panels in the Shaft. The majority of the animals depicted at Lascaux show seasonal characteristics that could have functioned as calendars. For example, deer are represented in their rutting season at the start of autumn, horses at the time of mating and foaling in late winter/early spring, and ibexes at the time when they congregated during late summer/early autumn in same-sex herds. Paintings of animals accurately represent their seasonal coat colors, and indications of particular seasons are sometimes enhanced by drawings of stylized plants. The 'Chinese horse' in the Axial Gallery is shown in its summer fur, pregnant, and surrounded by stylized branches, illustrating the time of foaling around summer solstice.

Some abstract designs associated with seasonal animals may be like almanacs. It's been argued that a set of dots, and another of 26, that appear beneath a roaring stag and a pregnant horse (representing autumn and spring respectively) in the Axial Gallery represent the 13 and 26-week intervals from summer solstice and then to spring equinox, each spot counting seven days. Two pictograph panels in the Shaft have been interpreted as the sky panorama that would have been seen by the Magdalenian people from the top of Lascaux Hill around midnight at the time of summer solstice circa 14,500 BCE.

Herodotus, a Greek historian from the fifth century BCE, claimed he received his material from Egyptian priests, who in turn claimed that their Egyptian history was at least 14,000 years old. Charles Berlitz, in his book *Atlantis*, quoted Diodorus Siculus, writing in the first century CE, who said, "The Egyptians were strangers who, in remote times, settled on the banks of the Nile, bringing with them the civilization from their mother country, the art of writing and a polished language. They had come from the direction of the setting Sun and were the most ancient of men." Authors Graham Hancock, Dr. Carmen Boulter, and others believe that what we call "Atlantis" was not merely an island nation in the Atlantic Ocean but was instead a number of sophisticated cultures around the globe that were destroyed by a series of ancient cataclysms.

According to the famous psychic Edgar Cayce, Atlantis was destroyed by volcanic and earthquake-like explosions on three distinct and widely-separated occasions. Cayce said in trance sessions that each of these destructions lasted over a period of months, or years, not just in a single day and night. The first of these disasters appear to have taken place about 50,700 BCE and the second about 28,000 BCE. The third and last destruction occurred around 10,000 BCE, which is the most familiar time frame in Atlantis lore. If there were multiple destructions over a 40,000-year time span, it makes sense that colonists and survivors would go to great lengths to preserve and protect knowledge that was critical to their survival, as they may have done at Lascaux and elsewhere.

The site of Gobekli Tepe in Turkey, which upended the conventional view of "hunter-gatherers," has been dated at about 11,700 years ago. This date corresponds with eerie precision to the end of what is called the Younger Dryas (named for an alpine tundra wildflower that is an "indicator genus"), a geological period from circa 12,900 – 11,700 BCE. The Younger Dryas saw a sharp decline in temperature over most of the northern hemisphere at the end of the Pleistocene epoch, which is often colloquially referred to as the Ice Age. This geological epoch lasted from about 2,588,000 to 11,700 years ago, spanning the world's most recent period of repeated glaciations. The end of the Pleistocene also corresponds with the end of the so-called Paleolithic Age. The change was relatively sudden, taking place in decades, and resulted in the extinction of most of the large mammoths and the rapid demise of the North American Clovis culture. The Younger Dryas ice age lasted for about 1,200 years before the climate warmed again.

Could at least parts of the zodiac we think originated in Babylon be instead a legacy of Atlantis? It is possible to imagine, based on growing evidence of the antiquity and sophistication of Cro-Magnon and Neanderthal cultures, that the spread of civilization may have come from Atlantis thousands of years ago and affected ancient cultures in Europe and Asia as far back as 40,000 years ago.

It seems natural that before artificial light the night sky was a canvas upon which the shining dots of light were connected into star pictures, and tales were told to mark the passage of the seasons. What ancient stories might have been shared by fires, and inside caves, to bring meaning to a universe that must have seemed remote, unpredictable, and sometimes dangerous? A change in the sky could portend disaster. It is both humbling and inspiring to imagine that some of the paintings on cave walls such as those at Lascaux, like the Bull of Heaven, have survived as art and symbolism for many thousands of years. We have much in common with our ancient forebears. We still gaze at the stars and study the constellations, reflecting on their mythic stories and decoding their symbolic meaning.

Atlantis Rising #122 January 2017

CHAPTER 4

THE ZODIAC OF PETRA: DECODING THE NABATEAN SCULPTURE

"By the salt and by the fire, and by Al Lat, who is greatest of all."

Ancient Arabian Oath, *Encyclopedia of Religion and Ethics,*

James Hastings

Zodiac of Petra (© S. Beaulieu)

At its height around 100 BCE the Nabataean empire included parts of Jordan, Egypt, Israel, Syria, and Saudi Arabia. The heart of the kingdom was Petra, "rock" in Greek, that was known as *Naqmu* to the Nabataen culture. It was a fabulous city carved into living rock that poet John William Burgon described as "a rose-red city half as old as time." Petra was established as early as 312 BCE but was unknown to the modern world until its discovery by Swiss explorer Johann Ludwig Burckhardt in 1812. When Indiana Jones was searching for the Holy Grail in the 1989 film, *Indiana Jones and the Last Crusade,* he galloped on horseback through a thin split in the red mountains in southern Jordan. Called the *Siq*, the only way into Petra is a dramatic tunnel-like gorge of towering red rock, nearly a mile long, that suddenly opens onto the city.

Scholars believe the Nabataean script was developed from Aramaic during the second century BCE and was in use until around the 4th or 5th century CE. Nabataean is considered the direct precursor of Arabic script. One of the earliest inscriptions in the Arabic language was written in the Nabataean alphabet, found in Namarah, modern Syria, and dated to 328 CE.

Archeologists have been puzzled by how a simple culture was transformed into a wealthy urban lifestyle in such a short time, excelling in art, architecture, engineering, and stone masonry. The answer seems to be that the Nabataeans became involved in the lucrative trade in South Arabian frankincense and myrrh, the same commerce that led the Queen of Sheba to visit the court of Solomon some five centuries earlier. Around 106 CE Petra was peacefully taken over by Rome's voracious appetite for empire, and the Roman culture was overlaid on the Nabataean. That is evidenced by the enigmatic Nabataean zodiac discovered at *Khirbet et-Tannur*, high on a hill near Petra, at the site of a ruined goddess temple.

Worship of the heavenly bodies was central to Nabataean religion, and zodiac figures were popular in Nabataean architecture. The zodiac found at Petra has been dated to about 120 CE and is at first both familiar and puzzling. The zodiac is a sculpture composed of a round wheel containing zodiac symbols in the outer portion with an image of the Greek goddess Tyche, the Roman Fortuna, inside the wheel. This in turn is supported by the figure of Nike, the Greek winged goddess of victory. The Nabataeans tended to represent their deities in *betyls*, "houses of god," that were aniconic blocks of stone--symbolic rather than literal representations. So this zodiac reflects the later Greco-Roman influence--but with a twist. It is an ingenious juxtaposition of the Greco-Roman overlay that retains unique elements of Nabataean culture.

The zodiac statue was originally built into a temple wall and was likely damaged by the earthquake of 363 CE. It was found in halves--one half is owned by the Antiquities Department in Jordan and the other by the Cincinnati Art Museum. Fortunately for history and culture the two halves were re-joined for the first time since antiquity for a stunning exhibit at the American Museum of Natural History in New York in 2003-2004. The Nabataean zodiac is unique in a number of interesting ways. Instead of a conventional continuous sequence, the figures proceed as mirror images in opposite directions from the top down, perhaps showing a reflection of relationship between the opposite signs rather than a linear sequential relationship. The zodiac begins with Aries at the top, moving counter clockwise down the left side in the expected direction, but the mirror image of the next six zodiac signs begins again at the top, where Libra is next to Aries, and the remaining signs move clockwise down the right side of the wheel. (Image credit Stephane Beaulieu, used with permission, from an article originally published in www.matrifocus.com)

The zodiac also uses a combination of familiar Greco-Roman figures but includes several intriguing substitutions for Aries, Sagittarius, and Capricorn, retaining Nabataean deities within the overlay of the conquering Roman symbolism. Rather than the familiar ram, Aries seems to be represented by the main, male god of Petra, Dushara, "lord of the mountain." He was seen as the protector of the royal house. This zodiac figure wears rather strange headgear that might have been intended as stylized, curved ram's horns. Sagittarius appears to be a jovial, youthful figure with a spear, rather than a centaur, but seems a good match for the Jupiter-ruled sign. Capricorn is shown as a now-damaged bust of a human figure rather than the traditional sea-goat familiar to Greco-Roman symbolism. The figure is female and has a crescent moon over her head.

Long before Islam, the Sabeans in Arabia worshipped a moon god named *Ilumquh* who was married to the sun goddess *Dhat Hamymand*. They had three daughters: Al Uzza, Al Lat, and Al Manat, who were widely worshipped from Petra in the North to the legendary Kingdoms of Arabia Felix in the South, including Saba, the Biblical

Sheba, and as far east as Iran and Palmyra. The three goddesses were very popular in Mecca at the time of Mohammed. These goddesses survived into Islam, where in the Koran they are called the daughters of Allah. They were worshipped as uncut aniconic stones, and the "idols" of Al Uzza and Al Lat were two of the more than three hundred pagan statues at the *Ka'aba* that were later viciously destroyed by Mohammed. They are also the source of the so-called *Satanic Verses*, discussed in the book of the same name by Salman Rushdie. These goddesses are related to the ancient triple goddess archetype that includes the Greek Fates and the Norns from Norse mythology.

Al-Uzza, "most mighty," was seen as the planet Venus, a virgin warrior riding astride a camel, and youngest of the three. Al Uzza is mentioned on many aniconic *betyls*. She was considered a goddess of the city of Petra as noted by Epiphanius of Salamis and was the consort of Dushara. She had a sanctuary at Nakhlah in a valley on the road from Mecca, with acacia trees into which she was said to descend. Some scholars believe she may even have been the patron deity of Mecca itself. Isaac of Antioch, a writer of the 5th century CE, called her *Beltis*, "Lady," and *Kaukabta*, "the Star." Al Uzza was associated with water and springs, and a votive fountain in the form of a lion carved into a rock face has been associated with her. She also guarded ships on ocean voyages. Although Arabia is a land of deserts and nomads, they did make ocean voyages to trade. In this aspect Al Uzza was symbolized as a dolphin, whose habit of swimming alongside ships made her a guardian and protector. This connects her to Atargatis, a mermaid goddess, who was a chief deity of ancient Syria. Large felines were also sacred to her, and the Temple of the Winged Lions at Petra is thought to be hers. This links her to the Semitic and Akkadian goddess Asherah, who is shown on the back of a lion.

Meteorites have been venerated as sacred objects by different cultures and ancient civilizations. Al Uzza was worshipped in the form of a black meteorite stone, which was inscribed with a mark or indentation called the "impression of Aphrodite." It has been suggested by several researchers and scholars that this same stone is the sacred Black Stone of Islam that was placed on the *Ka'aba*, the shrine in Mecca.

Al Lat, whose name means "goddess," as Al Lah means "god," was the mother figure and symbolized by the Sun. In Arabia the Sun was called *Shams* and considered feminine. Al Lat had a sanctuary in the town of Ta'if, east of Mecca, and was known from Arabia to Iran. Her symbol was a sun disk resting in a crescent, similar to the crowns of Isis and Hathor in Egypt. She wore a gold necklace, the solar metal, and sometimes she held a sheaf of wheat and a small lump of frankincense. Her emblem has been found carved on many incense holders.

Al Menat, "time," was the grandmother goddess of fate who was often shown holding a cup with a waning crescent moon above her head. Her name derives from the Arabic *maniya*, "fate, death," or *menata*, "part, portion, that which is allotted." She is similar to the Greek *Atropos*, one of the three Fates, who determined the length of life. She is known from inscriptions and tombs that were placed under her protection. *Maniya* is mentioned in poetry as bringing a person to the grave, holding out the cup of death. Al Menat is a very ancient deity, and her cult may have preceded both Al Uzza's and Al Lat's. Her worship was widespread, though she was particularly worshipped as a black stone at Quidaid, near Mecca and was connected with the great pilgrimage. Her sanctuary was the starting point for several tribes.

In 629 CE Mohammed sent twenty armed horsemen to destroy the statue of Al Menat at *Qudayd* on the road between Mecca and Medina. For eight years he had tolerated the coexistence of the pagan deities. Al Uzza was the favorite goddess of the Quraysh, the tribe to which Mohammad belonged, but Al Manat was the most popular in the region, and was idolized by three key Meccan tribes that Mohammad had been desperately trying to win over to his new monotheistic religion. The destruction of the goddesses' shrines, likely all on the same day, was bloody and final. Veneration of the divine feminine went underground until modern times.

The unique Nabataean zodiac of Petra makes the symbolism personal and specific to the site and culture of the period. This stone monument has survived for twenty centuries, silently expressing the voices and beliefs of a culture that was destroyed by conquest and religious persecution. Archeologists have discovered two main festivals that were celebrated at Petra each year: the "birthing of the lambs" festival at spring equinox and the harvest grain festival at autumn equinox. The arrangement of the Petra zodiac emphasizes the six opposite pairs of the twelve signs rather than the traditional sequence of individual expression. The unusual mirror image arrangement of the zodiac figures suggests that these two significant religious / seasonal festivals celebrated at the equinoxes were represented by the two figures at the top of the wheel. The zodiac of Petra was likely a festival calendar, showing the importance of the two main events in the sacred calendar. The temple where the zodiac was found would have been the location of the celebrations.

Dushara, substituting for Aries the ram, would hold the place at the top of the zodiac representing the spring festival. I believe it would be Al Uzza, goddess of Petra and consort of Dushara, who would be beside him, holding the place of Libra, autumn, and the harvest or grain festival. As consort of Dushara her rightful place would be at his side at the top of the wheel. Placing the mated pair of deities next to each other, and beginning the seasonal cycle of each, bestows equal rank.

Although some sources believe it is Al Uzza at the center of the wheel, I believe the Greek goddess of good fortune, Tyche, is instead a representation of Al Lat, the Sun. This shows the role of the Sun at the center of the zodiac wheel. Also, in Nabataean myth, Dushara was sometimes seen as the son of Al Lat, so his mother, rather than his mate, seems better placed inside the wheel.

Al Menat, goddess of time and fate, with the waning crescent moon above her head, is the elder goddess placed in the space of Capricorn. This also links her to the ancient pre-Hellenic Titan goddess Rhea, who wielded the sickle and was "Mother Time" long before Saturn dethroned her. With Nike holding up the wheel of fortune to assure victory, and the Sun in the middle represented by Tyche, goddess of good fortune, the Nabataean zodiac of Petra could have acted like a talisman, casting a magic spell to ensure good fortune through the year. Although it lay buried for centuries, that magic seems to have protected Petra, unlike Palmyra, which has been desecrated in our time by militant zealots.

As *Atlantis Rising* readers know, ancient knowledge and forgotten wisdom that has lain buried for aeons is re-emerging in our time thanks to the tireless efforts of alternative scholars. As we work to bring this knowledge to light we should also labor to use that light to banish the darkness of ignorance.

Atlantis Rising #118 June 2016

CHAPTER 5

ANCIENT ASTROLOGY: THE ROUND ZODIAC OF DENDERA

"The lips of Wisdom are closed except to the ears of Understanding."

The Kybalion, by Three Initiates

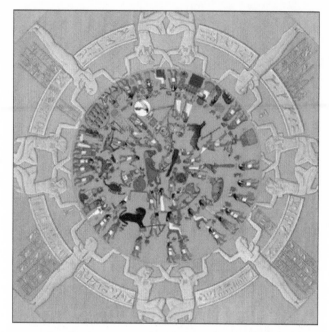

Round Zodiac of Dendera (Artist Alice-astro CC BY-SA 3.0)

Ancient hieroglyphic texts affirm that Egypt was seen as the mirror of heaven. As above, so below was not merely an aphorism but a way of life. The quest of individual, king and country was to express divine harmony, the principle of goddess Ma'at, and thereby literally reflect heaven on earth. To mirror heaven the skies must be known. The ancients carefully watched the cycles of the heavens because changes above portended changes below.

To orient toward a particular sky or star on a specific date we might paint that image on a ceiling. By rotating beneath that "sky" we could watch the stars apparent motions through the year, our painting functioning as a star dial. In just such a manner the ancient Egyptians replicated a sky in the round zodiac of Dendera. Astronomer priests could have viewed cyclical changes in the sky by positioning themselves in a certain way relative to the sculpture overhead. The ceiling of the temple-observatory would have mirrored the heavens, enabling them to anticipate important dates.

What remains today of the Hathor temple at Dendera is a Roman relic (circa 100 CE), but the site is much older and reconstruction on top of earlier structures is evident. Numerous references to stars, zodiacs and lunar cycles are etched into tomb and temple walls throughout Egypt, but as far as we know, this is the only circular zodiac. The original is in the Louvre, but a copy remains, and was painstakingly drawn by Lucie Lamy, stepdaughter of Schwaller du Lubicz. (The image is from Wikipedia CC BY-SA 3.0)

Zodiac is Greek and means "circle of animals" and describes the twelve constellations of the ecliptic (apparent path of the sun) where the planets move. The round zodiac of Dendera is actually a star map, portraying the heavens overhead at a certain moment in time.

In ancient Egypt a spiritual reciprocity existed between the people and the land. The cyclical relationship between the river and the desert was obvious and ever present. New Year's Day, which occurred on or near summer solstice, was heralded by Sirius, brightest star in the sky and great benefactor of Egypt, rising before the Sun. This momentous event "opened the year," announcing the annual inundation of Egypt as the life-giving waters of the Nile flood, gift of Isis, returned to renew the parched valley after the season of dryness. New Moon festivals were also significant at this time.

Each year the sun returns to the same place in the sky a quarter of a day later. We employ a leap year, adding a day every fourth year to adjust this lag. The ancient Egyptians used two cycles: a "vague" civil year of 365 days, and a "fixed" sacred year that marked the return of Sirius to the same place in the sky, in exactly 365 1/4 days.

A Great Year, or Sothic cycle of 1,460 years, marked the point when the vague year coincided with the Sothic year. Some texts indicate two dates, one in each cycle, which have allowed scholars to date events. Schwaller du Lubicz lists four such conjunctions in *Sacred Science*: 140 CE, 1320 BCE, 2780 BCE, and 4240 BCE , which he believed to be the inauguration of the Pharonic calendar.

Before computers star charts, which track how the sky changes through the year as a result of earth's annual journey around the sun, were manual computations. Ironically, at a time when Egyptian inscriptions were largely untranslated, astronomers spoke volumes about stellar knowledge, sky charts, and temple alignments. Jean Baptiste Biot, an eminent French astronomer, presented papers to the Academy of Inscriptions in 1822 and 1844. Biot concluded that even though the round zodiac was sculpted in the Roman era it either referred to a much earlier time, or the background sky was copied from an earlier work that may have been rendered on parchment or stone. This could explain a puzzling feature of the round zodiac. The familiar constellations of the zodiac are drawn in a form that we recognize, but the rest of the star groups have a decidedly Egyptian character. The zodiac signs may have been overlaid and copied onto a more ancient drawing.

Biot pinpointed the sky drawn on the ceiling of Dendera at precisely 700 BCE at midnight on summer solstice. Sir Norman Lockyer stated in The Dawn of Astronomy that subsequent translated context from hieroglyphics related the round zodiac to the period of 1,700 BCE. He stressed what he felt were important dates when summer solstice and the helical (before the Sun) rising of Sirius coincided. These dates were 270 BCE, 1728 BCE and 3192 BCE.

Scholars are generally agreed that the circumpolar stars are the Jackal, Ursa Minor, containing Polaris, the Thigh is Ursa Major, containing the star Dubhe, and the upright Hippo is Draco, containing Thuban, which was the pole star during the so-called Pyramid age, circa 2,800 BCE. Additionally, the Cow with the star between her horns is Canis Major, containing Sirius, and the striding man is Orion, containing Betelgeuse and Rigel, two first magnitude stars.

With five potential dates to examine, I used the Skyglobe astronomy software and viewed the skies based on the calendar conjunctions mentioned by both Lockyer and Schwaller. I reasoned that a New Year, or summer solstice, would be represented by the prominent alignment of Sirius, and that an equinox by the presence of Aries on the eastern horizon. Since I have not yet located a reference with a translation of planetary glyphs, I looked for a match with constellations that held a planet.

Aries faces east on the round zodiac, so I chose the epoch of 1700 BCE, during the age of Aries, when the Ram was the equinox dawn constellation. There is an interesting composite figure aligned with the eastern arm of the wheel. A falcon perches on a baboon, which sits on the eye of Ra with a donkey adjacent to the baboon. This seemed a symbolic way to indicate a planetary conjunction or perhaps a New Moon. If the eye of Ra is the Sun, and the baboon is Thoth, the Moon god, The Horus Falcon might be Mars. The equinox dawn of 1728 BCE (April 7 Gregorian) proved to be a good candidate, and there was a new moon conjunction with Mars present in the dawn sky.

Because Sirius is prominent in the figure, aligned with true north, it occurred to me that two time frames might be indicated on the sky map. After considerable searching to match the given years, I viewed the summer solstice prior to the 1,728 BCE equinox since the Egyptian new year began then. Based on the relative positioning of the circumpolar stars in Skyglobe on that date, the midnight solstice sky of 1727 BCE (July 7, Gregorian), yielded another promising result.

Ancient star gazers watched through the nights, just as their modern counterparts do since that is when the stars and planets are visible. The ancients didn't have super malls, super bowls, or electricity to mask the stars. The sky was an enduring source of divine inspiration. Nighttime sky watchers would have been rewarded with a momentous night of skywatching on summer solstice, New Year's Eve, in 1728 BCE, (July 7 Gregorian), building toward a spectacular dawn event.

Overhead at midnight, looking northward, the orientation of the circumpolar stars mirrors the sky map as they align with the cardinal directions. Sirius would have shone brightly in a northerly orientation, moving eastward as earth's rotation advanced toward dawn.

At midnight, the sixth hour of night, the Pleiades rose in the east. By one AM the Hyades rose over the eastern horizon. By 3:00 AM the stars of Orion crested the east, and by 4:00 AM, in a still-dark sky, Procyon, alpha Canis Minor, rose to join Mars, burning bright in Gemini, slightly southeast. At dawn a remarkable spectacle greeted those who persevered. Sirius, rose on this day before the Sun, welcoming a new day, a new year, and the onset of a "Great Year" of 1,460 years duration.

On this date Procyon, which rose well ahead of Sirius, appears almost due east on the horizon, Sirius is roughly eighteen degrees to the northeast, and sunrise occurs at the southernmost point of the year, twenty-three and one-half degrees southeast. This grand spectacle heralded the annual flood.

The axis of the temple of Dendera aligns with the figure of a Horus falcon atop a papyrus stem on the zodiac. Biot believed this indicated two representations of Sirius, but because of the relative positions of Sirius and Orion, I believe this figure portrays the star Procyon. In our modern skies Sirius, Procyon, and Betelgeuse (alpha Orion) form what is called the Winter Triangle, a familiar beacon to winter sky watchers.

Procyon means "before the dog," and Sirius is known as the "dog star." Due to the importance of the event it seems likely that the priests would have employed an early warning system and that the helical rising of Procyon, which occurred days before that of Sirius, and would have allowed time to sound the call and prepare for the celebrations. I believe thousands would have gathered along with the priests to watch the star of Isis rise and to prepare for the imminent innundation.

Sir Norman Lockyer, in *The Dawn of Astronomy*, demonstrated repeatedly how the Egyptians moved and reconstructed temples to align with certain stars. Why did they choose to do this when solar alignments remain reliable for thousands of years? In Egyptian cosmology stars were goddesses and the goddess Nut, the starry sky, was feminine. Sun god variants were male and reborn at dawn, "birthed" from the womb of the sky goddess. Perhaps the Sun was seen to influence earthly life and the stars to be the realm of eternal life.

Do the stars draw us by their beauty, or is there some inherent power to which we respond? Schwaller described the "living sky," a celestial Neter (Divine Archetype) at Memphis and a metaphysical, supra-celestial Neter at Heliopolis. Did the ancient Egyptians understand something about stellar influences that we have yet to rediscover? Was there a profound metaphor encoded by the stellar myths that was enacted inside the temples of initiation?

On such a day, surely the priests would have cast the charts and endeavored to divine the significance of the next cycles. Based on Skyglobe's images, and if I am correct in my planetary correlations, a brief forecast might have read as follows: The Sun and Mercury were in Leo on opposite sides of the notable star Regulus, indicating the importance of the kingly function and perhaps an imminent proclamation from Pharaoh. The Moon occupied Capricorn, the Sea Goat. This is not a strong place for lunar energies and would have portended a possible weakness in the structures and form of the realm, thus alerting Pharaoh's advisors. Venus in Virgo could have been read as a cycle of plenty, fruitful harvests, like the Biblical fat calves. Mars in Gemini energizes mental processes and makes the pen seem mightier than the sword—good news for a monarch. Jupiter in Aquarius expands the higher mind and might have ushered in a period of heightened learning and widened sharing of education with the masses. Saturn is said to be exalted in Libra. Pharaohs of this time might have seen fit to reform the legal system and the way discretions were judged.

Contemplating the so-called zodiac of Dendera is like peering through a window to the past, capturing a precise moment in the sky for all time. Hopefully more research will shed additional light and understanding on this priceless relic.

Atlantis Rising #30 October 2001

CHAPTER 6

THE ZODIACS OF DENDARA, EGYPT: WHY IS CANCER OF CENTRAL SIGNIFICANCE?

"May we die each night and be born each morning that the wonder of life should not escape us."

The Egyptian Book of the Dead,
Translation by Normandi Ellis

Ceiling of Dendera Temple Egypt (photo by author)

Ancient Egyptian astronomy reaches far back into prehistory. As discussed in AR #133 (Chapter 8 in the volume), the stone circle at Nabta Playa in the western desert of southern Egypt has sophisticated astronomical alignments dating back at least 7,000 years, very likely much longer, including a primary connection to summer solstice sunrise. Ancient Egyptians fixed dates for religious festivals, determined the hours of night, and divided the time between two successive risings of the Sun into twenty-four hours. The main axis of the Karnak temple aligns with winter solstice sunrise, and the main axis of the Luxor temple aligns with winter solstice sunset. Temple sky watchers observed lunar phases, planetary conjunctions, and the rising and setting of planets and stars.

By the time of the dynastic period of Egypt, around 3,000 BCE, the 365-day Egyptian calendar was already in use and observation of certain stars was key to determining the timing of the annual Nile flood. The flood occurred at the time of summer solstice and was heralded by the heliacal (before the Sun) rising of Sirius, brightest star in the sky, and star of the goddess Isis.

Priests and priestesses served Egyptian deities within temple precincts where ordinary people were typically not permitted. The people outside the temples lived more in resonance with the land and the agricultural cycles of the year. Seasonal festivals and ceremonies marked important points in the annual wheel of time and included ordinary people in temple life through extravagant celebrations, likely providing financial support through tribute and taxes.

Ancient Egyptians lived in a realm of magic similar to the Shinto religion that still thrives in Japan. Nature was experienced as alive and filled with conscious spirits who must be honored in order to maintain balance. The Egyptians, like the Hindu and Shinto, believed that the deities lived in the shrines and embodied the statues. Rituals and fertility festivals that related to the agricultural year, like the perennial mysteries of Osiris, had to be timed and the sky was both clock and calendar.

Ceremonies and celebrations maintained a critical balance between heaven and earth, above and below. The goddess Ma'at (pronounced May-et) was seen as the abstract principle of order that held the world together and without which everything would descend into chaos. Her name meant "that which is straight." Ma'at was born from the sun god Ra by *heka*, the power of magic, when he spoke the first word at the beginning of creation. She had no temples or priests but was worshipped by living a life in accordance with her highest principles of truth, order, harmony, and justice. Temples of other deities had small shrines to her as her principles of order were understood to infuse everything.

The Egyptians performed rituals to "Keep Ma'at on Earth," restoring and sustaining harmony by attuning to cosmic order. Acting according to Ma'at's principles included the organization of sacred space, orientation of life in time, creation of the calendar, and mapping the celestial landscape. In a similar manner, astrology seeks to find meaning and balance through correspondences between heaven and earth—timing is everything.

The temple of the goddess Hathor at Dendera is stunning. Hathor was an ancient goddess of fertility and beauty. Archeology dates the present form of the temple to the Ptolemaic period (332-30 BCE). The present Greco-Roman structure is built over an ancient site and is the last construction of an immensely older and influential temple. Dating of the existing building is known from specific mention of the building efforts of various historical rulers; their "signatures" appear in areas of the temple they completed or expanded.

Two extraordinary "zodiacs" were incorporated into the beautiful and extensively painted reliefs in the Dendara temple. The older zodiac, which is circular and generally dated to the middle of the first century BCE, forms roughly half of the ceiling in the eastern room in a series of small chapels built on the roof of the temple. The second zodiac, conventionally dated around eighty years later, is high up in the hypostyle hall of the temple and is part of a series of rectangular sections known as the astronomical ceiling of Dendera. The zodiacs are really star maps since they contain much more imagery than the twelve zodiac constellations. Because of the historical time frame, the zodiac characters are the familiar Greco-Roman figures with a decidedly Egyptian flair.

The round zodiac is unique as a circular design as other astronomical designs on walls or ceilings are linear. It's also puzzling that Cancer, the Crab, is almost at the center of the circle, appearing overhead with the circumpolar stars. Leo and Virgo follow in a clockwise direction around the inner part of the circle, moving in the direction of precession rather than the annual sequence. As Earth orbits the Sun each year the Sun appears to move through the zodiac constellations in a "right to left" counterclockwise direction. Because of its circular shape, and the enigmatic depiction and direction of the constellations, this zodiac has been the subject of intense speculation and scholarly debate.

The rectangular zodiac is formed of two sections, each containing half of the zodiac figures depicted as the familiar Ram to Fishes. Both sides of the rectangular zodiac have the elongated starry body of Nut, goddess of the sky, arching across the top. Nut symbolically swallows the solar orb at sunset, and the Sun was imagined to move through her body at night and be reborn from her at sunrise. The constellations of Capricorn, Sagittarius, Scorpion, Libra, Virgo and Leo are clearly seen on one half of the rectangle. On the other side Gemini, Taurus, Aries, Pisces and Aquarius can be seen, but Cancer does not follow Gemini, and the Crab seems to be missing. What does immediately follow Gemini is the Egyptian Holy Trinity--Isis, Osiris, and Horus--key players in the annual resurrection drama. Their placement indicates that they have risen before the Sun.

The zodiacs are believed to contain the mysteries of Osiris, which was the most important festival celebrated to assure the annual fertilization of the land. The *Web Renpet* festival opened the sacred year at the time of the annual flood at summer solstice. The star Sirius (Sopdet/Isis) and the constellation of Orion (Sah/Osiris) had disappeared for seventy days at the time of spring equinox. Osiris had descended into the underworld, and at summer solstice, which coincided with the flood, he reappeared in early morning darkness, rising ahead of the Sun. This was perceived as a symbolic death and resurrection, and the mysteries of Osiris were reenacted in the temple to attune to the mystery of Nature's cycles. The star Procyon, alpha Canis Minor, shown as the god Horus, divine son of Isis and Osiris, announced the imminent ascension of Sirius in the dawn sky, which heralded the flood. The stellar holy family had returned, bringing the waters of life to renew the land.

The constellation of Cancer, the Crab in modern symbolism, has central emphasis and significance in both zodiacs. At the time these zodiacs are believed to have been created, summer solstice aligned with Cancer and the annual flood. At summer solstice the Sun is directly overhead of the Tropic of Cancer and appears to stop, *sol sistere*, "sun stands still," and then seems to change direction and head south again. This moment is the onset of the zodiac sign of Cancer in the Greco-Roman zodiac. The key figures of Osiris, Horus, and Isis are strongly represented in the round zodiac, and I believe placing Cancer at the center in the round zodiac fixed a moment in time when the Osiris mysteries were celebrated.

In the rectangular zodiac Cancer is significant because of its apparent absence. However, a closer study of the area around the feet of the goddess Nut in both halves of the zodiac, where the Sun is reborn, reveals a scarab beetle. The beetle that is close to Gemini, the Twins, where Cancer should appear in the sequence, is closer to her feet. The newborn Sun shines on the countenance of the goddess Hathor. Further down her legs is the scarab beetle, symbol of the rising Sun, and the gaze of the goddess Hathor seems to look at the scarab, highlighting its importance.

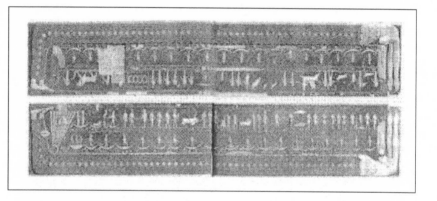

Moving to the other half of the zodiac the scarab beetle has one wing, perhaps representing that the Sun has almost completely risen, and Leo the Lion follows in the correct zodiac sequence. I believe the designers of the rectangular zodiac represented Cancer, the Crab as a scarab beetle, the newborn rising Sun at summer solstice. Cancer is not missing, it is represented by a profoundly Egyptian symbol.

The scarab, or dung beetle, was an ancient Egyptian symbol with importance in textual references and iconography. The scarab represented the god Ra Khefer, self-created father of the other gods, who was related to the idea of "becoming" and was depicted as the rising Sun, coming forth from the darkness of night. If these zodiacs commemorated an annual sunrise festival, and perhaps also a specific point in time, depicting the birth of the summer solstice Sun as a scarab beetle, in the place where Cancer falls in the zodiac, would have had obvious symbolic meaning to astronomer priests of the time. This was not only the daily rebirth of the Sun but also the rebirth of the year.

All cultures place a symbolic overlay on the wheel of time and add ritual to give it power. In the same way that the Christmas season is a celebration of the return of light in the northern hemisphere at Winter Solstice, the festival of Osiris in ancient Egypt celebrated the annual flooding of the Nile that brought life back to the desert at the Summer Solstice. This was the new year since without the flood waters there would have been no life in Egypt. This was experienced as an annual resurrection. Easter sunrise services in Christian churches, and spring festivals in many other cultures for thousands of years, have served the same purpose in the same way.

We can take a lesson from the ancient Egyptians. Invoking the principles of the goddess Ma'at, we should strive to move through our lives attuned to the seasonal cycles of light and dark, learning to live in accordance with the principles of truth and justice, bringing divine order into our lives.

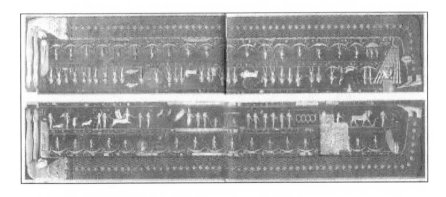

Atlantis Rising #134 February 2019

CHAPTER 7

GOBEKLI TEPE: AN ANCIENT STAR TEMPLE BUILT AT A RESURRECTION OF CIVILIZATION

"There is only one day left, always starting over: it is given to us at dawn and taken away from us at dusk."

Jean-Paul Sartre

Gobekli Tepe site (author Zhengan CC BY-SA 4.0)

Around 12,900 years ago, at the end of the Pleistocene period, which corresponds to the end of the Paleolithic Age, temperatures had been steadily rising and ice caps had been melting for 10,000 years. Then, Earth suddenly and dramatically dipped into a mysterious mini ice age. The Northern Hemisphere saw temperatures nearly as cold as the peak of the Glacial Maximum. The change was relatively sudden, taking place in decades, and resulted in the extinction of most of the large mammoths and saw the rapid demise of the North American Clovis culture. In Europe, the period was characterized by advancing glaciers and a vegetation shift to cold-tolerant plants. Called the Younger Dryas, named after an alpine tundra wildflower that flourishes in cold conditions, the mini ice age lasted for about 1,200 years from 12,900 -11,700 BP (Before Present) before the climate warmed again.

According to one increasingly tenable hypothesis, comet fragments striking Earth triggered the sudden climate change. What is termed the Younger Dryas Impact Hypothesis is a comprehensive effort to explain the cause of the cold period. Collaborating as the Comet Research Group, the project is the work of sixty-three highly-qualified scientists from fifty-five universities in sixteen countries and is headed by physicist Richard Firestone. The theory radically changes the long-held traditional view of a slow and gradual development of Earth's relatively recent geology. According to the Younger Dryas Impact Hypothesis, dust and gasses caused by the explosion, or the impact of a comet or meteorite in Earth's atmosphere absorbed sunlight, causing the American continent to cool dramatically. The heart of the explosion also melted parts of the Laurentide ice sheet that covered parts of North America. As a result, freshwater flowing into the Atlantic Ocean caused shifts in marine currents, slowing down the warm Gulf Stream.

The hypothesis has caused the debate between gradualism and catastrophism to reach a fever pitch. Catastrophism holds that Earth has been shaped by sudden and violent events that might have been global in scope. Gradualism contends that Earth has developed in slow incremental changes, such as erosion. We now realize it's ridiculous to believe that the cosmos revolves around us, but it was serious business in the 17th century that resulted in Galileo's house arrest. The argument of a sudden catastrophe nearly 13,000 years ago is of no less significance in the evolution of knowledge than the Copernican revolution, and the scientists who are in opposition to the mounting evidence appear as dogmatic as the church fathers of Galileo's time.

The team's evidence focused on sediment samples that contained several different types of debris that could only have come from an extraterrestrial source, such as a comet or an asteroid. The debris included nano diamonds, created by the shock and heat of impacts, tiny carbon spherules that form when molten droplets cool rapidly in air, and carbon molecules containing the rare isotope helium-3, far more abundant in the cosmos than on Earth. The team believes the agent of destruction was probably a comet, since the key sediment layer lacks both the high nickel and iridium levels that are characteristic of asteroid impacts.

Adding to the excitement of shattering paradigms, Gobekli Tepe, a remarkable site in southeastern Turkey, has upended the conventional view of the beginnings of civilization. Dubbed the "oldest temple in the world," the site is 6,000 years older than the accepted age of Stonehenge and pre-dynastic Egypt. The traditional view of pre-history asserts that civilization arose roughly 6,000 years ago around the fertile crescent of the Tigris and Euphrates rivers. The complex site of Gobekli Tepe, also located between the two great rivers, has been reliably dated to 11,700 years ago. This corresponds with remarkable "coincidence" to the end of the Younger Dryas.

Now considered to be one of the most important ancient sites discovered so far, Gobekli Tepe is located some six miles from Urfa, an ancient city in modern Southeastern Turkey close to the border of Syria. Pious Muslims believe this is Ur of the Chaldeans and the birthplace of the patriarch Abraham. A large fishpond is a refreshing gathering spot today, but in local lore, it is where King Nimrod attempted to burn Abraham on a pyre. His plan was foiled when God turned the fire to water and the coals to fish, and it's believed they remain in place as a reminder of this early miracle and a testament to the power of faith. However, it's tempting to see this story as a mythic description of the end of the fiery age of Aries and the beginning of the age of Pisces, the Fishes.

Archeologist Klaus Schmidt worked at Gobekli Tepe until his untimely death in 2014. Dr. Schmidt mapped the entire summit using ground-penetrating radar and geomagnetic surveys, charting where at least sixteen other megalithic rings remain buried across twenty-two acres. The one-acre excavation area covers less than five percent. Professor Schmidt said archaeologists could dig for another fifty years and barely scratch the surface, but what has already been uncovered is stunning. Archeologists believe the site was active for almost three millennia before being deliberately backfilled and abandoned about 9,000 years ago.

Schmidt believed that Gobekli Tepe was like a pilgrimage site since there isn't evidence of a major permanent populace. By contrast Catal Huyuk is a thirty-two acre Neolithic site in south-central Turkey, dated to circa 8,500 – 7,700 years before the present, just at the time Gobekli Tepe was abandoned. Catal Huyuk is about 300 miles west of Gobekli

Tepe. The site has been described as "one of the first true cities," and is characterized by fully developed agriculture and extensive trading, particularly in obsidian, frescoed temples, mud-brick fortifications and houses, and mother-goddess figures. Perhaps Catal Huyuk was the next evolution after Gobekli Tepe had been abandoned. Although the Minoan culture on the island of Crete is dated much later, the iconography and appearance of the two cultures bears a striking similarity. It's possible earlier versions of that culture will be unearthed at some point.

The main part of the Gobekli Tepe site consists of twenty round enclosures that are up to twenty meters (65 feet) in diameter with low stone walls. Two hundred T-shaped pillars that average twenty feet in height and weigh up to twenty tons are embedded in the walls of the enclosures. Larger T-shaped pillars, consisting of a large rectangular piece of stone with another smaller stone balanced on top, stand in the center. The larger stone blocks weigh about seven tons. One pillar that is still attached to the native rock where it was being quarried would have been thirty tons and seven meters (30 feet) high.

Within enclosure D, which is the oldest, the sides of the pillars are elaborately carved with images of animals, people, and geometric designs. Most carvings represent wild animals such as felines, foxes, boars, vultures, spiders, snakes, and scorpions. Pillar #43, called the Vulture Stone, has become famous because of its reliefs. Using astronomy software, researchers have realized that 11,700 years ago the summer solstice Sun was in what we now call the constellation of Scorpio. A scorpion on pillar #43 raises the question of the antiquity of some zodiac symbols. The mostly-circular enclosures can be thought of as "circles of animals," reminding us that the English word zodiac comes from the Greek *zoidiakos*, meaning "cycle or circle of animals." Perhaps elements of the zodiac had a much earlier origin than we have supposed.

Some of the interior pillars are topped, or otherwise adorned, with carved animal statues that include lizards and lions. The large central pillars have hands and "belts." Archeologists believe the enclosures were not covered and were open to the sky. Researchers can only speculate, but many of the speculations are compelling, based on astronomy, and strongly suggest that Gobekli Tepe was an observatory —a star temple.

If indeed the site functioned as an observatory, how was it oriented, and where they did they primarily direct their gaze? It's beyond the scope of this article to discuss the scholarly opinions in detail. However, researchers have analyzed sky-ground relationships with astronomy software, shifting the view of the sky back in time to look at possible connections to the figures on the pillars and potentially match them to stellar asterisms. Their opinions also link the origin of Gobekli Tepe to the time frame of the Younger Dryas.

Graham Hancock, in *Magicians of the Gods,* notes that the alignment of true north, not magnetic north, is a significant detail of Gobekli Tepe that is agreed upon by mainstream scientists and is not in dispute. Hancock says, "For the ancients to know about the spinning axis of the earth and construct a site in sync with the stars classifies it as legitimate knowledge of astronomy and should be considered more than just mere coincidence." He favors an astronomical orientation to the southern sky as he feels a northern view would be obstructed by the hill.

Robert Schoch, in *Forgotten Civilizations,* also looks south and finds a correlation to the rising of Orion's Belt in the southeast. Italian archeoastronomer Guilio Magli sees an intriguing connection to the reappearance of the helical rising of Sirius after a long absence due to precession.

M.B. Sweatman and D. Tsikritsis of the School of Engineering at the University of Edinburgh in Scotland have provisionally matched animals on Pillar #43, the Vulture Stone in Enclosure D, with stellar asterisms. Their abstract in *Mediterrean Archaeology and Archaeomety* titled "Decoding Gobekli Tepe with Archaeoastronomy: What Does the Fox Say?" outlines their theory that the Vulture Stone is a date stamp for 10,950 BC ± 250 years, which corresponds closely to the proposed date of the onset Younger Dryas.

Andrew Collins, in his book *Gobekli Tepe: Genesis of the Gods*, looks north instead and draws a powerful connection to the setting of Deneb, the alpha star in Cygnus, the Swan. He bases his opinion in part on the positions of the hands on the large central T-shaped pillars in enclosure D. Both face south toward the entrance and not each other. His rationale is that someone entering the enclosure from the south would face, and be faced by, the large pillars in the center. If the central pillars are seen as "deities," Collins likens this to a church or temple where the focus of attention would be in the opposite direction of the entrance, in this case north.

Who built this amazing site and tended it for three thousand years? Did they bury Gobekli Tepe as a "message in a bottle" for a future time on the other side of the wheel of precession? Graham Hancock posits that Gobekli Tepe was constructed by survivors of a high civilization (that we call Atlantis), which was lost to a cosmic impact event. Hancock suspects that a transfer of technology and / or knowledge occurred at this site between hunter-gatherers and survivors of a lost culture, mainly because agriculture sprang up in the same time period and area of the world.

The antiquity of Gobekli Tepe provides a context that makes the question of the actual age of the pyramids of Egypt, theorized by alternative scholars such as John Anthony West, Graham Hancock, and Robert Bauval, open to re-examination. Likewise, sites like Pumapunko in Bolivia are pushing back the origin stories. Clearly, humans were performing amazing feats far earlier than has been credited by academia.

Atlantis Rising #129 April 2019

CHAPTER 8

NABTA PLAYA: ANCIENT SOURCE OF EGYPTIAN COSMOLOGY

"People living more than seven thousand years ago may have possessed technical knowledge in astronomy and physics more advanced than our current understanding of the same subjects."

Robert M. Schoch, geologist, 2002

Nabta Playa Stone Circle (Author Raymbetz CC BY-SA 3.0)

In 1972 a group of archeologists were crossing the Egyptian desert, tracking by compass in an area known as Nabta Playa, when they arrived at the shores of a long extinct lake. Stopping for a break, they noticed potsherds at their feet. Intrigued, they returned later to investigate. Following several seasons of digging they realized that in the area where they had noticed the potsherds, what they had assumed were merely outcroppings of rock were in fact an enigmatic circle of standing megalithic stones. Years later, in March of 1998, a team led by anthropologist Fred Wendorf of Southern Methodist University, one of the original discoverers, officially announced discovery of the site. Wendorf's team presented their research in *Holocene Settlement of the Egyptian Sahara*, in 2001.

Nabta Playa is located in Nubia, west of Abu Simbel in Egypt's Western Desert, and is the only known megalithic stone circle in Egypt. The circle is formed from Nubian sandstone slabs of varying sizes, enclosing an area of about twelve feet (four meters). The circle of standing stones, according to the stellar alignments, dates at least as far back as six thousand years, and may be the first evidence of ancient skywatching in Egypt.

The western Egyptian desert is totally dry today, but this was not always the case. There were several humid periods in the past that saw levels of annual rainfall of nearly twenty inches (500 mm). This fact is also related to the work of Robert Schoch and the water weathering of the Sphinx, indicating its much older age based on past levels of rainfall. The most recent period of more rainfall was during the last interglacial and early last glaciation periods, stretching between 130,000 and 70,000 years ago. Around 10,000 BCE the area around Nabta flooded seasonally, creating a lake that was surrounded by grasslands that attracted Neolithic nomadic tribes. The area would have been a savanna, a large open grassland with widely spaced trees, supporting extinct buffalo and large giraffes, and varieties of antelope and gazelles. Around 7,500 years ago the researchers saw a notable change in the culture of the peoples of Nabta Playa that exhibited a degree of social organization not previously seen in ancient Egypt, as far as we know.

The stone circle at Nabta Playa has two pairs of stone slabs. There are six upright slabs set along two lines. There is also an east-west alignment that connects one megalithic structure with two stone megaliths about a mile away. There are two other geometric lines that involve about a dozen additional stone monuments that lead both north-east and south-east from the same megalith, and there are other large megalithic stones nearby. The overall design and potential significance of the site is larger than the stone circle itself.

During the seasons of digging, Wendorf's team unearthed numerous cultural artifacts that were carbon dated to the Holocene period around 10,000 BCE to 3,000 BCE, although most of the dates clustered around 6,000 BCE, when the climate was much wetter. Because other stone configurations were present in the area, Wendorf's team dug down through twelve feet of sediment to bedrock, expecting to find burials. What they discovered instead were strange and unexplained carved sculptures and etchings in the bedrock that had been buried intentionally.

According to researcher Kim Malville of the University of Colorado, his colleagues, and the excavators of the site, who have authored articles and scientific abstracts, some of these slabs seem to organize in a series of what they call "gates" that may have served as a calendar, using the sky. Astronomical calculations indicate that alignments pointed to stellar constellations that are known from ancient Egyptian writings. Six stones in the center run northeast-southwest, marking summer solstice, which would have been the beginning of the rainy season. According to Malville and Wendorf, the most important alignments were to Dubhe in the Plough, the ancient Egyptian constellation of *Meskhetyu*, and Sirius, the ancient Egyptian *Sopdet*, when this bright star rose before the Sun at summer solstice and heralded the annual flood.

Meanwhile, NASA physicist Thomas Brophy, who holds a PhD in physics and has worked with the NASA Voyager Project, the Laboratory for Atmospheric and Space Physics, and the Japanese Space Program, had also been studying the site. After designing his own astronomy software adequate to the task, he analyzed the alignments and published his conclusions in 2002 in the *The Origin Map*. His book has a Foreword by Robert Schoch PhD, and an Afterword by the late John Anthony West.

According to Brophy, and his colleague P. Rosen, if Sirius is identified in the alignment it would have to have been 8,000 years ago. Brophy and Rosen's work indicates another alignment with the helical (before the Sun) rising of Orion's Belt at the spring equinox, and the other three center stones showed Orion's "head" as it rose. *Atlantis Rising* readers will be familiar with the sky-ground link between this asterism in Orion and the three main pyramids of Giza that was identified by Robert Bauval and Adrian Gilbert in their book *The Orion Mystery*.

Brody has proposed that the alignments corresponded with a date of around 4,800 BCE or 16,500 BCE. He suggested a connection between the southernmost alignment of stones and Sirius with a date of around 6,088 BCE. He also proposed that the larger stones set at various distances to the stone circle were also aligned to center stones and other stars in Orion, setting a date of around 6,270 BCE. Brophy demonstrates a truly amazing linkage to the vernal equinox helical risings of six stars in Orion that only occur once in approximately

26,000 years. And not only do the center stones in the circle align with other megaliths at various distances, but the distances on the ground show the actual distances to these stars. Finally, he proposed that the table rock that was uncovered was a map of the Milky Way galaxy at around 17,500 BCE and that the stars mapped Orion at around 16,500 BCE.

Malville and Wendorf have a more conventional approach that the three northernmost alignments point to Arcturus, the brightest star in the northern celestial hemisphere, a fourth alignment links with Sirius and Alpha Centauri, the brightest and third brightest stars at that time, while a fifth alignment points to Alnilam in Orion's Belt. They note that it is difficult to be certain of astronomical alignments because of the shifting of sand and significant damage to the stones in the thousands of years since they were erected. They point out that there is no evidence of settlements outside the Nile Valley before 9,000 BCE. However, that same argument was used to discredit the age of the Sphinx, but now Gobekli Tepi and Catalhoyuk in Turkey have challenged traditional views about earlier settlements and cultural context.

Malville and Wendorf believe that Nabta Playa became an important ceremonial and cultural focal point for the Neolithic people of the Sahara between 6,100 and 5,600 BCE. People came from miles around to perform sacrifices, evidenced by the presence of hearths, but did not settle in the area. They believe that around 4,800 BCE the stone circle was erected to mark the summer solstice, and further megalithic structures followed until around 3,600 BCE. The rich burials of the Gebel Ramlah cemetery nearby are dated with a reasonable degree of certainty to around 4,400 BCE, and it is these prehistoric herdsmen who Malville and Wendorf consider to be the likely builders of the stone circle and associated megalithic structures.

But the situation is more complex. John Anthony West has commented that only in the last few decades have we gained enough astrophysical ability to comprehend the advanced knowledge encoded at Nabta Playa. Another stunning aspect to this unfolding story is Brophy's belief that the carvings in the uncovered bedrock appear to be a scaled map of the Milky Way, indicating the position, scale, and orientation of the Sun and the spiral arms. Brophy used Wendorf's accurate diagrams and maps to conclude that the central point of the sculpture was directly above and correctly placed the Sun on the galactic map. Even more startling is Brophy's discovery that a site line of one of the megaliths was in correct relation to the spring heliacal rising of the Galactic Center around 17,700 BCE.

If Brophy is right, it is difficult to imagine that nomadic Neolithic herdsmen possessed the knowledge, or had the need, to design a complex that showed distances to stars in Orion or carve a map of the galaxy and encode it with such sophisticated astronomical knowledge, and then bury the map with sand. Nabta Playa appears to be much more than a circle of standing stones that mark seasonal alignments, and there may be layers of meaning that were buried in successive periods.

Nabta Playa is at the southern end of the country, called Upper Egypt by the ancient Egyptians, since the Nile flows from south to north from its source in central Africa, so the site is at the root of Egypt. The enigmatic site may hold the key, the conceptual blueprint, to what became the massive ground plan of Giza with the three main pyramids mirroring Orion's Belt. The complex might also contain an over-arching cosmology whose theme persisted throughout Egyptian history.

The intentionally buried carvings and sculptures could be a message in stone from the distant past, encoding technical knowledge that was a legacy of Atlantis, or somewhere else. Nabta Playa may contain advanced knowledge that was lost in a great cataclysm. If survivors of a cataclysm suspected the event was triggered cyclically, they may have tried to send a warning across time. Graham Hancock suggested a similar idea relative to the intentionally buried stone circles at Gobekli Tepe and their stellar alignments.

John Anthony West often remarked that ancient Egypt was a legacy culture from an advanced civilization that came long before. He believed Egypt's origins stretched back nearly 30,000 years. We are also reminded of the mystery of the Dogon of Mali and their sophisticated knowledge of Sirius and its dark companion. Their fascinating knowledge may also be a legacy.

The haunting question that remains is "Why Orion?" What is the symbolic significance of this part of the sky that the ancient Egyptians took such care to create lasting sky-ground connections? Stepping out of the realm of traditional science is the legend that long ago in the epoch *Zep Tepi*, the "first time" Osiris (Orion) and Isis (Sirius) came from the sky and brought their wisdom to Earth, creating the Egyptian civilization.

It is always wise to keep an open mind—Troy was also once only legend. What seems certain is that as our technology advances our paradigm of the past keeps shifting and widening, radically altering our formerly narrow view of "history." Perhaps one day we will reclaim the truth of our past.

Atlantis Rising #133 December 2018

CHAPTER 9

HAMLET'S MILL: GRIST FOR
THE WHEEL OF HEAVEN

 " A thought ruled by time can only be expressed in myth."

Giorgio de Santillana, *Hamlet's Mill (Introduction)*

A Flour Mill (Snappygoat.com)

For millennia, people have found meaning by watching the night sky as it changed over time, looking for repeating patterns and searching for changes that could portend danger. Sparkling points of light in the dark sky could be tracked and named. For example, the stars of Ursa Major became a dipper, a plough, a wagon, or the hind leg of an ox to different cultures. The sky "moves" every day because of Earth's rotation on its axis. The sky also changes each month as Earth orbits the Sun through a different slice of sky, progressing through the twelve zodiac constellations, and the Moon also goes through its monthly phases. The Sun's apparent daily motion is divided into dawn, noon, dusk, and midnight. Like the four phases of the day, the Moon's cycles are also four-fold, new, the quarters, and the full Moon. The year is divided into four by the seasons, marked off by the equinoxes and solstices. In this way time can be seen as circular and its frame as a sphere where the four seasons intersect the circle of the year.

But there are much longer cycles that generations of sky watchers were able to perceive. One of these cycles is called axial precession, or nontechnically, precession of the equinoxes, since the spring and fall equinoxes move very slowly westward along the ecliptic (apparent path of the Sun) relative to the stars at the rate of one degree of arc every seventy-two years. This slow motion causes a different part of the dawn sky to appear relative to the seasons, or cardinal points, of the year. Precession occurs because Earth wobbles as she spins, tracing imaginary circles in the sky, like two styluses on a spinning top. Moving in the opposite direction to the solar zodiac, the astrological ages "precess," or inch backward through the more familiar sequence of signs. This cycle of precession is called a Grand Year, or Platonic Year, and lasts roughly 26,000 Earth years.

Hamlet's Mill, by Giorgio de Santillana & Hertha von Dechend, is a scholarly work and a daunting piece of research, accumulating myths from around the world that demonstrate similarities of theme and imagery, showing how knowledge of the stars was encoded into the stories. The thematic myth has Norse Icelandic origins with a character named Amlodhi, who owned a mill. In his time the mill ground out peace and plenty, but as time passed and circumstances declined, the mill ground out salt. Finally, the mill sunk to the bottom of the ocean where it ground out rocks and sand, creating a whirlpool that was a vast *maelstrom*, the "grinding stream."

The metaphor of the mill describes the polar axis, piercing the center of the earth, and the frame of time, and points toward the northern and southern axes of the sky. A dust jacket comment from *Hamlet's Mill* explains that numerous myths from cultures as diverse as "Iceland, Norway, Finland, Italy, Persia, India, Mexico, and Greece, to name a few," have a churning mill as their central theme. Much care was taken, with the assistance of gods, goddesses, and tremendous forces of nature were sought, to assure that the mill of heaven ground smoothly and without incident. Santillana and von Dechend believe the persistence of this image and the mill's motion provides a cosmic timepiece.

The authors' thesis is that this symbolism represents precession, the slow movement of the Sun through the stars of the zodiac, which determines the world ages. Each age is said to have a characteristic era, or dispensation, followed by a "twilight of the gods." At the end of an age the supporting pillars of that aeon collapse and floods and cataclysms trumpet the unfolding of a new age. The subtitle of *Hamlet's Mill* is "an essay on myth and the frame of time." Because we have four clearly defined seasonal events, two equinoxes and two solstices, the year is automatically divided into four. This quartering of the circle is an ancient and worldwide practice. The fourfold division of time seems to lead naturally to a four-fold division of space.

This mythical earth is conceived as a flat plane intersected by the "frame" of the equinoxes and solstices, the cardinal points of the year. This is why the earth is often said to be quadrangular. The intersections are the four seasonal points, the four directions, and the four winds. "The four zodiacal constellations rising heliacally at both the equinoxes and solstices form parts of the frame and determine the 'earth' or age." There is a conceptual "hoop" of four signs of the same modality that form seasonal signposts at the cardinal points of the year.

"Every world age has its own 'earth.' It is for this very reason that 'ends of the world' are said to take place," the authors say. A new age causes a new 'earth' to arise when another set of zodiacal constellations move into the seasonal framework and determine the year's four points. However, the zodiacal constellation that rises heliacally (before the Sun), at spring equinox in the northern hemisphere constitutes the overarching mythic theme of the current age. In our time, as the age of Pisces ends, it is the omega star of the constellation of Pisces that rises before the Sun on spring equinox dawn. Soon, stars of the constellation of Aquarius will take its place.

Peering back in time to earlier ages, such as the Age of Gemini, there were many "twin" deities, like Isis and Osiris. Looking even further back, convincing evidence has also been presented by authors such as Robert Bauval and Graham Hancock that since the lion-bodied Sphinx of Egypt gazes due east at equinox sunrise, 12,000 years ago during the Age of Leo the Sphinx would have looked at its heavenly counterpart —the constellation of Leo, the Lion.

As we look for other evidence of markers or icons of past ages we can see in Old Kingdom Egypt that during the Age of Taurus, 6,000-4,000 years before the present, bulls were the primary symbol. At the end of that age Moses cast down the golden calf to end the age of Taurus. In Middle Kingdom Egypt 4,000-2,000 years before present the ram was the symbolic animal for the Age of Aries, the Ram, and sacrificial rams were also the choice for offerings in the Bible. As the wheel turned to the Age of Pisces 2,000 years ago, Jesus, the symbolic lamb of god became the fisher of men for the Age of Pisces, the Fishes. The fish has been a predominant symbol of the Christian religion.

We are now poised at another such juncture on the turning wheel as the Age of Pisces gives way to the dispensation of the Age of Aquarius. Aquarius is the Water Bearer, and it certainly seems apt that water would be the symbol of transforming energy for a new age at a time when water may well be our most precious natural resource. During the Age of Aquarius, the famous Royal Stars of Persia will once again move into the seasonal marker positions.

Hamlet's Mill relates that the time when the cogs of the great mill shifted, heralding the beginning of a new age, was seen as especially fraught with peril. How did the ancient knowledge of those who watched the skies in long ago times determine that this was true? What could be the mechanism driving the timing, character, and overarching lessons of the ages? Perhaps there is some inherent magic in the geometry of twelve that relate to music, vibration, and frequency. Or perhaps it is the stars themselves and their unique energies that drive the influences of the ages and of astrology itself? The Tibetans are custodians of star knowledge that includes awareness of the "personalities" of certain bright stars and the nature of their frequencies. These are mysteries we may well be unable to penetrate, but if we are wise, we will pay attention.

The authors make a compelling case in their monumental work for sophisticated knowledge among the ancients, and their contribution to our understanding of antiquity is inestimable. The authors demonstrate repeatedly that myth was never intended to be fiction or fable, but rather to serve as a clever mnemonic device, enabling people to recall and transmit complex astronomical information through stories. In other words, using sky lore as the mechanism, and the night sky as the canvas, myth became a brilliant device, an astronomical allegory, for teaching and transmitting sky lore over vast periods of time.

As I was finishing this article a science news post reported that the observable Universe contains about two trillion (that's twelve zeroes) galaxies — more than ten times the number previously estimated. I find that an impossible number to conceive. This stunning announcement was the result of the first significant revision of the galaxy count in two decades. The research team was led by Christopher Conselice of the University of Nottingham, U.K. The Hubble telescope allowed researchers to directly observe only about 10% of the two trillion galaxies, but Conselice says "that will change in 2018 when Hubble's successor, the James Webb Space Telescope, is deployed. That telescope will peer much further back in time to see how galaxies started to form."

In November of 2013, based on Kepler space mission data, astronomers reported there could be as many as forty billion Earth-sized planets orbiting the habitable zones of stars in the Milky Way. Eleven billion of these planets may be orbiting sun-like stars, and the nearest planet may be only four light-years away. Astronomers now estimate there are roughly two thousand stars at a distance of up to fifty light-years from our Solar System. Sixty-four of them are yellow-orange "G" stars like our Sun.

As science and technology advance, and we are able to view more of the Cosmos, we can't help but be awed by the size and fantastic potential for other life among the stars. The narrow scope of what we were able to observe just a short time ago is expanding at what seems to be an exponential rate. How do we find additional meaning, living on the "pale blue dot" that Carl Sagan showed us during the Voyager I mission in 1990?

Author and teacher Joseph Campbell spoke of a "magic ring of myth" that flows through every culture. He said that a "mythology is a system of images that incorporates a concept of the universe as a divinely energized and energizing ambience within which we live." Myths are single stories in this grand scheme that interlock in some way to create a tapestry. Campbell explained that myths are not created or invented in the way stories are. He said they are inspired, and arise in the same way dreams do, and that they speak to the deep mysteries of both the individual and all that is. As we face a juncture in our own time of shifting cogs on the Great Wheel, I believe we desperately need new myths, new archetypal stories of a cosmos too big to imagine, in which we are not diminished by its size but are rather ignited by the understanding that we are part of a magnificent creation that can be known. As the Age of Aquarius begins in earnest, so does our journey of exploration.

Atlantis Rising #121 December 2016

CHAPTER 10

THE SUN AT MIDNIGHT: ENTERING THE GATES OF HEAVEN

"May we come and go in and out of heaven through gates of starlight."

Awakening Osiris, Egyptian Book of the Dead

Translated by Normandi Ellis

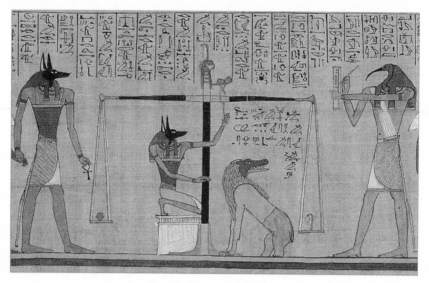

Scene from Papyrus of Ani (Public Domain)

Egypt's conventional timeline dates pre-dynastic Egypt to approximately 8,000 years ago, and what is termed the Old Kingdom dates to more than 5,000 years before the present. The Middle Kingdom period was about 4,000 years ago and the New Kingdom, the most familiar period that includes the famous 18th dynasty, lasted from about 1550 BCE to 1077 BCE, and included the 19th and 20th dynasties. Ancient Egypt came to an end with the Roman conquest and suicide of Cleopatra in 30 BCE. However, although it is not yet acknowledged beyond alternative scholarship, the story is much older—three times as ancient.

People naturally imagine pyramids when they think of Egypt, but many are also fascinated with the diverse pantheon of deities that populated temple and tomb walls. Ancient Egyptian cosmology is complex, and except for the brief Amarna period during the 18th dynasty, the paradigm remained remarkably consistent over time. Ancient Egyptian funerary texts include the Pyramid Texts, the *Amduat*, the Book of the Dead, the Book of Gates, the Book of Caverns, the Coffin Texts, the Litany of Re, the Book of Aker, the Book of Day, and the Book of Night.

All derive from the earliest Pyramid Texts and describe similar aspects of the nightly journey of the Sun and the deceased, traveling through the *Duat,* a particular part of the sky, which was viewed as the underworld and the afterlife. Gates marking twelve hours of night have been found in the earliest texts. The sun god's journey through the twelve hours of this realm also represented the belief that the soul of the deceased pharaoh took the same journey to become "an Osiris" and live in eternity. The ancient Egyptians did not have a word for death—they used the expression "westing." Just as the Sun set each day on the western horizon and rose again at dawn the eternal soul was believed to likewise rise again in an ongoing cycle of rebirth and renewal.

In *The Traveler's Key to Ancient Egypt,* author John Anthony West described Egyptian funerary texts as "manuals of spiritual instruction" and said the *Duat* is the "field" in which the transformation of the soul occurs. The theme of transformation and reclamation also runs through other ancient mystery traditions. Many ancient gods were seen as solar fire, and many rites represented the redemption and regeneration of this spiritual energy. The ineffable mysteries they sought to unveil, and the hidden knowledge the rites contained, held and transmitted this wisdom. Manly P. Hall, in *Secret Teachings of the Ages* said, "Mysteries were the channels through which this one philosophical light was disseminated."

The Eleusinian Mysteries of Greece took place from 1,600 BCE to about 400 CE, although most scholars believe their origin is much earlier in the Mycenean period. They were contemporary with, and bear strong resemblance to, the Egyptian mysteries of Isis and Osiris. In the Greek mysteries the goddess Demeter, carrying two torches named "intuition" and "reason," searched the world for her daughter Persephone, who symbolically represented the lost soul. She had to be rescued from the underworld, where she had been abducted by Hades, and reunited with her "mother."

The Tibetan word *bardo* means "intermediate," "transitional," or "in-between." Bardo refers to the state of existence between two lives on Earth. The *Bardo Thodol* is a text from a larger body of teachings revealed by Karma Lingpa (1326–1386) that are known in the West as the *Tibetan Book of the Dead*. Although this work is modern its origin is likely much older. It is similar to Egyptian funerary books as the text is intended to guide the soul through the experiences in the *bardo* after death. For those who are prepared, and who have been appropriately trained, the *bardo* offers a great opportunity for liberation. For others it can become a place of danger.

The Pyramid Texts are a collection of ancient Egyptian texts from the Old Kingdom; the oldest have been dated to 2400–2300 BCE. They were carved on walls and sarcophagi at Saqqara during the fifth and sixth dynasties more than 4,000 years ago. Unlike the later Coffin Texts, and the Book of the Dead, the Pyramid Texts were not illustrated and were reserved for pharaohs. Following the earlier Palermo Stone, the Pyramid Texts are the oldest known mention of Osiris, who would become the most important deity associated with the afterlife.

The *Amduat*, the Text of the Hidden or Secret Chamber, was written on the inside of royal tombs during the New Kingdom around 1,500 BCE. The earliest known complete version was found in the tomb of Thutmose III in the Valley of the Kings (KV34). The text describes the twelve hours of night, and the sun god's journey through underworld, beginning at sunset in the west and ending when the Sun rose again in the east. The *Amduat*, "what is in the Duat," names the gods and monsters that would be confronted along the way. The purpose was to provide names of these underworld denizens so the spirit of the deceased could call upon them for aid or use their names to defeat them. By knowing the names of the guardians, the sun god Ra triumphed over the challenges he faced.

The Book of the Dead, literally the Book of Coming Forth by Day, was derived from the Pyramid Texts and dates from the New Kingdom to the Late Period, roughly 1580 – 712 BCE. The text consists of one hundred chapters of varying lengths that were found only on scrolls, or in mummy swaths, which were buried with the deceased. The *Papyrus of Ani* is a well-known version.

The Book of Gates is usually dated from the New Kingdom; however, Dr. Eric Horning, professor of Egyptology and author of several books including, *The Ancient Egyptian Books of the Afterlife,* believes the text originated during the Armana period with Akhenaten. Like the Book of the Dead, the Book of Gates describes the passage of a newly-deceased soul into the next world, corresponding to the journey of the Sun during the hours of night. The Book of Gates was painted on tomb walls and gave the name of the hour, its gate, and the part of the underworld where it was located. The scenes appeared in three registers: in the upper register, along the upper banks, were the "blessed dead," and in the lower register were the "damned."

The banks of the underworld were also populated with helpers and hinderers. The text implies that some people would pass through unharmed, but that others would suffer torment in a lake of fire. Between the banks the Sun, and the soul of the deceased king, traveled in a solar boat on the celestial river, which was a symbolic journey through stages of initiation and transformation.

A many-coiled serpent symbolized time, and the gate guardians were goddesses and daughters of the sun god Ra, who embodied the hours. They had different titles and wore different colored robes, but were identical in all other respects. Each was crowned with a five-pointed star. Most of the goddesses are specific to the *Book of Gates* and do not appear anywhere else in Egyptian mythology. A recurrent declaration is pronounced by the deceased in front of the gates, "Make way for me, since I know you, I know your name, I know the name of the goddess who guards you."

Some researchers believe that the *Book of Gates* originated as a system for determining the time of night with the goddess at each gate representing a bright star, or pattern of stars, appearing during the hour. These are very likely the Zodiac constellations. Egyptologist Dr. Thomas Mudloff believes one purpose of the gates was to accurately time sunrise rituals, celebrating the resurrection of the solar principle and to function as a celestial timepiece or yearly calendar. To accomplish this the rising, setting, and apparent motions of bright stars were noted through the year. Each star, or star group, marked the "gate" or "hour" for fifteen days before a new star moved into position due to Earth's orbit.

Although the Egyptian Osiris was usually identified as the god of the afterlife and the dead, he is more appropriately the god of transition, resurrection, and regeneration. The Judgment Hall of Osiris occupied a critical moment in the funerary texts, just before the sixth hour, and halfway through the night. This was the turning point when the soul of the deceased pharaoh who had passed through the judgment became an Osiris--an illumined god. In a similar motif, mythologist Joseph Campbell described a universal theme in global myths that he called the "hero journey" that was characterized by a descent, a crisis, and an ascending return. Like the Egyptian pharaoh, the hero became a "god" at one stage of the journey.

Another theme running through mystery traditions, ranging from Sufism to esoteric Christianity, is described as the "Sun at Midnight." This was symbolized in esoteric rituals by a brilliant light that emerged slowly from complete darkness at midnight and then grew to shine like the Sun. As the deceased pharaoh became an Osiris, this represented the turning point in spiritual development when the soul infused the personality. Sun at Midnight initiation rituals symbolized the awakening of spiritual light shining within the soul. Rudolf Steiner held a dramatic ritual at midnight on Christmas Eve for his students. After meditating in silence for several hours, at the moment of midnight a light slowly emerged from a sphere that represented the Earth and ordinary consciousness. Steiner said this was a moment of grace where the light of the Sun at Midnight blazed forth, and the person awakened to the reality of the eternal soul and the true nature of existence, experiencing a profound reorientation of consciousness.

Egyptian funerary texts proclaimed that when the sun god arrived at dawn, the twelfth and last hour of the night, the miracle of rebirth occurred through the gate "with the mysterious entrance." Poet Khalil Gibran said, "One may not reach the dawn except by the path of the night." This is true, but there have always been those who hold lanterns to guide our way through the darkness to the mysterious entrance of initiation. We can take heart that this universal path of spiritual teaching has permeated spiritual traditions throughout time. Often called the Underground Stream, the spiritual wisdom of ages is always present, even though hiding in the shadows at times. Our job is to prepare ourselves to receive this knowledge.

Atlantis Rising #124 June 2017

PART II
PROPHECY & PREDICTION

CHAPTER 11

THE LORE OF A SHAMAN

"What's really important about shamanism is that there is another reality that can be personally discovered; we are not alone."

Michael Harner, *Cave and Cosmos*

2005 Powwow of Indian tribes (Snappygoat.com)

Anthropological orthodoxy assures us that history began in Sumeria six thousand years ago, and modern humans are the pinnacle of culture and evolution on the planet. Circa World War II, humanity shattered the rails of our technological playpen, sporting new atomic bombs. Space-faring ETs suddenly took notice, and a proliferation of silver saucers filled the skies. The UFO era was born; Roswell was a defining moment. Or so the story goes.

But an emerging, alternate view is compelling. Mobilized by fulfillment of long-heralded warning signs of prophecy, indigenous elders from around the world are breaking their vows of silence and sharing their secret stellar wisdom. While we slept for millennia in Western egocentricity, the indigenous peoples of the planet guarded the hidden history of humanity, quietly maintaining contact with our visiting and resident stellar family.

Native Americans, such as the Lakota Sioux, have a beautiful expression, *Mitakuye Oyasin*, which means "all our relations." Four-leggeds, winged ones, crawling ones, plant and stone nations are greeted as relatives. The Lakota Medicine Wheel is composed of four colors: red, black, white, and yellow - four races of humanity. Within Native cosmogony, it is not confusing to include and respect the Star Nations from other worlds among our extended family members.

Standing Elk, Dakota elder and Sun Dance chief, recently came forward with an open letter to the Elders of Turtle Island, the people of Earth. His heart told him to speak of the secret knowledge of his people concerning the Star Nations, since the time of their prophecies is at hand. Believing the knowledge belongs to the world, Standing Elk created Star Knowledge Gatherings, a forum to share this information. Sharing these secrets is controversial and unpopular with some Native peoples; history painfully demonstrates our track record with the Red Nation.

At Standing Elk' gatherings, Native Elders share the conference podium with prestigious researchers in the UFO field. "Alien" contactees speak openly of their experiences. Indigenous Elders do powerful ceremony and give candid testimony of their knowledge and relationship to the Star Nations. Humanity was seeded from the stars, and we have a profound genetic kinship with humanity's stellar brethren.

At a recent Star Knowledge Gathering in Las Cruces, New Mexico, Quiche Mayan Elder, Grandmother Windrider, talked of her visions and her challenging personal path. When she spoke, a hush fell over the room, and the air was filled with a stillness and electricity like the calm before a storm. Her words were carefully chosen, flying straight to the heart as do the arrows of a brave warrior. She challenged women to step into their power and help men to balance and heal the planet.

Across the world, on the continent of Africa, a similar phenomenon unfolds. In South Africa, Vusamazulu Credo Mutwa, renowned Zulu elder and author of *Song of the Stars: The Lore of a Zulu Shaman*, has courageously taken the same path. He has come forward to share the secret star lore of indigenous Black Africans in an effort to unite thinking people in the world and diminish the severity of African prophecies. Credo Mutwa is a master storyteller who has traveled to more than twenty countries sharing his wisdom. His openness resulted in great personal loss; his son was brutally murdered by those who want him silenced.

The Dogon tribe's startling knowledge of Sirius and its dwarf companion is well known, thanks to the work of Robert Temple in his book *The Sirius Mystery*. Credo Mutwa affirms that this knowledge is the tip of the iceberg. Indigenous knowledge of stellar relations is vast and complex, often dwelling at the heart of sacred ceremony. Rich oral traditions, including protocol for contact and how to distinguish friendly off-earth visitors from those who are potentially harmful, have been handed down from one *sangoma* (shaman) to the next for thousands of years.

According to Credo, "In every language in Africa, the meaning of star is 'bringer of knowledge' or 'bringer of enlightenment.'" Credo has traveled the continent of Africa, sculpting haunting images of visitors from the stars which were described to him by African shamans.

Cradled in South Africa's Krueger National Park lies a private game reserve called Timbavati. This emerald jewel of the African bush is almost mythical in reputation. White lions are born in Timbavati. Credo Mutwa continues, "A very long story is told about a chieftainess called Numbi. Many generations ago, she and her people saw a burning white light like a star fall out of the sky right where Timbavati is today.

The story is, that it was not a star; it was a shining ball of metal, brighter than the Sun. And when this ball came down to the ground, Queen Numbi, who was a sick old woman at that time, went towards the light and was swallowed by the light. And in that light, very faintly seen, were strange beings with very large heads. These beings received Numbi into the light, and for some hours she remained inside. When Numbi emerged from the light, and she walked towards her people, she had become a much younger woman than she had gone into the light.

After that star fell, stayed on the ground for some days, and then rose back into the sky, strange things started happening there. Cattle with two heads were born repeatedly. Lions, leopards and even impalas with snow white fur and green eyes were born, until to this very day. This story is one of the most amazing stories in Africa. It is one hundred percent true because even to this day, white animals are still being born in Timbavati. Some years ago, a snow white elephant with beautiful blue eyes and long tusks used to roam that place, until white adventurers shot it."

Credo said that when a tribe of invaders appeared at Timbavati many years after Numbi's experience they brought sacred stones that had been taken from Zimbabwe, a sacred location to the Zulu, and erected and enshrined the stones in Timbavati in honor of that place. Timbavati, whose name means 'the falling down of a star,' is also one of the holiest places in South Africa. But now he said its story is lost and has been overshadowed by a lot of nonsense.

The standing stones of Timbavati, brought from Zimbabwe to honor Numbi's visitors, are reminiscent of megalithic sites around the world and give mute testimony to the power and antiquity of the site. I stood among these stones at the March Equinox, beginning of Autumn in the southern hemisphere. The stones have a resonant quality when struck with a smaller stone, similar to Egyptian monoliths. Adjacent to Timbavati is a powerful and enigmatic place known as *Manyeleti*, which means "Gateway to the Stars." A community of nearly thirty shamans lives there.

In Credo's book, he relates a prophetic vision. He sees four great leaders emerging in the world: red, black, white and yellow. The colors are the same as the Lakota Medicine Wheel and four races of humanity. These leaders will work to unite the planet. One of these, a female leader, will arise in America. She will be called the Red Savior, because of the fiery color of her hair.

From Central America, Guatemalan Mayan Elder, don Alejandro, speaks eloquently of vast and repetitive cycles of time, noting that the Mayan calendar never has to be altered, because it is based on the stars. Our unwieldy western counterpart has been changed many times and is still not very accurate. This knowledge was bequeathed to the Maya by the *abuelos*, the grandfathers, who came from the stars.

Don Alejandro enigmatically links the origin and destiny of the Maya with the Pleiades, who he says were called May. Astronomically, Maia is one of the named stars in the Pleiades, the Seven Sisters.

Don Alejandro told us of a circle of indigenous Elders from around the world who gathered recently at Palenque, Chiapas, in Mexico to perform sacred ceremony and share their visions. Grandmother Windrider also entered that circle. "We worked in silence," Grandmother said. "Each of us walked to one of the four directions where we were called through inner guidance." Don Alejandro is organizing another circle to be held in the four corners area of America, which he hopes will draw even more people to pray for planetary healing.

December 21, 2012, is the end of the current Mayan long count. According to scholars, this "Great Cycle" began August 11, 3114 BCE. In Mayan terms this time period is equal to thirteen *baktuns*; in Gregorian terms, this equals 5125 years. Five Great Cycles, or suns, equals 25,625. Modern astronomers count one cycle of the precession of the equinoxes as 25,920 years. Maya say we are living in the time of the fifth sun, approaching the end of a major cycle. Mayan prophecies point to this time as filled with earth changes and transformation.

On December 21, 2012, Winter solstice, a unique astronomical event will occur. This event may occur only once in 26,000 thousand years. From the vantage point of earth, looking through the constellation of Sagittarius toward the center of our Milky Way galaxy, our Sun will conjoin the Galactic Center. What might be the nature of potent energies emitted by the Galactic core and beamed in our direction?

Ancient prophets and modern seers speak with one voice and see with a single eye. The Bible, Nostradamus, Edgar Cayce, Hindu texts and Hopi prophecies predicted this time on earth would be profound -- marked by miracles and cataclysms -- the storm before the long prophesied golden age. What is required of humanity to step through that portal in divine grace? Before crossing the threshold, we must purify ourselves and our planet.

Modern voices such as Credo Mutwa, Grandmother Windrider, Gordon Michael Scallion, Annie Kirkwood, and Robert Ghost Wolf sound a clarion call, echoing earlier harbingers. Robert Ghost Wolf recently shared Hopi prophecies about the "Seven Thunders" with millions of listeners on the Art Bell radio program Coast to Coast. He said, "The Seven Thunders roll through the heavens like the four horsemen of the apocalypse."

Credo Mutwa told me, "Anyone who investigates will come upon this amazing fact. In South America, in Brazil, in Peru and in Bolivia, different Native American tribes are expecting a world-wide cataclysm in this coming century. They have been expecting this cataclysm for centuries, and they knew it would occur early in this coming century."

If every tradition on earth concurs that we are at the culmination of their prophecies, how did they know the specific time frame thousands of years ago? If the triggering event of global cataclysm is an external object like a comet, with a cyclical orbital period, its return would be predictable and monitoring the movements in the sky would be vital. The last such juncture was the previous ice age roughly thirteen thousand years ago. I believe this story, and that of our progenitors, was recorded in legend and star lore and passed by oral tradition through shamans and elders.

Megalithic monuments around the globe contain critical stellar alignments, conveying messages and timing significance when understood, as researchers like Robert Bauval have shown. Profound physical evidence may have been left on Mars, as Richard Hoagland and others suggest. Other civilizations, perhaps many, have preceded us; their life cycles and attainments terminated by a cataclysmic mechanism which destroys the evidence.

In our time, we have lost touch with our celestial roots. To grasp our peril, and our opportunity, we must eliminate our egocentric arrogance that the present state of western humanity is the most developed civilization that has lived on this planet. We must heed the voices of our elders and ancestors. The indigenous guardians of our past assure us that we were seeded from the stars, and to the stars we will return.

A common thread binds the clarion call of the prophets and sages. Love and healing can make a difference. We must awaken from our collective amnesia. Corruption and greed must be eliminated, and the common good of all instilled in every heart. Once that recognition is accepted, the rest becomes story line in a celestial drama of infinite antiquity and cyclical repetition. Stars and galaxies are born, flower, decay and die in vast rhythms we can scarcely stretch our human minds to conceive. Sometimes, on some worlds, sentient beings emerge and ultimately seek their origins and their relations in the stars.

Mitakuye Oyasin!

Atlantis Rising #23 April 2000

CHAPTER 12

2012 GALACTIC ALIGNMENT: DOOMSDAY OR THE DAWN OF A GOLDEN AGE?

"We shall not cease from exploring, and at the end of our exploration, we will return to where we started and know the place for the first time."

T. S. Elliot, *Little Gidding V*

Milky Way Galaxy (Snappygoat.com)

The spectrum of scenarios expressed about December 21, 2012 ranges from apocalyptic "end of the world" rhetoric to the promise of a golden age or a mass ascension of humanity to a higher state of consciousness. Famous prophets and prophecies such as Nostradamus, Edgar Cayce, the Hopi Blue Star, South African Zulu shaman Credo Mutwa, and certain interpretations of the Bible, to name a few, are often cited as evidence for major events in this time frame.

The Prophecy of the Popes, attributed to Saint Malachy, is a list of 112 short phrases in Latin. Arnold de Wyon, a Benedictine historian, as part of his book, *Lignum Vitæ*, first published the prophecy in 1595. They describe each of the Roman Catholic popes, along with a few so called anti-popes, beginning with Pope Celestine II, elected in 1143, and concluding with the successor the current pope, Benedict XVI. The last pope is described as "Peter the Roman," whose pontificate will end in the destruction of Rome.

Misinterpretation of the Mesoamerican Long Count calendar seems to be the basis for the belief that a catastrophe, or epic event, will occur on December 21, 2012. Sandra Noble, executive director of the Foundation for the Advancement of Mesoamerican Studies states, "For the ancient Maya, it was a huge celebration to make it to the end of a whole cycle." She considers the portrayal of December 2012 as a doomsday or cosmic-shift event to be "a complete fabrication and a chance for a lot of people to cash in."

What does happen on 12/21/2012, according to most Mayan scholars, and based on a start date of August 11, 3114 BCE, is the close of one of the ancient Maya calendar cycles--the end of b'ak'tun 13. One b'ak'tun is a period of 144,000 days, equal to 394.26 tropical years. Thirteen b'ak'tuns is roughly 5,125 years. But in a similar manner to our New Year, a new cycle begins and goes to the next b'ak'tun, at Long Count 13.0.0.0.0. The full long count has seven more b'ak'tuns, before the odometer turns over. The next big phase, a p'ik'tun, a complete series of twenty b'ak'tuns, will occur on October 13, 4772, which is 2,760 years from December 2012. In other words, the ancient Maya weren't expecting the end of time but the continued turning of calendar wheels.

Other indications of potentially big changes come from astrophysicist Dr. Paul LaViolette, author of *Earth Under Fire*, who first alerted the scientific community to the existence of what he calls superwaves, or cosmic pulses, in 1983. His principal area of research at the Starburst Foundation is the investigation of intense cosmic ray particle barrages that travel from the center of our galaxy and can last up to several thousand years. Astronomical and geological evidence indicates that the last major superwave impacted our Solar System around 12,000 to 16,000 years ago, producing abrupt changes in Earth's climate. This is also the time that researchers say Atlantis was destroyed. It's estimated that approximately one or two superwaves strong enough to trigger an ice age are presently on their way to us.

There is evidence that the Galactic Center has erupted as many as ten times in the past two millennia, the most recent event occurring about 700 years ago. According to LaViolette, the electromagnetic radiation pulse accompanying such a superwave would be far more intense than any gamma ray pulse we have experienced in modern times, which would knock out electrical power grids and global communication networks.

Another theory that impacts the 2012 scenario is the possibility that our Sun is in a binary system with a brown or red dwarf star. Astronomers first postulated the hypothesis for this still-theoretical object in 1987 to account for cycles of mass extinctions that appear in the geological record. In 1984 paleontologists David Raup and Jack Sepkoski examined 250 million years of fossil records and observed that massive species extinction occurred at 65 million year intervals. Two independent teams of astronomers, Davis, Hut, and Miller, and Whitmire and Jackson, examined the data and suggested that the Sun had an as yet undetected companion star in a highly elliptical orbit.

Additional support for a binary companion comes from the Hindu *Vedas*, the ancient wisdom of India. Walter Cruttenden, founder of the Binary Research Institute, popularized the idea in his award-winning documentary *The Great Year*. Hindu cosmology includes an explanation of the phenomenon of Precession of the Equinoxes, through a cycle of ages called *Yugas*, which are echoed in the description of the Greek ages. The mechanism for this is a binary companion of the Sun whose periodic appearance ushers in a golden age and whose disappearance plunges the world into unconsciousness. In this view, the closer our companion gets, the more light and wisdom increases. The Rishis, Hindu sages, taught that this cycle was about 24,000 years, close to a full cycle of the astrological ages. Discovery of our Sun's companion would symbolically indicate an increase in light and the potential to reclaim ancient knowledge.

Ancient Indian astronomers also gave a physical reason for how the dual star, or binary motion, might facilitate the rise and fall of human consciousness. They said that as the Solar System traveled along its set orbital path with its companion star, it would cyclically move close to, then away from, a point in space referred to as *Vishnunabhi*, a supposed magnetic center or "grand center."

The Sun is one of hundreds of billions of stars in our Milky Way galaxy, and a gargantuan Black Hole lives at the heart. All the matter in our galaxy -- gas, dust, and stars -- rotates around a central axis perpendicular to the galactic plane. The galactic plane is an imaginary horizontal line that bisects the Milky Way. The Milky Way is about 100,000 light years across, and the Sun is located in the outer part of the galaxy. Our Solar System is about 30,000 light years from the center, and is currently traveling within the inner rim of the Orion Arm.

Our galaxy is one of fifty-four galaxies of various sizes that comprise our local group. Astrophysicists say that these galaxies are all moving toward something called the Great Attractor. A candidate for this role is a galactic conglomerate called the Shapely Supercluster, the largest concentration of galaxies in our nearby Universe, which is located in the constellation of Centaurus. Perhaps the Great Attractor is also the Grand Center the *Vedas* mention.

All the stars and stellar systems in the galaxy rotate around the galactic center at the same rate, which led to the premise of dark matter. Based on the distance from the center of 30,000 light years, and the estimated speed, the Sun completes one clockwise orbit, as viewed from the galactic North Pole, in about 225-240 million "terrestrial" years. One circuit of the Sun around the galactic center is called a Cosmic Year, or Galactic Year. Based on estimates of the Sun's age our star has made that journey twenty times.

Closer to home, as Earth orbits the Sun, every year around December 21 the Sun rises against the backdrop of stars at the center of our galaxy. This creates a vertical alignment of the Sun with the Galactic Center. In addition, as the Sun slowly circles the Galactic Center, the whole Solar System oscillates above and below the galactic plane like a sine wave. What is said to be significant now is a horizontal alignment with the galactic plane. When the Sun conjoins the galactic center at winter solstice there will be both a vertical and horizontal alignment. However, due to the slow movement of the Solar System, this is not just a one-time occurrence, and we have already experienced this alignment for some time.

Using the wheel of the zodiac as a frame of reference, the Galactic Center is at 26 degrees 51 minutes of the sign of Sagittarius. Also in this same location of the sky, peering deep into the heart of the Milky Way, is the youngest Supernova Remnant in our galaxy. Supernova explosions are the death of massive stars and release tremendous energy. Jupiter, who was a god of light and wisdom, rules Sagittarius. This phase of astrological experience searches for wisdom through experiences of expanded vision and widened horizons. In the northern hemisphere this is the dark time of the year and has always been celebrated with festivals of light. At a minimum, the intensified energies of a galactic alignment can offer a wider lens into the Universe and a reminder of how big Creation really is. If our minds are open they can be filled with light.

Whatever our opinions about 2012, we do seem to be riding the crest of exponential change, and those who study this subject see the acceleration as intrinsic to the nature of change itself. Futurist and inventor Ray Kurzweil says, "The whole 20th century, because we've been speeding up, is equivalent to twenty years of progress at today's rate of progress, and we'll make another twenty years of progress at today's rate of progress equal to the whole 20th century in the next fourteen years, and then we'll do it again in seven years. And because of the explosive power of exponential growth, the 21st century will be equivalent to 20,000 years of progress at today's rate of progress, which is a thousand times greater than the 20th century."

Kurzweil also insists "The single most necessary component of any attempt to make predictions about the future is a deeply internalized understanding of the accelerating, exponential rate of change." He popularized the idea of a critical mass of technological changes called a singularity. The specific term "singularity," as a description for a phenomenon of technological acceleration causing an eventual unpredictable outcome in society, was coined by mathematician and physicist Stanislaw Ulam as early as 1958. He wrote of a conversation with John von Neumann concerning the "ever accelerating progress of technology and changes in the mode of human life, which gives the appearance of approaching some essential singularity in the history of the race beyond which human affairs, as we know them, could not continue."

Proponents of the singularity typically state that an "intelligence explosion," where super-intelligences design successive generations of increasingly powerful computing minds, might occur very quickly and might not stop until the cognitive abilities greatly surpass that of any human. The technological singularity is the hypothetical future emergence of greater-than-human super-intelligence through technological means. Since the capabilities of such intelligence would be difficult for an unaided human mind to comprehend, the occurrence of a technological singularity is seen as an intellectual event horizon, beyond which events cannot be predicted or understood. Advocates of the theory expect the singularity to occur sometime in the 21st century--a very Aquarian Age idea.

Whatever happens on December 21, 2012 everything in the Universe is moving in vast orbs of time, and the wheels of astrology allow us to experience some of those nested cycles. If we are paying attention to the current acceleration of change, and the intensifying complexity of information, we will realize that we may indeed be approaching a point of no return, an event horizon, and that evolution takes leaps. Awake and aware, we can poise ourselves to catch the wave, or singularity, and make the quantum jump in consciousness. If something sudden and remarkable does happen on December 21, 2012, I choose to believe it will be cause for a grand celebration.

Atlantis Rising #96 October 2012

CHAPTER 13

THE BIBLE AND ASTROLOGY: WHAT DOES JUDEO-CHRISTIAN TRADITION OWE TO ANCIENT CELESTIAL LORE?

nd there shall be signs in the sun, and in the moon, and in the stars. On the earth, nations will be in anguish and perplexity at the roaring and tossing of the sea."

Jesus, Luke 21:25-26

The Pleiades (Snappygoat.com)

On February 15, 2013 a meteor raced across the skies of central Russia, shattering violently about fifteen miles above the ground, the lowest level ever recorded. The thundering explosion created fireballs and rained down thousands of tons of debris, destroying property and injuring more than a thousand people. The object careened into the atmosphere at about 40,000 mph, detonating with the force of a 500-kiloton bomb. By comparison, the Hiroshima bomb had the force of 15 kilotons. Ironically, the Russian meteor explosion happened on the same day that an asteroid, Near-Earth Object 2012 DA14, passed by Earth. Identified in 2012, many telescopes were trained on its path while no one detected the approach of the meteor, although it's estimated it was one-third the size of the asteroid, and its effect was dramatic.

It is tempting to equate such occurrences with Biblical prophecy such as the verse in Revelation 8:10-11, "And the third angel sounded, and there fell a great star from heaven, burning as if it were a lamp, and it fell upon the third part of the rivers and upon the fountains of waters."

What are we to make of signs in heaven, prophecy, and the role of astrology in the Bible?

Zondervan's *Pictorial Bible Dictionary* states, "There are hundreds of references to stars, sun, moon and planets." A well known verse from Genesis 1:14 proclaims, "And God said, 'Let there be lights in the firmament of the heaven to divide the day from the night; and let them be for signs, and for seasons, and for days, and years.' " Job 38:31-33 is a well known phrase, "Canst thou bind the sweet influences of the Pleiades, or loose the bands of Orion? Canst thou bring forth *Massaroth* (zodiac) in his season or guide Arcturus with his sons? Knowest thou the ordinance of heaven? Canst thou set the dominion thereof in the earth?" In Judges 5:20 we read, "They fought from heaven; the stars in their courses fought against Sisera." Sisera was a Caananite commander who oppressed the Israelites. In Psalm 136: 7-9 the author says, "To him that made the great lights; the sun to rule by day; the moon and stars to rule by night."

The story of the Magi, or wise men, and the star of Bethlehem is a favorite Christmas story that only appears in the book of Matthew(2:2). The Magi ask Herod, "Where is he that is born King of the Jews? We have seen his star in the east, and are come to worship him." And later in Matthew 2:10, "When they saw the star, they rejoiced with exceeding joy." Different authors have tried to identify the star, but it's likely it was symbolic. The *Catholic Encyclopedia* informs us that "Magi is usually translated as 'astrologers' as the magi were thought to be priest-astrologers from Persia. The historian Herodotus (5th century BCE), attests to the astrological mastery of the Persian Magi." Accounts vary as to the number of Magi, but the oldest tradition says there were twelve.

The practices of stargazing and divination were well known and respected in biblical times; divination means, "to be inspired by the divine." There were Roman augurs, Sybiline oracles, the Chinese I-Ching, the Tibetan State oracle, the Oracle of Delphi, and of course Joseph, who interpreted dreams for the Egyptian pharaoh in the Old Testament. Through most of its history, astrology has been considered a scholarly tradition and was accepted in political and academic contexts. Astrology was connected with astronomy, alchemy, meteorology, and medicine. The Chinese, Indians, and Maya developed elaborate systems for predicting terrestrial events from celestial observations. Among Indo-European peoples, astrology has been dated to the third millennium BCE with roots in calendar systems used to predict seasonal shifts and to interpret celestial cycles as signs of divine communication.

Early forms of astrology emerged from Bablylonia, Assyria and Egypt and entered Greece after 323 BCE when Alexander the Great's conquests spread Greek culture throughout the Mesopotamian and Roman world. Egypt has star charts that go as far back as 4,200 BCE. The earliest known evidence of astrology are markings on cave walls and bones, dated to 25,000 years ago, showing lunar cycles. Babylon, or Chaldea in the Hellenistic world, was so identified with astrology that "Chaldean wisdom" became synonymous with divination through the stars and planets. In these cultures astrologers like the Persian Magi were astronomer priests with considerable power.

The Zodiac of twelve constellations is one of the oldest conceptual images and began as a way to mark time. The twelve zodiac constellations are the backdrop for the Sun's apparent path through the band of sky above and below the equator over the course of a year. The zodiac also reflects the twelve months of the year, the four seasons, and the solstices and equinoxes. The term Zodiac, "circle of animals," indicates that constellations were personified as figures or animals. Scholars often conclude that the figures depicted in the constellations suggest what's happening on earth at the time. For example, lambs are born at the time of Aries, and harvest occurs at the time of Virgo, who holds a sheaf of wheat.

Rupert Gleadow, in *The Origin Of The Zodiac,* says the idea of dividing the circle into 360 units originated independently in Babylon, Egypt, and China as an approximation of the number of days in the solar year. Further dividing the year into twelve months is an outgrowth of the lunar cycle as months have always been "moon periods." Albert Churchward, in *The Signs and Symbols of Primordial Man,* states, "The division is in twelve parts: the twelve signs of the Zodiac, twelve tribes of Israel, twelve gates of heaven mentioned in Revelation, and twelve entrances or portals to be passed through in the Great Pyramid, before finally reaching the highest degree, twelve Apostles in the Christian doctrines, and the twelve original and perfect points in Masonry."

Revelation 21:12 says that the new Jerusalem, "had a wall great and high with twelve gates, and at the gates twelve angels, and names written thereon, which are the names of the twelve tribes of the children of Israel." The origin of our twelve birthstones comes from Revelation 21:19-21 and is rooted in the twelve colored stones in the breastplate of the High Priest of ancient Israel as recorded in the Book of Exodus. The breastplate is sometimes called the breastplate of judgment because the *Urim* and *Thummin*, which were used for divination, were placed inside. Although the books of Deuteronomy and Leviticus condemn divination, Exodus 28 gives *Urim* and *Thummin* to the priestly class to "divine the will of Yahweh."

In the first book of Ezekiel (1:10) he has a vision and describes four living creatures above the wheels of the chariot he sees, "the four had the face of a man and the face of a lion on the right side: and the four had the face of an ox on the left side, the four also had the face of an eagle." That's a confusing desciption to be sure, but these symbols can be compared to the four fixed signs of the astrology: Leo the lion, Aquarius the man with a water pitcher; the Calf is Taurus the Bull, and the Eagle is one of the symbols of Scorpio.

There are many references to the idea of an "age" in the Bible that seem related to astrology. For example, In Matthew 28:20 Jesus tells his disciples, "I will be with you even to the end of the world." The Greek word *aeon* is translated in the King James Version as "world," but the actual meaning of the word is "age." The period of roughly 2,160 years required for the precession of the Sun through one zodiacal constellations is called an age and was named for the constellation in which the Sun rose as it crossed the equator at the vernal equinox. Approximately six thousand years ago was the Age of Taurus the Bull, the Age of Aries the Ram followed, and then the Age of Pisces, the Fishes, about two thousand years ago. We are near the end of that aeon, and the Age of Aquarius the Water Bearer will come next.

During these ages religious icons took the form of the appropriate celestial symbol. For example, the Bull of Heaven and Golden calf in the Age of Taurus, the Passover lamb and the ram-headed god of Egypt, Amen-Ra, in the Age of Aries. In the earlier Age of Gemini, the Twins there are examples, like Isis and Osiris, of deities who are both twins and siblings. In the Age of Pisces, Jesus the Lamb of God became the Fisher of Men as he was born at the juncture of two ages. The sign of the fish was one of the earliest symbols of Christianity. Jesus' early disciples were fishermen, he fed the multitude with two small fishes, and Jesus ate a baked fish after his resurrection (Luke 24:42).

When Jesus' disciples asked him where the next Passover would be (Luke 22:10), he replied, "A man will meet you carrying an earthen pitcher of water; follow him into the house where he goes in." This has been interpreted as the natural sequence of precession where Aquarius, the Water Bearer will follow Pisces, the Fishes. Understood in this way, Jesus' reign as the "Son of God" for an age will end when the Age of Aquarius begins.

As early Christianity became the Church of Rome, in 321 CE the emperor Constantine issued an edict that threatened Chaldeans (astrologers), Magi, and their followers with death. Not surprisingly, astrology went underground for a time. Constantine then convened the famous Council of Nicea in 325 CE in what is now Turkey as part of his plan to make Christianity the official religion of the Roman Empire. Among the subjects debated and decided was the divinity of Jesus, making him a "Son of God," which put him on a par with Pagan gods and made Christianity more attractive to converts.

Astrology did not remain hidden after Constantine. Ptolemy's work *Tetrabiblos,* written in the second century, became the basis of Western astrological tradition. The *Catholic Encyclopedia* reports that the emperors Charles IV and V and Popes Sixtus IV, Julius II, Leo X and Paul III followed astrology. In fact, papal and imperial court ambassadors were not received until the court astrologer had been consulted. Lucas Gauricus, who published a number of treatises, was the court astrologer of Popes Leo X and Clement VII. Men of the Renaissance, including Nicholas Copernicus, who observed that the

Earth orbited the Sun, asserted that astronomical research was valuable only to the degree that it advanced the discipline of astrology.

The powerful Medici family of Florence produced four popes. Catherine de Medici, who married a French king and wielded enormous power as regent for her son Charles IX, popularized astrology in France. She built an observatory near Paris, and her court astrologer was none other than the celebrated Michel de Notre dame, Nostradamus. He published his work on astrology in 1555, and it is still considered authoritative.

In Hebrew, astrology was called *hokmat ha-nissayon*, "the wisdom of prognostication," in distinction to *hokmat ha-hizzayon*, the wisdom of star-seeing, or astronomy. The Jewish Talmud identified the twelve zodiac constellations with the twelve months of the Hebrew calendar, and astrology became predominant in some books of Kabbalah. Although on the surface Jewish tradition discredits astrology, the zodiac has appeared as a central motif in at least six synagogues dating to early centuries after the destruction of the temple. That has led scholars to imagine that the Jerusalem temple was decorated in a similar way where the temple represented the cosmos. This stellar theme was discussed by the historians Josephus and Philo of Alexandria, and the idea is being confirmed by new discoveries in the field of biblical archeology.

At the beginning of the 17th century, great scientists like Tycho Brahe, Galileo Galilei, Johannes Kepler and Pierre Gassendi, who are now remembered for their roles in the development of modern physics and astronomy, all held astrology in high esteem. Astrologer William Lilly's comprehensive book, entitled *Christian Astrology*, was published in 1647 in three separate volumes. It is considered one of the classic texts of traditional astrology from the Middle Ages and has never gone out of print.

By the end of the 17th century, new scientific concepts in astronomy and physics, such as heliocentrism and Newtonian mechanics, caused a growing division between the emerging science of astronomy and its mother discipline astrology. Likewise, the divide between science and religion continued to widen. In our time psychoanalysts like Carl Jung caused a popular revival of astrology with a more psychological approach.

Astrology, the Church, and the Bible have a relationship that has shifted over centuries. Likewise, science and religion often seem at odds as we witness the ongoing debate over evolution and creationism. The struggle between facts and faith, measure and meaning continues to this day. One aspect of the conflict between the Bible and astrology is the literal interpretation of biblical texts. There is also a religious premise of an external creator, who exists apart from creation and must be worshipped with priests acting as intermediaries. Ironically, early followers of Jesus, whom we now call Gnostics, believed that every person had both the right and responsibility to develop their own relationship with the divine, without intermediaries.

Other belief systems, like Buddhism, Hinduism and certain indigenous traditions, do not see creation as existing apart from a creator. Rather, the universe itself is seen as a divine being, and therefore, reverence for its cycles and expressions is honoring of the sacred whole. This view perceives that every phase and function of the Universal Body has a correspondence in humans—as above, so below. To the ancients, the study of the stars was a sacred science, for they saw in the movements of the celestial bodies the ever-present activity of the Infinite Parent. In my research, I actually didn't find negative comments in the Bible about astrology itself. Rather, the fault was with practitioners who might be viewed as untrustworthy. That charge could be leveled at any occupation, as sadly there are always people who will misuse their knowledge. To quote Cassius in Shakespeare's *Julius Caesar*, "The fault dear Brutus, is not in our stars, but in ourselves . . ."

Astrology, not unlike the Bible, is an aspect of perennial wisdom that seems to wax and wane in widespread favor over periods of history. This might have been forseen by astrology. After all, if there had never been any demonstrated effective applications, astrology would not have developed in the first place, let alone persisted and thrived for six thousand years, inspiring many great minds. For its congregations, tt seems that the Church may have replaced astrologers with priests, and now the Church, in the name of God, holds the power to direct these believers. Either way, if the result uplifts the spirit and provides wise counsel, the changing roles will serve the greater good.

Atlantis Rising #99 April 2013

CHAPTER 14

TWELVE GATES OF HEAVEN

 nd the twelve gates of heaven were adorned with twelve pearls, one for each gate."

The Book of Revelation 21:21

Breastplate of the High Priest of Israel (author Dr. Avishai Teicher Pikiwiki Israel CC BY 2.5)

Whether or not someone gives credence to astrology, the idea that each month of the year has a "birth stone," a special gem related to it, is a familiar notion, and wearing an item of jewelry containing a birth stone is commonplace. The idea of wearing birth stones as jewelry originated in Poland in the eighteenth century, but the origin of the practice is rooted in more ancient traditions.

The architecture of the "holy Jerusalem, descending out of heaven from God" (Rev 21:10), was magnificently bejeweled and corresponded to the twelve tribes of the children of Israel. "The city had a wall great and high, and had twelve gates, and at the gates twelve angels, with names inscribed thereon, which are the names of the twelve tribes of the children of Israel. On the east were three gates, on the north three gates, on the south three gates, and on the west three gates. And the wall of the city had twelve foundations, and on them the twelve names of the twelve apostles of the Lamb . . . and the foundations of the wall of the city were adorned with all kinds of precious stones . . . and the twelve gates were adorned with twelve pearls, one for each of the gates, and each gate was made of a single pearl; and the great street of the city was of pure gold, as it were transparent glass." (portions of Revelation 21:12-21)

In *The Curious Lore of Precious Stones*, George Frederick Kunz says, "It is easy to trace in this description the substitution of the twelve apostles for the twelve tribes in connection with the precious stone enumerations. And we also have the twelve angels, associated at a later date with the months and the signs of the zodiac."

A vision of Saint Peter, guarding the entrance to the Pearly Gates of heaven, is familiar iconography. Saint Peter was seen as the leader of the twelve apostles and was therefore awarded the first position as Gatekeeper of Heaven. Likewise, the first birth stone (Jasper), was assigned to Saint Peter, and to the month of March, as spring equinox is the symbolic beginning of the year. Perhaps the original practice dated back four thousand years ago when the year began at the spring equinox when the first sign Aires, the Ram rose before the equinox sun.

Kunz also says, "The foundation stones were inscribed with the names of the apostles (and therefore twelve tribes and zodiac signs) is expressly stated (Rev 21:14), but it was not until the eighth or ninth century that the commentators on Revelation busied themselves with finding analogies between these stones and the apostles. At the outset, the symbolism of the stones was looked upon from a purely religious standpoint." One of the earliest writers to discuss these correspondences was Andreas, bishop of Caesara. "The jasper, which like the emerald is of a greenish hue, probably signifies St. Peter, chief of the apostles . . . as the sapphire is likened to the heavens, I conceive it to mean St. Paul, since he was caught up to the third heaven, where his soul was firmly fixed," and so on . . .

When the Jews fled Egyptian captivity during Pharaonic times, among the items they were instructed to craft, or take with them, was a sacred garment which later became a holy relic. "And you shall make the breastplate of judgment with the work of a craftsman . . . and you shall set in it setting stones, four rows of stones; the first row shall be a sardius (red jasper), a topaz, and an emerald. . . " Exodus (28:15-19)

Called the breastplate of the High Priest, or the breastplate of judgment, this sacred vestment of twelve stones was said to confer the power of God upon the Old Testament patriarch, Aaron. Several Old Testament stories describe how the stones on the breastplate of judgment turned cloudy or murky when someone did not tell the truth. The power to discern truth from falsehood was somehow bestowed on the priest by the behavior of the stones themselves.

As the twelve tribes wandered in the desert, each tribe carried a standard and displayed it as a flag or insignia while camping in the wilderness. The colors of the flags, and each tribe's symbols, were based on gem colors from the High Priest's breastplate.

We are likewise told that the stones themselves carried the power of the twelve tribes, "And the stones shall be engraved with the names of the sons of Israel, twelve, according to their names, like the engravings of a signet; every one shall be engraved with his name according to the number of the twelve tribes." (Exodus 28:21). The potency of these tribal stones has survived ancient Egypt and the Hebrew Exodus, still thriving today as birth stones, gemstones of the month.

To the ancients power was contained in the stone's color as well as the geometry of the crystal. Minerals are formed in the earth through the forces of fire or water, ancient elements of alchemy. Igneous rocks are formed through dramatic fiery events while sedimentary minerals accumulate over time through water's influence. Metamorphic stones form through a combination of influences.

Crystals grow in accordance with mathematical law, according to principles of what is sometimes called Sacred Geometry. The external geometric form of a crystal is the outward, visible expression of the mineral's internal atomic structure. This matrix is at the heart of any crystal and also determines other characteristics such as hardness, fracture, and cleavage and its relation to every specimen of the same mineral. Because crystals hold a numeric frequency of shape and form their atoms vibrate in accordance with the characteristic and significance of that number.

In earlier times the power of the stones were believed to embody certain qualities or an archetypal energy that was used to heal an ailment or illness, strengthen a weakness, or perhaps to counterbalance an excess. The belief that gems and stones have special qualities, relating to the time of year and perhaps also containing a special virtue of talismanic power, can be historically traced to the writings of Josephus, in the first century of the Current Era (AD), and to Saint Jerome in the early fifth century. In *The Curious Lore of Precious Stones,* George Frederick Kunz informs us that both Josephus and St. Jerome assert the connection between the twelve stones of the High Priest's breastplate, the twelve months of the year, and the twelve zodiacal signs.

The order of the foundation stones in Revelation corresponds with the tribes and signs, this determined subsequent gems of the months. In the beginning, the "stone of the month" was worn by everyone during the period that particular "tribe" or sign was thought to have the most efficacy. Later when the zodiacal signs were engraved on gems to endow them with special virtue, the Hebrew letters designating the sign (or at least the initial character), were often cut upon the gem. Engraving a sacred letter upon a gem, and wearing the stone with intention, imbued the object with talismanic potency.

Today, the signs don't move in concert with the months of the Gregorian calendar, so while modern birth stones are assigned to the calendar month, the signs range from roughly the twenty-first of one month to the twenty-first of the next. Over time, substitutions and changes have been made in the order to arrive at the familiar list of birth stones in use today. However, it is interesting to note that when changes to the calendar are accounted for, the modern list of gems and months still holds true for the most part to the original foundation stones from Revelation.

A diagram of the new Jerusalem from the Book of Revelation bears striking resemblance to an astrology chart with its twelve divisions or "houses" which outline the signs and contain the wandering planets. The twelve jeweled gates of heaven can also be seen as portions of the ecliptic occupied by the archetypal twelve signs, stages of the hero's journey.

The architecture and ancient power of twelve shown by gates, angels, apostles and zodiac signs also relates to the mystery of our spiritual anatomy, the heavenly city within. In Qabalah the Tree of Life exists in four worlds simultaneously and symbolism is multi-layered. In Qabalistic lore, Jerusalem, "Bride of the Lamb" is also a metaphor for the sacred anatomy of the spiritualized human.

To the initiate, the sacred geometry encoded in these attributions is a reflection of the accomplishment of what is termed the Great Work, the successful transmutation of lead into gold and the attainment of mastery. When the "Great Work" is accomplished, the new city is built and the Bridegroom, literally the Anointed One, may enter and reside. From a three-dimensional perspective, perhaps the heavenly Jerusalem is a symbolic dodecahedron - a solid figure with twelve faces - meant to be built from within.

In a modern sense, the twelve jeweled gates of heaven are also the months of the year, marking the apparent passage of the Sun through the sky (ecliptic) on its annual journey. By converting the Biblical Foundation Stones to monthly birthstones we can partake in this passage more consciously, honoring ancient wisdom.

In the New Testament gospel of Luke, a much-quoted passage appears, "For the Kingdom of God is within you." (Luke 17:21). Perhaps if we wear a birth stone, or zodiacal stone of the month with intention, we can invoke the archetypal energy of the angels, setting the foundation stones for the inner temple.

Atlantis Rising #43 December 2003

CHAPTER 15

PLANETARY HARMONICS: THE MUSIC OF THE SPHERES

"Venus draws a pentagram around the Earth every eight years. The Moon squares the circle. Everything in the heavens moves around everything else, dancing to the Music of the Spheres."

John Martineau, *A Little Book Of Coincidence*

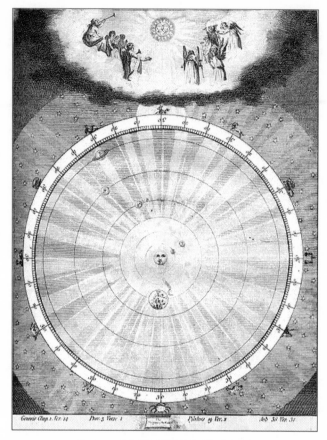

Harmony of the World 1806 (public domain)

Musica Universalis, or the "Music of the Spheres," is an ancient
philosophical concept that sees the proportions of the movements of
celestial bodies--Sun, Moon and planets--as a form of *musica,* the
Medieval Latin name for music. This music is not audible but is
understood as a mathematical concept. The Greek philosopher
Pythagoras is usually credited with this idea, which stemmed from his
mystical and mathematical philosophy and its associated system of
numerology. The discovery of the geometric relationship between
mathematics and music within the Classical Period is also attributed to
him. Pythagoreans believed this relationship gave music powers of
healing as it could "harmonize" the out-of-balance body.

There is a legend that Pythagoras could hear the Music of the Spheres, enabling him to discover that consonant musical intervals can be expressed in simple ratios of small integers. In an effort to win their confidence, Pythagoras told Egyptian priests that the god Thoth gave him the ability to hear this "music." He believed that only Egyptians of the right bloodline, passing successful initiations, could enter the temples and learn the mysteries set in place by divine beings at the beginning of time. Plato and others transferred Pythagoras' concepts into structural models of the universe assigning the Platonic solids to the planets and alchemical elements: Earth-tetrahedron, Water-cube, Air-Octahedron, Fire-dodecahedron, and Quintessence-icosahedron. The spheres were thought to relate to whole-number ratios of pure musical intervals, creating harmonies.

Johannes Kepler used this concept in his *Harmonice Mundi, the Harmony of the Worlds,* in 1619. Kepler was convinced "that geometrical things have provided the Creator with the model for decorating the whole world." He attempted to explain the proportions of the natural world, particularly astronomical and astrological aspects, in terms of music. The central set of "harmonies" was the *musica universalis*. Kepler noticed that the ratios between planets' extreme angular velocities were all harmonic intervals, and he attempted to precisely calculate these "world harmonies." He said, "The heavenly motions...are nothing but a continuous song for several voices, perceived not with the ear but with the intellect, a figured music, which sets landmarks in the immeasurable flow of time."

Pythagoras identified that the pitch of a musical note is in proportion to the length of the string that produces it, and that intervals between harmonious sound frequencies form numerical ratios. Later, Plato said astronomy and music were twin studies of sensual recognition— astronomy for the eyes and music for the ears—both requiring knowledge of numerical proportions. In antiquity the seven notes of the octave, in which the eighth note is a doubling of the vibration of the first, were assigned to the seven visible and moving heavenly bodies: Moon, A, Mercury, G, Venus, F, Sun E, Mars, D, Jupiter "Middle C", and Saturn B. There are five black notes on the piano keyboard between middle C and the C above it. If we add those pitches, the sharps and flats, to the seven white notes already mentioned, we have twelve pitches (the Chromatic scale) that are the same as the number of signs in the zodiac, showing the relationship between the two systems.

One axiom upon which the Hermetic principles of astrology are based comes from *The Kybalion*. This is the Law of Vibration, which says, "Nothing rests; everything moves; everything vibrates." Hermetic teachings state that not only is all matter vibrating, but our emotions are also a manifestation of vibration. Therefore, emotions and desires are accompanied by vibratory rates, which may be lowered or raised at will by adepts.

Modern science suggests that ordinary people can accomplish the same thing. According to research by University of Missouri scientists published in *The Journal of Positive Psychology*, people can successfully improve their moods and boost their overall happiness in just two weeks, simply by listening with intention to specific mood-boosting music. Researchers at McGill University in Montreal say the response to music comes from the chemical dopamine. When we listen to a rhythm, our heartbeat actually synchs with it. A slow heartbeat with a strong diastolic pressure tells our brain that something sad or depressing is occurring. Fast beating is related to excitement, and a dreamy rhythm with occasional upbeats can signify love or joy. Hitler used martial music to stir aggression. Churches use hymns to inspire and comfort, while rock music energizes and activates people in various ways. It's likely that types of music correspond to planets and signs; marches to Mars and Aries, waltzes to Venus and Libra, for example.

Tones are equally as important as rhythm. A major key sends a cheerful communication to the brain, while minor keys mirror sadness. Research shows that this has a powerful effect on the brain, directing our psyches to resonate with the type of music and to actually feel what's being communicated, thereby altering our emotional state.

When a note is played on any instrument, the number of vibrations per second determines the pitch. If the octave to any note is played or sung, it has twice the number of vibrations per second. Therefore, the ratio between notes is 2 to 1 (or 2:1). In an intriguing parallel a formula stated in the *Tao-te ching* says, "One has produced two, two has produced three, and three has produced all the numbers by its cyclic repetitions."

As for the planets, Mercury is gravitationally locked and rotates in a way that is unique in the Solar System. Astronomers once thought Mercury always kept the same side towards the Sun, like the Moon, meaning one rotation on its axis was the same as its orbital period, but this is not true. As seen relative to the fixed stars, Mercury rotates on its axis exactly three times for every two revolutions around the Sun. As seen from the Sun, in a frame of reference that rotates with the orbital motion, Mercury appears to rotate only once every two Mercurian years--a 2:1 ratio.

There is also an inherent geometry between Mercury and Venus, the first and second planets from the Sun. If the three points of Mercury's "sunrise" are plotted on a circle they form an equilateral triangle. If circles are drawn around the center points that are large enough to touch each other's circumferences, the orbit of Venus exactly encloses the three circles.

In Atlantis Rising #69 (Chapter 13 in Volume Two of these anthologies) I wrote about the amazing geometry of Venus's orbit. From Earth's point of view Venus traces a perfect five-pointed star over a period of eight years. Each time Earth and Venus "kiss," at the time of Venus's inferior conjunction, or when Venus is in alignment with the Sun and closest to Earth, one point of the star is formed. The conjunctions of Jupiter and Saturn form an equilateral triangle every twenty years. The oppositions likewise form another equilateral triangle, so a six-pointed star is formed over a period of about 120 years. The orbits of all the planets have amazing geometric relationships in an exquisite synchrony of celestial mechanics.

Ernst Chladni was a German physicist and musician. Chladni's technique, first published in 1787 in his book, *Discoveries in the Theory of Sound*, consisted of drawing a bow over a piece of metal whose surface was lightly covered with sand. The plate was bowed until it reached resonance, and the sand formed a pattern showing the nodal regions. The results became known as Chladni Figures.

Two centuries later, Hans Jenny, a Swiss doctor, artist, and researcher, published the bilingual book, *The Structure and Dynamics of Waves and Vibrations*. Jenny, like Chladni, showed what happens when materials like sand, spores, iron filings, water, and viscous substances are placed on vibrating metal plates and membranes. Shapes and patterns appear that vary from nearly perfectly ordered and stationary to those that are turbulent, organic, and in constant motion. Jenny called this new area of research Cymatics, from the Greek *kyma*, which means wave. The mystery of "solid matter" appears to be contained in sound and vibration.

A modern composer, Greg Fox, wrote *Carmen of the Spheres*, a composition that attempted to literally "hear" the planets as they orbit the Sun. His approach was to halve the planetary orbital period until he found the "pitch" of a planet orbiting the Sun. He created his music by raising that pitch 36 to 40 octaves.

Jim Bumgardner, a Los Angeles software engineer specializing in visualizations, created *The Wheel Of Stars*, a visualizer that utilizes data from the Hipparcos mission. Hipparcos was a satellite launched by the European Space Agency in 1989 that accurately measured over a hundred thousand stars. Bumgardner downloaded data that contains position, parallax, magnitude, and color information, among other things. The program puts the stars to an ethereal music of their own making, creating something magical.

A number of active spacecraft, including the "planet hunter" Kepler Space Telescope, use asteroseismology, which is the science that studies the internal structure of pulsating stars by interpreting their frequency spectra. Different oscillation modes penetrate to different depths inside the star. This technique turns tiny variations in stars' light into sounds, measuring minuscule variations in a star's brightness that occurs as sound waves bounce inside the star. Using resonances, a picture is created of what the inside of a star looks like. The Kepler telescope studied thousands of stars in its field in this manner.

In *A Little Book Of Coincidence* John Martineau says, "The planets have long been suspected of hiding secret relationships. In antiquity students of such things pondered the Music of the Spheres, the heavenly bodies singing subtle and perfect harmonies to the adept." Martineau asks if it is all just a coincidence? If not, what are we to make of these exquisite harmonies and geometric proportions?

In 1968, Russian scientist A.M. Molchanov's research for the Institute of Applied Mathematics in Moscow resulted in a paper where he argued that the entire Solar System is a tuned quantum resonant structure, with Jupiter, largest of the planets, as the orchestra conductor. He wrote, "oscillating systems that have attained evolutionary maturity are inevitably resonant, and their structure is given by sets of integers, just as in quantum systems." He also remarked "Even if every one of the billions of stars in our galaxy had a planetary system, it would not be able by chance to produce even one resonant system such as our Solar System."

Plato said, "God ever geometrizes," and like mathematics, music was discovered, not invented. It does seem as though harmony and proportion are the foundation of Creation. Music can be simple or complex, ranging from a solo voice to a symphony orchestra. Melody involves the consecutive playing or singing of notes, while harmony involves the simultaneous playing of notes like in a chord or multi-part singing. Duration, which is the length of time a note is played or sung, creates rhythm, or "beats" per measure. Different instruments playing different rhythms can create a multi-faceted musical experience. This might be compared to the durations of the planets' orbits as well as their differing axial rotation periods, which through their mathematical relationships does create a sort of symphony that the ancients perceived and we are beginning to measure.

If the planets geometric relationships and resonances create, or result in, vibrations or frequencies, an astrologer who is equipped with knowledge of planetary harmonics, could identify what was "out of tune," or imbalanced, in a birth chart. The ancient art of musical healing might then be used to harmonize the vibrations. What might the implications be for harmonizing the energies of an individual or even the Earth itself?

Atlantis Rising #114 October 2014

CHAPTER 16
ASTROLOGY & ALCHEMY

"Thou shalt separate the earth from the fire, the subtle from the gross, suavely and with great ingenuity."

Hermes Trismegistus, *The Emerald Tablets of Thoth*

William Fettes Douglas The Alchemist (SnappyGoat)

According to legend, Alexander the Great found the Emerald Tablets
when he discovered the tomb of Hermes/Thoth. The words on the
magical tablet had been etched into green stone and were clasped
between the hands of the entombed master magician. Most scholars
believe the story to be myth, but the tale speaks to the archaic origins
of what is commonly associated with alchemical laboratories and
cryptic treatises in Medieval Europe. Although attributed to the
legendary Hermes Trismegistus, the "Thrice Great," the Emerald
Tablet is likely a more modern work that probably originated in Greek
Alexandria.

To trace the origins of alchemy we must follow a trail that has gone
cold in the outer world, but still runs pure and true as an ancient

underground stream. The waters of this stream originate at least five millennia past in the head waters of the mother cultures of Earth, including China, India, and Egypt, flowing into the present as tributaries of the Perennial Philosopy.

The word Egypt derives from the Greek *Aigyptos,* which is how the Greeks rendered Het-Ka-Ptah, the temple of Ptah at Memphis. But Khem, or Khemit, was what Pharonic Egypt called their own country, and they carved the names as heiroglyphs into temple walls. These heiroglyphs are written as K-M-T and written in English as Khemit, (sometimes Khem), and translated as "Black Land." There is a graphic picture of these heiroglyphs in Stephen Mehler's book, *The Land of Osiris* (Fig 10, pg 41).

Later, invading Arabs added the Arabic article "Al" which means "the," resulting in Al Khem. So the origin of the word alchemy was rooted in the hieroglyphic and symbolic name of the ancient land. Alchemy has come down to us through time as the body of hidden wisdom and spiritual transformation that was once practiced in the temples of Khemit.

The glyphs are still visible on temple walls and are comprised of three ideograms: a bent knee, meaning "slope," which we pronounce like the letter K. Hieroglyphics can be interpreted on several levels, and this glyph carries the deeper significance of "high" or "exalted." The second image is an owl, with the suggestion of keen sight in the darkness. This glyph is pronounced like the letter M.

The third component is a half-circle, described as a loaf of bread, which is like the letter T. The loaf glyph is a feminine suffix, indicating the "gender" of the word. This last glyph carries the symbolism of the pregnant, primordial mound out of which all was born as well as the leavening process of baking bread. The composite hieroglyph usually contains an equal-armed crossed at the end which designates a dwelling place. It is also interesting that Author Moira Timms has noted that the Hebrew word for the Pleiades in the Bible (Job 39:31), is spelled KMH, spelled Kimah in English.

Some scholars believe the name represented the dark, alluvial soil that bordered the Nile. Symbolically blackness cloaks and conceals, and the path of spiritual mastery has ever been about hiding and revealing. In alchemical language, the first phase of transformation is called *Nigredo*, "black earth," and is symbolized by a black raven. The majestic temples of the Black Land stood along the rich banks of the river Nile, and great secrets were taught inside these walls.

The hidden wisdom that has flowed faithfully in the underground steam is often called the Hermetic Tradition because the Egyptian god of this province was Thoth, Hermes to the Greeks, and Mercury to the Romans. Thoth-Hermes was god of wisdom and consciousness and also measurement and choice. Thoth was the guardian of wisdom itself, but Isis was revered as queen of magic. Magic is the application of knowledge and principles to achieve specific results. Egypt was a land of magic and goddess Isis ruled supreme in this art, bringing her dead husband Osiris back to life long enough to conceive their divine son Horus.

Understood alchemically, the Egyptian myth of Isis, Osiris, and Horus tells the perennial story of spiritual transformation and immortality, incorporating the recurring themes of alchemical and mythical literature. The journey of transformation always includes death and rebirth, descent and return from the underworld, struggle with a monstrous adversary (serpent, dragon, etc.), quest for a priceless treasure, sacred marriage, and the birth of a divine child. Joseph Campbell, the great scholar of myth, observed that spirituality is like the flowering or fulfillment of human endeavor rather than a supernatural virtue artificially imposed upon us. We are meant to invoke and participate in this flowering, cultivating the plant in a crucible.

Some of the stupendous claims of Medieval alchemists, which include transmutation of metals, prolonging life and the miraculous cure of diseases, are true as genuine alchemists who have accomplished the Great Work do possess extraordinary power over physical conditions. And yet this picture is misleading and incomplete for the Great Work must first be performed on the alchemist. The athanor, the alchemist's furnace, is the human organism, and the transformation that occurs in this furnace is said to take place through the "essence of fire."

Likewise, the Philosopher's Stone, which is the symbol for what is accomplished by the Great Work, is the perfected human personality and not a substance produced in a chemical laboratory. However, by means of this transformed personality, sometimes called the Stone of the Wise, works of power are achieved as the true alchemical adept commands the forces of nature.

There are actually three kinds of alchemists. First there are authentic magicians who have accomplished the Magnum Opus or Great Work. Second, are those who have read the works of authentic alchemists and attempt to perform chemical experiments, mistaking metaphor for meaning. In the second category are students of genuine alchemists who may have been given a quantity of transmuting agent but are not able to produce this on their own. It is likely that those in this category were the ones who were revered, feared, and tortured for their efforts at turning lead into gold. Lastly are the charlatans, motivated only by greed, who attempt to fool or impress people.

Numerous alchemical treatises survive. Some have been written by "those who know," while others are clouded attempts to understand the veiled words. The cryptic and confusing language of alchemy is written in code, intending to conceal meaning from the "profane" or truly dangerous and reveal meaning to true seekers or those who already know. For the sincere student the exercise of reflecting on the strange language stretches the mind and increases receptivity to intuition. Slowly, significance dawns.

Alchemy is inseparable from both astrology and magic when understood as a process of personal transformation. Astrology's relationship to alchemy and spiritual growth is both diagnostic and magical. The component symbols of astrology correlate with the symbols of alchemy in the west and Yoga in the east, and astrology is one means of working consciously with our own transformation.

Alchemy accelerates the process of spiritual growth, forcing the process like a hothouse plant. True alchemy is not about turning physical lead into gold. Likewise true astrology is not about attaining fame, riches, or romance. Both relate to a spiritual discipline in which the transformation is inner and the gold is the crown of the spiritual adept.

The wisdom of the East remains today in the discipline of Yoga, and the tenets of Yoga are parallel to the principles of alchemy and astrology. First there is one, all-encompassing energy that pervades existence. This energy is seen to manifest as three qualities that describe how energy moves in form. These qualities are Sulfur, Mercury, and Salt in alchemy; Rajas, Sattva, and Tamas in Yoga; and Cardinal, Mutable, and Fixed in the language of astrology. In terms of human personality these qualities manifest as desire, intelligence, and form.

The one energy is also described as having five modes of expression. In alchemy and astrology these are the four elements Fire, Earth, Air, and Water and the mysterious fifth element called Ether, Quintessence, or Akasha in Yoga philosophy. The elements reveal how condensed in matter the energy has become from the relatively free state of fire to the fixed and grounded state of solid matter. In Yoga the same principles are described as Tattvas, and these symbols are expressed in terms of geometry.

Next are the seven metals or "interior stars of alchemy," which relate to the physical planets known to the ancients and to the seven chakras of Yoga philosophy. The interior "planets" act like transformers. Saturn correlates with the alchemical metal lead, Mars with the metal iron, and Jupiter corresponds with alchemical tin. The metal of the planet Venus is copper, the Moon is silver, and Mercury corresponds with the metal Mercury, often called Quicksilver.

The Sun is alchemical gold and corresponds to the heart chakra. Considering the stated goal of the alchemist, turning lead into gold, reflecting on this correlation can bring insight. According to the ancient Egyptians the seat of true wisdom and the principle of Ma'at, right relationship to all things, resided in the heart. The heart was weighed against Ma'at's feather of truth after death. The fate of the soul depended upon what hung in the balance.

Astrologically there are twelve signs of the zodiac, and there are said to be twelve stages in the process of alchemical transmutation, beginning with "calcination," which corresponds to the first and fiery sign of Aries. Each stage of the alchemical process can be understood as a phase on the path of the zodiac wheel.

To the true alchemist the chemical vessel known as the retort was like a mirror for the inner transformations occurring within. If each stage corresponds to both a chemical substance and a zodiac sign the alchemist knows and can interpret the battleground of inner change required. For example, the eighth stage called Putrefaction, is said to correspond to Scorpio and to Sodium Chloride. Understood correctly each outer chemical experiment reflected the transformation occurring within the consciousness of the experimenter.

An occult aphorism states, "Equilibrium is the basis of the Great Work." Bringing balance and harmony to our nature is key to realizing alchemical gold. Astrology can be practiced as alchemical magic because a deep understanding of the birth chart reveals strengths, weaknesses, and karmic patterns. Learning to work with planetary energies as real frequencies can increase inherent strengths and talents, balance difficult areas, and develop traits which are missing.

Observing the planets ongoing motions (transits and progressions) can further provide a sort of "weather forecast," which shows the likelihood that certain "experiments" will succeed or fail, according to timing and conditions. Learning to temper these influences within the crucible of the personality is the real purpose of astrology and the ultimate golden fruit of alchemy.

Atlantis Rising #50 February 2005

CHAPTER 17

ECLIPSES — PROMISE OR PERIL?

"The wise man looks not at the finger, but rather at the Moon to which it points."

John Milton, *Paradise Lost*

Solar Eclipse with flare (1115920 snappygoat.com)

On December 4, 2002, at the New Moon, a total eclipse of the Sun will occur. Totality of the solar eclipse will be visible in Africa, except the northern portion, occurring at 7 AM GMT (Greenwich Mean Time).

Eclipses have fascinated and frightened humanity since ancient times. Astronomer priests of antiquity tracked these dramatic sky events, searching for meaning and gleaning portents. Ancient history tells how eclipses ended battles and signified the birth of kings or saviors. Historical records of eclipses date to around 800 BCE (Before Current Era). A large stone from Nineveh is displayed in the British Museum which enumerates a lineage of kings and the eclipses which occurred during their reigns.

Although the Sun is nearly four hundred times the size of the Moon it is almost that many times as far from Earth, so from our viewing perspective the Sun and Moon appear to be the same size. The Earth and Moon are tilted on their axes, so eclipses happen when the horizontal alignment of Sun, Moon and Earth is exact enough to cast a shadow on the Sun or Moon.

There are two kinds of eclipses, solar (eclipse of the Sun), and lunar (eclipse of the Moon), and they range from partial to total. During a solar eclipse a portion, or the complete solar orb as viewed from Earth, is temporarily blacked out. Because of the dramatic size difference of the Sun, Moon, and Earth our perception of a solar eclipse is based on our location on earth. Due to shifting orientation, a total eclipse of the Sun may be visible only once in three hundred years from the same place on Earth.

Because the Moon's orbit is more elliptical than circular, when the Moon is farther away its distance prevents it from completely eclipsing the sun. An annular eclipse of the Sun occurs when the Moon's shadow does not quite cover the entire solar disc. During an annular eclipse a halo of sunlight surrounds the darkened Moon. Annular eclipses occur about as often as total solar eclipses, and each year one annular and one solar eclipse usually happens somewhere on Earth.

The phase of the Moon called the New Moon cannot be seen from Earth because the Moon is between the Earth and Sun and the lighted side of the Moon is pointed away from us. The New Moon rises and sets with the Sun because from our perspective they occupy the same place in the sky. During a solar eclipse, the darkness that temporarily conceals the light of the Sun is the Moon, passing between the Earth and Sun. The Moon creates a shadow that falls on Earth, and we experience this as an eclipse of the Sun. A solar eclipse is only visible in the daytime (when we see the Sun), and can occur only when the Sun and Moon appear to be in the same place in the sky, or in conjunction.

The Moon's shadow has two parts. The Penumbra is a faint outer shadow. Partial eclipses are seen within this shadow. The Umbra is the dark inner shadow and total eclipses of the Sun are seen inside this shadow. The track of the Moon's shadow across Earth's surface is called the Path of Totality and defines the parameters where a total eclipse can be seen.

When the Moon is on the opposite side of the sky from the Sun, with the Earth in between, the Moon is said to be Full, or opposed to the Sun. The Full Moon fully reflects the Sun's light and is a brilliant, silvery orb in the night sky. The Full Moon rises in the east at sunset, is visible all night long, and sets in the west before sunrise. A lunar eclipse, or eclipse of the Moon, can occur only at a Full Moon and is visible only at night. When the Sun, Earth, and Moon are aligned in space in a straight line, with the Earth in the middle, sunlight traveling toward the surface of the Moon is blocked. During a Lunar eclipse the black circle which moves across the surface of the Moon is actually Earth's shadow, being cast upon the Moon.

Unlike a solar eclipse, everyone on the night side of the Earth can see an eclipse of the Moon because Earth's shadow is so much larger than the shadow of the Moon. During a partial Lunar eclipse, only a portion of the Moon passes through the Earth's umbral shadow. During a total lunar eclipse the Earth blocks all direct sunlight from the Moon as the entire Moon moves through the umbral shadow of the Earth. As the Moon is eclipsed it appears a coppery-red color, and during a total lunar eclipse the Moon displays a vibrant range of colors during totality.

Because of the alignment of Sun, Moon, and Earth, eclipses are new or full moons with extraordinary alignment or focus. Therefore, extraordinary insight is available. Eclipses can also be viewed as keys to the lunar cycle of the year. It's possible to grasp the archetypal and symbolic energies of the Sun, Moon, Earth alignment, sustaining focus for spiritual work for the whole year.

Eclipses of the Sun (New Moons) represent vision into the nature of our life and offer insight into our personal worldview. Solar eclipses occur in the daytime, so our ordinary perception of day-to-day reality is impacted. Our waking consciousness has access to what is generally hidden within the realm of the dark of night, and we see stars in the middle of the day. The experience of a solar eclipse is the emergence of memory or subconscious knowledge, overtaking the sense of the present. The light of the self-conscious mind is temporarily overshadowed by subconsciousness and what is normally hidden from view becomes uppermost.

Astrologer R. C. Jansky states, "During the period of totality (of the solar eclipse) darkness falls and the electrical character of the Earth's near cosmic field is drastically altered. Birds fly about excitedly, night creatures come out of their dens, predators howl, roosters crow, diurnal animals go to sleep, and flowers close their blossoms." Certainly a total solar eclipse must affect the biomagnetic systems of humans too.

Because lunar eclipses are visible at night subconsciousness and the dream state are activated. The darkness of night, which has been illuminated by the Full Moon, becomes completely darkened by the Earth's shadow. Too much focus on the concerns of Earth can prevent the full reflection of our spiritual light. Eclipses of the Moon (Full Moons) represent a waking experience in the dream of our life. We can perceive where we have placed too much emphasis on worldly things. The energies of a lunar eclipse might represent dominance or conquest of materialism over instinct and memory as the Earth obstructs the Sun's reflection. Viewed another way this represents the conscious mind overcoming instinct or habitual behavior.

R. C. Jansky reports "It has been shown that at the time of the Full Moon, and especially during a lunar eclipse, the surface tension of all fluids is increased (the molecular cohesive forces at the surface of any fluid). " Since our bodies are mostly fluid, we can surmise that there must be some corresponding physiological response in our bodily system.

Ptolemy examined the sign in which an eclipse occurred in terms of its potential effect on the whole Earth and believed the effect of a solar eclipse lasted as many years as the eclipse lasted in hours, and the effect of a lunar eclipse lasted as many months as the eclipse lasted in hours. Ptolemy then looked at which star or planet the eclipse occurred closest to and described this heavenly body as the ruler of the eclipse. He also took the time of year into account. If an eclipse happened near the Spring Equinox, then the potential germination of seed might be impacted. If the eclipse occurred near the Autumn Equinox the yield of the harvest was considered.

At totality of a solar eclipse the air takes on a mysterious quality, and the sky becomes a strange twilight as complete, and temporary darkness falls, and stars become visible in the heavens. The bright orb of the Sun is replaced by the black disk of the Moon, and the Sun's normally invisible corona spreads out around the black Moon as a translucent halo. Totality can last for as long as seven and a half minutes. The average time is four to five minutes, but the memory lasts a lifetime.

The December 4, 2002 total solar eclipse occurs in the sign of Sagittarius at 11 degrees 58 minutes of the tropical zodiac. Sagittarius is the sign of truth and the higher mind, offering a chance to take higher ground. The fixed star which occupies this degree of celestial latitude, and is the ruler of the eclipse, is the beta star of Draco, the Dragon, named Rastaban, "the head of the Dragon." The nature of this powerful, yellow star brings the mystical serpent power into the head. This is an influence of illumination. The Dragon is also the ancient symbol of China so we might expect that country to play a prominent role in unfolding events.

The planets that align with the eclipse (Sun and Moon) are Pluto and Mercury, forming a stellium in Sagittarius, bringing hidden things to light. This focuses considerable power on issues of communication, hidden agendas, and the use of force. Anti-war sentiment may increase, becoming more strident. In August an Earth Summit was held in South Africa, and the US was called on the global carpet for environmental negligence. Since the path of totality happens in Africa, that may be where revelations or further accusations originate. The eclipse occurs before the winter solstice in the northern hemisphere, offering the potential to begin a new cycle with the awareness the alignment offers.

If the chart of the December eclipse is overlaid on the accepted birth chart of the US the eclipse falls in the twelfth house of the US chart, in conjunction with America's ascendant at 12 Sag 28, further highlighting hidden matters. Previously held secrets may come out of the closet, and American citizens may see truth unveiled about power-related issues. Power might be interpreted as oil interests.

This eclipse could bring an awakening experience from behind the scenes which will break forth from the collective consciousness of America, changing our worldview, and expressing in a new and transformed manner in America's personality. What have we forgotten as a nation about our ideals and who we are in the world?

Individually and collectively we can consciously accept a new stage of experience in readiness for the opportunity the eclipse will present. I find this promising, but it may feel uncomfortable. As we each own our personal hidden agendas and misuses of power, we create the space for healing the collective. Americans may have to accept increased accountability for certain attitudes and behavior. As we pass any threshold, leading to a new realm of experience, we can choose to meet certain requirements and adjustments willingly or perhaps face a more difficult awakening.

Atlantis Rising #36 October 2002

PART III
MYTHIC THEMES

CHAPTER 18

GODDESS SIGNS: ASTROLOGY OF THE SACRED FEMININE

"She is so bright and glorious that you cannot look at her face or her garments for the splendor with which She shines."

Hildegard of Bingen

Goddesses for Every Day: Exploring the Wisdom & Power of the Divine Feminine Around the World

Someone once asked me, "What would your life be like if you had grown up imagining the Divine as feminine?" The question haunted me and became a quest that resulted in my book *Goddesses for Every Day*. Marking time by the motions of the Moon and planets against the background of the zodiac has been part of every culture--Egyptian, Mayan, Babylonian, Celtic, and many others. This circle of stars, which has also been called The Girdle of the Goddess, is divided into twelve constellations, and seemed an appropriate way to frame the 366 goddesses that are included in the book.

Sacred feminine symbols, such as birds, trees, serpents, and spirals are found in cultures around the world, and I perceived an alignment with these icons and the familiar twelve zodiac signs. They came together in a magical and mysterious way. I called the result of this inspiration the Goddess Signs©. They are: Aries, the Cretan Axe or Labrys; Taurus, the Tree of Life; Gemini, the Honey Bee; Cancer, the Clam Shell; Leo, the Cobra; Virgo, the Sheaf of Wheat; Libra, the Dove; Scorpio, the Spider;

Sagittarius, the Bow & Arrow; Capricorn, the Spinning Wheel; Aquarius, the Spiral; and Pisces, the Chalice or Grail.

In addition, the ancient trinity of the Triple Goddess--Maiden, Mother, and Crone-- can be linked with seasonal cycles. Goddesses of dawn and new beginnings can be aligned with spring, goddesses of birth and mothering with summer, goddesses of the harvest with autumn, and goddesses who preside over death, portals, and the wisdom of age, can be matched to the dark time of year in the northern hemisphere. The many facets and myriad manifestations of the Goddess embody a seeming paradox that is complex and sometimes contradictory. Like life itself, her expressions can be alternately gentle or fierce, loving or cold, creative or destructive, so the circle of goddesses who live in the pages of the book are a diverse spectrum of expression.

Aries - The Cretan Axe The *labrys* of Crete was a ritual implement wielded by a priestess. The Cretan Axe was a symbol of royal power and not a weapon, although it may have been an implement of sacrifice. The word comes from the same root as labyrinth. Aries are pathfinders, and walking the sacred path of a labyrinth, wielding the Double Axe, seems a fitting metaphor for the pioneers of the zodiac. Aries goddesses include gentle goddesses of Spring who embody new beginnings, the light of dawn, cyclical renewal of the Earth, and the rebirth of life. Aries goddesses are also pioneers who blaze new trails, and courageous leaders and fierce warriors who have the will to do battle. The quality of vision enables them to move forward in the direction of the new path. These goddesses are often independent, possessing a keen sense of adventure.

Taurus - The Tree of Life Trees, especially those that bear the fruit of immortality, are connected with the Goddess in cultures around the world where she typically lives in a western garden with a serpent who guards the tree. The energy that sinks sustaining roots deep into the Earth describes the grounding and stabilizing nature of Taurus.

These goddesses embody the element of earth, and many are also symbolized by cows or other strong, protective mammals. Qualities of Taurus goddesses are abundance, sustenance, manifestation, security, growth, establishing roots, and fertility.

Gemini - The Bee Like curious Gemini, the bee flies from flower to flower, drinking nectar and preparing to make honey. The Bee is an ancient symbol of royal power and the sacred feminine. Myths of Queen Bees, and priestesses who tend her hives and shrines, exist in diverse cultures. Bees pollinate flowers that bear fruit and yield seeds in a perpetual cycle of renewal. The industrious Bee, who is not supposed to be able to fly, is an appropriate symbol for the pollinating nature of mental Gemini. The goddesses included in Gemini encompass magicians, clever tricksters, and shape shifters, as well as those who are gifted with words and language. Gemini goddesses are animated, verbal, mental, versatile, and magical.

Cancer - The Shell is a symbol of the ocean from which Cancer's traditional symbol of the Crab emerges. Shells, which are containers of life, appear in numerous cultures as images of the Goddess. Sometimes it is the Cowrie shell, which is widely revered, and is suggestive of a woman's anatomy. The goddess Venus also mythically emerged from the ocean on a clam shell. Cancer is ruled by the Moon, so Goddesses that appear in the sign of Cancer include lunar goddesses. Cancer goddesses are nurturing, often creators, and are linked to the ocean, which is the source of all life. They are protective mothers who guard the home, keep the hearth fires burning, and honor their ancestors.

Leo - The Cobra is arguably the Queen of Serpents. Around the world serpents and dragons are connected with the wisdom of the sacred feminine. Many cultures also imagine the apparent motion of the Sun, the ruling planet of Leo, crossing the sky as a serpent. Dragons are creatures of fire, and in myth cobras are seen as "spitting fire" at their enemies. A cobra goddess named Wadjet, symbol of divine kingship, appeared on the brow of all Egyptian pharaohs. Leo goddesses include radiant solar goddesses and great cats from different cultures, and also those who represent the creative principle of fire in the form of dragons or serpents. Leo goddesses represent nobility, the principle of light, and the fire of the Sun.

Virgo - The Sheaf of Wheat is symbolically held in the hand of the goddess of the constellation Virgo. With rare exceptions Earth is seen as a goddess who sustains her children through the annual cycle of fertility and renewal of the land. The body of the Goddess feeds and nourishes her children, and many ancient goddesses embodied the perpetual motion of the agricultural year. Virgo goddesses include ancient goddesses of grain, agriculture, and the harvest, whose myths embody these seasonal cycles. Images of these goddesses often include vast fields of waving grain, overflowing cornucopias, or generous platters of fruits.

Libra - The Dove is an ancient emblem of the goddess Venus, the traditional ruler of Libra. Birds are connected with the Sacred Feminine around the world and viewed as messengers to heaven. In Hermetic tradition the Language of the Birds, or the Green Language, is the domain of the Goddess. White doves are ancient symbols of peace and purity; even the ancient Egyptians revered them. Doves are also symbols of love, "billing and cooing." Libra goddesses embody the idea of love, beauty, art, and elegance. Although Libra seeks peace and harmony, conflict is inherent in relationship, so goddesses included in this dual air sign can also appear as fierce birds of war. Libra is also the sign of marriage, so these goddesses learn to balance the challenges relationships present.

Scorpio - The Spider is the great weaver who spins creation, the literal web of life, from her own life force. Scorpio is traditionally represented by a Scorpion and represents the life force and how that energy is expressed, so this sign is connected to sexuality as well as healing. Serpent goddesses, when they are healing agents appear here, representing the life force directed toward transformation. In Scorpio the substance of the threads of life are spun out of the Spider's belly, creating the potential. Scorpion and spider goddesses are included as well as goddesses who embody passion and sexuality. Because Scorpio is the portal to the unseen realm beyond the Veil, goddesses of death and rebirth are also included.

Sagittarius - The Bow & Arrow relates to traditional astrology where Sagittarius is symbolized by the Archer, who is a centaur. Many goddesses, in fact some of the most ancient, are huntresses who live in primeval forests and guard the animals who live there. For these goddesses hunting is not sport but a sacred reciprocity that is represented in women's lives and the Earth herself. The Sagittarius hunt can also be seen more symbolically as the quest for wisdom, engaging the fire of aspiration that takes us into a larger view of the world. Goddesses included in Sagittarius represent wisdom, dreams, providence, fortune, and the voices of oracles. Because Sagittarius is ruled in astrology by the sky god Jupiter, a mythical latecomer, goddesses of light, wisdom, thunder and lightning are also included.

Capricorn - The Spinning Wheel represents Crone goddesses who are weavers of Fate. Spinning, weaving, and looms are the province of wise elder goddesses who pronounce destiny, measuring and cutting the threads of our lives. While Scorpio spins the threads out of the substance of the belly of the Goddess, it is in Capricorn, the sign of form, that the threads take shape and are woven into the tapestries of our lives. Mountains are symbols of this process in all spiritual traditions, so Capricorn has usually been symbolized by a mountain goat with the tail of a fish or dolphin. Ancient mountain goddesses are included in Capricorn along with goddesses who embody structure, organization, time or duration, as in measuring the threads of Fate, endings, the dark of winter, and the wisdom of old age.

Aquarius - The Spiral can be seen in the whirling galaxies of deep space, hurricanes, pine cones, and sea shells. This motion represents the spiraling nature of reality that eternally spins and evolves. The spiral represents the cyclical motion of Nature and the sky, including the arms of our Milky Way, inviting us to look up and beyond our limited scope to widen our view. Aquarius goddesses are connected to space and knowledge of the alchemical Above. Aquarius goddesses reach toward heaven, and the realm of the higher mind, connecting to the sky and stars, celestial themes, and the ancient wisdom of astrology.

Pisces - The Chalice, or Grail, contains the waters of collective consciousness and is a symbol of the quest toward immortality and conscious union with the Divine. Pisces is traditionally symbolized by two fish swimming in opposite directions in the ocean of existence, but tethered at the tails. Pisces can represent illusion, not seeing clearly, refusing to see, or divine inspiration. This stage of the journey requires faith. Pisces endows knowledge of the alchemical Below, the deep reservoir of collective existence, which engenders empathy. Pisces goddesses include mermaids, fish deities, and mother-creators from the sea, as well as those who embody the principles of sacrifice and compassion.

The Goddess Signs© offer a feminine lens through which the timeless energies of the zodiac can be expressed and experienced. Ancient Egyptians said every woman was a *nutrit*, a "little goddess," after the nature of the great goddess Nut, whose star-covered body arched over the Earth. Each dawn she gave birth to the Sun. I believe if every woman reclaimed that awareness we could heal the world.

Atlantis Rising #130 June 2018

Excerpted from *Goddesses for Every Day: Exploring the Wisdom & Power of the Divine Feminine Around the World*

New World Library, 2010

CHAPTER 19

ASTROLOGY AND THE HERO'S JOURNEY

"It is good to have an end to journey towards; but it is the journey that matters in the end."

Ursula K. Le Guin, *The Left Hand of Darkness*

Hero Path — the Beginning (SnappyGoat.com)

At the beginning of *The Hero with a Thousand Faces,* arguably Joseph Campbell's finest book, the author asserts, "It would not be too much to say that myth is the secret opening through which the inexhaustible energies of the Cosmos pour into human cultural manifestation."

In our time myth is considered to be more like a fairy tale or a fictional flight of fancy, but this was not always the case. In ages past myth was a mechanism for describing profound truths in a way that could be recognized and remembered. Myths are carefully crafted stories that transmit timeless truths through the language of archetypes. Linguistically the word myth equates with "mouth" and carries the meaning of truth transmitted orally, or through stories.

Campbell was the premier scholar of myth in modern times. Drawing on myths and traditions through time and across diverse cultures he demonstrated how the stages of the archetypal hero's journey had the same pattern everywhere. The hero's journey is structured as a circle or a cycle that is roughly divided into three phases: separation (departure), initiation, and return. The hero typically ventures forth from a world of safe and ordinary reality and enters a realm of supernatural wonder where strange forces are encountered. The journey penetrates the heart of some mystic power, and eventually the hero wins a decisive and life-enhancing victory, returning from the magical journey transformed and possessing power to bestow boons on those left behind.

Since this cyclic journey appears in stunning consistency in myths and sacred writings around the world it should come as no surprise that this archetypal pattern is also expressed in the twelve signs of the zodiac. We can view zodiac, the great wheel of astrology, as the circular frame of this familiar story.

In *Atlantis Rising* #62 (Chapter 23 in this volume) I examined how the span of the astrological ages, the Cosmic Months of Precession, might serve to affect the evolution of the collective consciousness of humanity. The ages are driven by a stellar mechanism, and at a macro level Precession acts like a massive clockwork. The astrological signs on the other hand are a function of time and the solar year and their mythic content influences our psyches in a more individual manner. Astrology is living myth. What follows compares the archetypal nature of the twelve signs to the stages of hero's journey as described by Joseph Campbell.

STAGES OF THE HERO'S JOURNEY

Stage One - Departure

1. Aries: Call to Adventure - A seminal trigger acts like a jolt and activates the impulse to begin the journey. Like birth itself the hero is expelled from Paradise into the cold, cruel world. Usually, the call comes in the form of a life crisis or loss which shatters the safe and bucolic nature of the hero's previous life. The resonance between the hero's call to adventure and the nature of the first sign, Aries, is easy to see. The rambunctious energy of new life and springtime and the "headfirst" character of the first sign propels energy into experience.

The hero responds to the ageless call and sets forth on the quest, signaling the onset of spiritual awakening.

2. Taurus: Supernatural Aid - As the hero or heroine sets out the first experience is an encounter with a guide. This figure may be an old man in the guise of a hermit, but is just as often a gnarly old crone who possesses wisdom or a key. Campbell says this meeting represents the "benign, protecting power of destiny," and like the wonder of a fragile green shoot pushing through a concrete highway, the force of new life is tremendous because sufficient power is required to sustain the initial impulse. To quote Campbell again, "Mother Nature herself supports the mighty task." The inherent wisdom of the forces of nature are embodied in Taurus. Fertility and growth are automatic processes and provide early support. Ponder the stability of a grazing cow and the power of a charging bull.

3. Gemini: Crossing of the First Threshold - Now supported in a mysterious way as a result of the guide, the journey moves into the realm of the unknown. Diverse experiences await and at this stage of the quest the hero, our psyche, is driven by Gemini curiosity to acquire as much knowledge as possible. In mythical tales this phase is filled with lures, traps, wily tricksters, and temptations to snare the unwary. The emphasis is on quantity and diversity. Likewise in astrology the paramount lesson of Gemini is gathering data and cultivating discernment.

4. Cancer: Belly of the Whale - Mythically this stage is often called the "belly of the whale" and stories involve being swallowed, experiencing a symbolic death, or entering a womb, with the implication of a potential rebirth. The previous sense of limited and separate identity is "swallowed up" and a sense of being part of something larger takes its place. The insular shell of Cancer and the womb it symbolizes acts as a nurturing container. Symbolically Cancer's lessons uncover the deep roots of being and the processes of creation and birth.

Stage Two -- Initiation

5. Leo: Road of Trials - The stage of the journey termed "road of trials" contains themes of bravery and courage as the hero faces trials and ordeals that test his or her mettle and build character. "Here there be dragons," as the old maps said. What is at stake is proving oneself, and along the road of trials the hero recognizes his true spiritual nature. The significance of this phase is gaining personal dominion. Disney's movie *The Lion King* wove these themes and this specific archetype into a powerful and timeless story that touched a deep chord.

6. Virgo: Meeting with the Goddess - Having attained awareness of his divine nature the questing hero is ready to meet the Goddess. A mystical marriage occurs as the hero, representing the soul, unites with the Queen, Goddess ,or Mother of the World -- the Cosmic Mother principle. The sacred feminine energy, called Kundalini in Sanskrit, represents the sacred mysteries and the power that must be embraced and embodied to achieve enlightenment. This transformation of love and metamorphosis occurs at the Virgo stage of the astrological journey. If the mythic sojourner is female it is here she becomes the consort of a god.

7. Libra: Atonement (At-one-ment) with the Father - The hero is now elevated to divine status and challenged to apply the experience gained thus far to the flesh-and-blood beings in his or her own life. How do the revelations apply to the dynamics of ordinary human relationships? Astrologically this is certainly a question for Libra and the lessons of the sign involve reconciling the pairs of opposites. Part of the deeper realization is the androgynous nature of the Divine, so the pairs of opposites have a new significance.

8. Scorpio: Ultimate Boon - The next stage is truly magical as the quester reaches a point where he or she now lives consciously in eternity. The psyche moves into a realm where duality is left behind. Finally free of all fear, the two dark masters of pain and pleasure no longer rule. Stories include drinking magic elixirs and eating the food of the gods. The sign of Scorpio likewise provides lessons of life, death, regeneration, and immortality. This segment of the zodiac is the gateway to the unseen and eternal realms.

Stage Three -- Return

9. Sagittarius: Magic Flight - By virtue of supernatural powers the hero returns to the realm of ordinary reality and back to the world left behind. It is now the responsibility of the enlightened and transformed hero or heroine to share their wisdom with still-slumbering humanity. The Buddha chose not to enter Nirvana but instead to remain and offer his enlightenment so that the souls of Earth could take the same journey. The sign of Sagittarius is the domain of dreams, shamanic journeys, and otherworldliness. All of these experiences are meant to widen our horizons and confer wisdom.

10. Capricorn: Crossing of the Return Threshold - At this stage our returning hero realizes that the two kingdoms are actually one. Although he seemed to travel in a magical realm peopled with gods and demons the journey was in fact an inner one. Appearances have been deceiving and an enlightened consciousness is a matter of degree of the same awareness. There is no separation and matter is actually crystallized light. Capricorn is the Seagoat who partakes of the sum total of the depths and heights of manifest existence and contains the entirety of evolutionary experience.

11. Aquarius: Master of the Two Worlds - Perceiving the true nature of reality the hero is now able to travel from the Above to the Below and back again like Hermes moving from Hades to Mount Olympus by virtue of his Caduceus wand. The hero now moves in a spiritual manner along the Mystical Caduceus at will and by choice. This represents the Aquarian realm of higher mind and ethereal states of consciousness and rarified energies that most of us have not yet glimpsed.

12. Pisces: Freedom to live - Campbell describes this last phase as "individual consciousness reconciled to universal will." Having come full circle the hero achieves the sublime surrender aptly represented by the twelfth sign of Pisces. This stage involves the capacity for sacrifice on behalf of others, which is not suffering but instead a complete alignment with the One through understanding. The hero or heroine now possess true compassion, which is the result of sharing the hearts of humanity and recognizing the essential unity of all life.

The heroic quest is the eternal quest that has been chronicled in every land and tongue. The hero represents the Soul of Everyone who journeys through space-time on an epic return to the Source. Heroes and heroines from the great stories stand out as shining examples, but sooner or later we must all place our feet on the "yellow brick road." As metaphor this journey contains a map of the inner quest we all embark upon; an ancient path of illumination. Life has a grand purpose and we are not meant to be merely spectators.

The Wheel of the Zodiac contains the blueprint of our becoming and is another symbolic map we all follow. Likewise the individual horoscope contains the archetypal focus for each lifetime, revealing lessons we must meet and master. At the dawn of the Aquarian Age the pathway into the forest seems more like a moving sidewalk.

Atlantis Rising #63 April 2007

Credit to Joseph Campbell, *The Hero with a Thousand Faces*, Princeton University Press, 1949 & 1968

CHAPTER 20

CHILDREN OF THE GODS: SKY GODS AND HUMAN DESTINY

"The gods may throw the dice; their minds as cold as ice . . ."

The Winner Takes It All, ABBA,
Super Trouper album July 1980

The Greek Olympian gods Wikia.org

Babylonian astronomer priests fixed the spring equinox in Aries four thousand years ago, and the Astrology we have inherited in the West is a legacy by way of Greece. In more ancient times the skies were interpreted on behalf of the collective with the king representing the destiny of the realm. Since the time of the Greeks horoscopes have been cast for individuals, assessing talents, gifts and pitfalls that were portended in the life.

The Greeks made the sky personal by giving the gods almost human natures and foibles, peopling the heavens with a host of heroes, animals, and monsters who enacted cyclical morality plays. While Egyptian gods seem more purely archetypal, the Greek gods inflicted the slings and arrows of outrageous fortune as archetypal energies interacted in finite and vulnerable ways with far-reaching consequences. In this way, the gods are often jealous, but they can also be kind.

In her classic work *Mythology*, Elizabeth Hamilton remarked, "The Greeks did not believe that the gods created the universe. It was the other way about: the universe created the gods." Before there were gods Heaven and Earth had been formed and were the first parents. The Titans were their children, and the Olympian gods were their grandchildren.

Ancient Greek cosmogony viewed the world as having passed through several ages from Creation in the dim mists of antiquity. The tradition belonging to the legendary poet Orpheus described the concept of Time as emerging first, seeming to exist from the beginning. Out of Time came Chaos, an infinite space that contained Night, Mist, and Aether. At Time's command Mist spun in the empty space, forming an egg. This is hauntingly familiar to the Qabalistic description of the origin of the Tree of Life as "the beginning of the whirlings." The being Phanes (Light), mated with Night, creating Heaven and Earth. Some sources say the egg split, with Eros (Love) emerging from the center, and Heaven (Uranus) and Earth (Gaia) being formed from two halves of the egg shell.

The Titans were Lords or Kings and as such the first divine race. Rhea was the earth goddess, daughter of Uranus and Gaia, and sister-wife to Cronus, with whom she bore Hestia, Demeter, Hera, Hades, Poseidon, and Zeus. These children of the Titans became known as the Olympians because of their heavenly dwelling place.

Cronus (Saturn), was the son of Uranus (heaven) and Gaia (earth). This eldest Titan castrated his father and threw the phallus into the sea, resulting in the birth of Aphrodite (Venus). Having rendered his father impotent, Cronus liberated his Titan siblings and is said to have ruled over a Golden Age.

Since Time devours all, not to be outdone by his own sky father, Cronus (Saturn and Time) swallowed every one of his children as they were born. Rhea tricked him into swallowing a swaddled stone instead of Zeus, the youngest, and then she helped Zeus trick him into vomiting up the rest of the godlings. So Cronus too was dethroned, and the Olympian era began.

The Hindu Yugas were named from an ancient Indian game of chance and implied, that at some level, existence itself is a game of dice. Similar to the Hindu Yugas, the earliest Greek age was also golden, descending into a time of strife and conflict. The first and Golden age was ruled by Cronus in a time when even humans were immortal. Zeus introduced the Silver age, instituting the seasons, *Horae*, along with work and labor. Another invention of Zeus was the Bronze age, which was characterized by war and violence. The so-called Heroic age, peopled by demigods, was filled with fabulous exploits. The Iron age, like the Hindu Kali Yuga, and sounding much like modern times, reeked with crime, suffering, and toil.

Olympus was said to include the "heavens" the sea, and the underworld. The entrance was described as a great gate of clouds kept by the seasons. To the ancient Greeks, Mount Olympus was a heavenly dwelling place, a twelve-roomed mansion in the skies, which was home to twelve Olympian gods and their consorts. Olympus corresponds to the Norse Valhalla. Zeus was declared supreme over all the Olympians, claiming the upper world of the heavens for himself, bestowing the sea and rivers to Poseidon, and relegating the lower world to Hades.

Today's astronomers use the term Celestial Sphere to denote the heavens. The skies have a "watery" section, an underworld inhabited by stellar water snakes and other mythical creatures, as well as the vault of heaven where the circumpolar stars rotate around the pole.

Hamlet's Mill is a scholarly work and a daunting piece of research, accumulating myths from around the world, demonstrating similarities of theme and imagery, and showing how knowledge of the stars was encoded into stories. The authors, Giorgio de Santillana and Hertha von Dechend, demonstrated repeatedly that myth was never intended to be fiction or fable, but rather to serve as a clever mnemonic device, enabling people to recall and transmit complex astronomical information through stories. In other words, using sky lore as the mechanism, and the night sky as the canvas, myth became a brilliant device, an astronomical allegory, for teaching and transmitting sky lore over vast periods of time.

The word myth derives from the Greek *mythos* and means "spoken word." Myths were orally transmitted stories. The root word is the Indo-Germanic Mu. In German the word "mutter" means mother. In earlier times myth was the language, the "spoken word," and provided the mechanism for communicating knowledge. In ancient times people watched the skies and told their stories in the same way we watch the evening news. Myths were a way to describe what occurred in the sky, so constellations were drawn, or dots connected between the stars to form pictures, facilitating stellar stories. In the Native American lore of the Wasco Indians Coyote drew the star pictures. As the "age of reason" expanded, and eclipsed older ways of knowing, this priceless legacy was unintentionally forgotten.

Myth functions on more than one level. Myth as metaphor teaches truths about our spiritual selves through the archetype of the hero's journey. Myth as sky lore was a mechanism to teach technical information about the stars in a manner that was easy to remember. Star pictures and characters made the yearly sky a familiar landscape.

The mythical earth is conceived as a flat plane intersected by the "frame" of the equinoxes and solstices, the cardinal points of the year. This is why the earth is often said to be quadrangular. The intersections are the four corners, the four directions, and the four winds. The four corners, or zodiacal constellations rising heliacally (before the Sun) at both the equinoxes and solstices, form parts of the frame and determine the "earth." This frame is one of time and is not to be confused with the physical globe that is the planet.

Hamlet's Mill states that " . . every world age has its own 'earth.' It is for this reason that 'ends of the world' are said to take place. A new 'earth' arises, when another set of zodiacal constellations brought in by the Precession determines the year points." The zodiacal constellation that rises before the sun at the equinoxes and solstices constitutes the frame of the current age. The conceptual image might be seen as a platter surrounded by two wire hoops, intersecting the platter at ninety degree angles. Time can be thus seen as circular and its frame as a sphere where the seasons intersect the circle of the year.

What we call science today has established a technical language of its own and maintains stewardship over knowledge that in the past was available to everyone through the magic of myth. The authors of *Hamlet's Mill* observed that "Magic material withstands change, just because of its resistance to the erosion of common sense." Rather than integrating and synthesizing "modern" knowledge with traditional ways of knowing, we have discarded earlier truths as primitive or invalid.

The familiar planets of our Solar System bear names that have come down to us from Greek and Roman myth. It's a testimony to the power of naming that the manner in which planets are interpreted in modern Astrology still carries the archetypal significance bestowed on their heavenly counterparts thousands of years ago.

The planets orbit (except Pluto's eccentric orbit) the Sun in a flat plane of space roughly fourteen degrees of arc wide. From our perspective on Earth the Sun appears to move through the sky on an annual trek. This apparent path of the Sun is called the Ecliptic, and this area of space is divided into twelve by the constellations of the zodiac. This twelve-roomed mansion where the sky gods interact is likely to be the mythical Mount Olympus.

The Twelve Olympians

Greek	Roman	Planet	Asteroid	Key word
Aphrodite	Venus	Venus		Attraction
Apollo	Apollo	Sun		Focus
Ares	Mars	Mars		Action
Artemis	Diana	Moon		Memory
Athena	Minerva/Sophia	Pallas-Athena		Wisdom
Demeter	Ceres	Ceres		Regeneration
Hephaestus	Vulcan			Metamorphosis
Hera	Juno	Juno		Sacred Marriage
Hermes	Mercury	Mercury		Communication
Hestia	Vesta	Vesta		Devotion
Poseidon	Neptune	Neptune		Sacrifice
Zeus	Jupiter	Jupiter		Expansion

There were twelve Olympians; six males and six females. The Olympians correspond in part to the planets of our Solar System and to the archetypes of Astrology. There are some exceptions. Uranus and Cronus (Saturn) were Titans who fathered and grandfathered their Olympian offspring. Hades (Pluto) was a member of the group by lineage, but did not reside in Olympus, rather ruling his underworld domain. The mythical stories showed how the archetypal pantheon of energies combined in love and war.

The gods and goddesses were energies that manifested in both genders. For example Iris, goddess of the rainbow, was the feminine messenger of the gods, but she does not get equal billing with Hermes (Mercury), her male twin. It was not until Greek (or Roman) law was established in Egypt that the feminine lost its equal status. In a fascinating manner, several of the female Olympians are staging a comeback, returning to mythic power in the form of asteroids.

On the first day of January of 1801 Astronomer Guiseppe Piazzi discovered what he thought was a new comet. The object was named Ceres and was to be the first of thousands of asteroid discoveries. Named Ceres, this now-classified dwarf planet orbits in what we now call the asteroid belt. The next three in sequence, Pallas (Athena), Vesta and Juno, were discovered in the next few years. Several hundred thousand asteroids have been discovered so far, which are categorized by their spectra (light signatures) and position in the Solar System. (At the time this article was written in 2001 only the four largest were included in interpretation—that interpretative pallet has expanded and is explored in Volume Two).

Mythologically Ceres (Demeter) is a grain and fertility goddess and represents the great Earth Mother in both her nurturing and withholding aspects. Pallas Athene (Minerva) is the archetypal daughter and goddess of wisdom who sprang from the head of her father Zeus. Vesta (Hestia) holds the archetype of virgin and sister, symbolizing femininity that is complete within herself. Juno (Hera), represents the sacred marriage, and indicates the balanced union of the feminine and masculine principles.

These goddesses, representing four aspects of the feminine experience, round out the missing spaces in the halls of Olympus. Increasingly these asteroids are used by modern astrologers to enrich interpretation and insight. If the correct birth time is known, the asteroid goddesses can be placed in the birth chart for expanded understanding.

Atlantis Rising #33 April 2001

CHAPTER 21

ASTROLOGY AND THE MYTHS
OF THE TWELVE SIGNS

"The early Greek mythologists transformed a world full of fear into a word full of beauty."

Edith Hamilton, *Mythology*

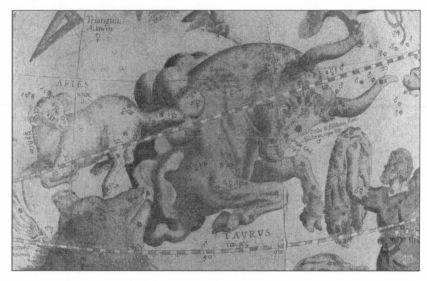

Aries & Taurus Mercator (SnappyGoat.com)

In our time a myth is considered to be like a fairy tale, or a fictional flight of fancy, but in ages past myth was a means for describing and transmitting profound truths in ways that could be recognized and remembered. Myths were carefully crafted stories intended to transmit timeless truths through symbols, metaphors, and archetypes. Linguistically the word myth equates with "mouth" and carries the meaning of orally transmitted stories.

The earliest references to the mythological significance of the Greek constellations are found in the works of Homer, dating to the 7th century BCE. In the *Iliad*, Homer describes the creation of Achilles's shield by the blacksmith god Hephaestus, "On it he made the earth, sky, sea, the weariless sun and the moon waxing full, and all the constellations that crown the heavens, Pleiades and Hyades, mighty Orion and the Bear." At the time of Homer most constellations were known as the objects or animals that they represented, such as the Bull or the Ram. Two centuries later, in works such as Eratosthenes, the constellations were associated with myths.

Most of the planets' names come from Roman mythology and reflect their characteristics: Mercury, messenger of the gods, revolves fastest around the sun; Venus, goddess of love and beauty, shines the brightest; Mars, god of war, looks blood-red; and Jupiter, king of the gods, is the largest planet in the Solar System. The planets were the gods and goddesses who traveled through the mythical starry realms of the zodiac constellations.

How astrology works is still a mystery. From Tarot cards to tea leaves and the I-Ching to the Oracle at Delphi, there are many systems of divination. It seems the nature of reality, and our place relative to it, can be discerned through systems that develop their own language and symbolism based on universal archetypes. Some have speculated that astrology is a revealed body of knowledge and partakes of the nature of reality itself. The zodiac is a description of sequential and repeating experience on multiple levels of simultaneous expression, and we travel this wheel as individual souls with brief life spans. But humanity also moves around this wheel as a collective consciousness, evolving and unfolding according to a pattern. Astrology is living myth, and the twelve constellations of the zodiac wheel tell a series of great stories. There are often multiple myths that were adapted over time. Where possible, I have chosen the older stories.

Aries is an ancient star group that has been seen as a Ram since Babylonian times 4,000 years ago. In later Greek myth Aries became associated with the golden ram that rescued Phrixos and Helle who were the son and daughter of King Athamas and his first wife. The king's second wife was jealous and wanted to kill the children, so she caused a famine and falsified a message from the Oracle of Delphi that Phrixos must be sacrificed to end the famine. Athamas was about to sacrifice his son when Aries, sent by Nephele, the first wife, arrived. Phrixos sacrificed the ram to Zeus in his stead, and the Golden Fleece was hung in a sacred place and guarded by a dragon. In a later myth, Jason and the Argonauts stole the Golden Fleece, but that's another story.

The mythology of Taurus began with a wandering bull known as Cerus that was enormous and powerful and had the unfortunate tendency to trample anything in his path. Most people assumed he was immortal because of his size and strength. One day the goddess

Persephone found him trampling a field of flowers. Though he couldn't speak, he seemed to understand her, and her presence calmed him. Persephone taught the bull patience and how to use his strength wisely. Every spring, when Persephone returns to the land, Cerus joins her. She sits on his back and they run through the fields, allowing her to cause the plants to bloom. In the fall when Persephone returns to Hades, Cerus returns to the sky as the Taurus constellation.

Gemini represents the twin brothers Castor and Pollux. Leda was their mother and Helen of Troy was their sister, but the twins had different fathers. In the same night, Leda became pregnant by Jupiter in the form of a swan and by her husband, king Tyndarus of Sparta. Pollux, the son of a god, was immortal and renowned for his strength, while his mortal brother Castor was famous for his skill with horses. The Twins were traditionally depicted with spears and riding a matched pair of snow-white horses. The most common explanation for their presence in the heavens is that Pollux was overcome with sorrow when his mortal brother died, and begged Zeus to allow him to share his immortality. Zeus acknowledged the heroism of the brothers and reunited them in the stars.

Cancer's origin was a giant crab named Crios who guarded the sea nymphs in the Greek god Poseidon's kingdom. He was enormous and strong, and Poseidon had blessed him with immortality. When the monster Typhon terrorized the Olympian gods, Poseidon, along with most of the other gods, went into hiding. He left Crios to protect the sea nymphs, who were Poseidon's daughters. After a time some of the nymphs became restless, and convinced that they were in no danger from Typhon, they escaped into the open sea. Crios could not chase them since he was protecting the others, so he enlisted the help of the giant squid, Vamari. However, Vamari had his own intentions and devoured them. Vamari told the crab that he could not find the missing sea nymphs, but Crios knew he was lying, and they battled until the crab finally won. But he sustained crippling injuries, and since he was immortal, he had to live in pain. Poseidon rewarded the crab's bravery by relieving his pain, but not his immortality, placing him in the sky as the constellation of Cancer.

Leo is one of the oldest constellations and was seen as a lion by
Sumerians and Mesopotamians 5,000 years ago. To the Greeks, Leo is
said to represent the Nemean Lion killed by Hercules during the first
of his twelve labors, which is itself a story of the hero in all of us
making a spiritual journey through the zodiac. According to the myth,
the Nemean lion had an impenetrable skin. Hercules overcame this
obstacle by wrestling the lion and strangling it. He removed one of its
claws and skinned the beast. Afterward, Hercules wore the lion's skin
as protection. Although being placed among the stars is generally a
reward, both Eratosthenes and Hyginus wrote that the lion was placed
among the constellations because it was the king of beasts.

Virgo represents many harvest goddesses of antiquity, such as
Demeter, and signifies the cycle of fertility and the harvest. She is
shown holding a sheaf of grain, usually wheat, which is the alpha star
in the constellation named Spica. Virgo is the only female figure among
the zodiac constellations. She is said to embody the fertility of the earth
and to announce the annual harvest.

Libra was equated with the goddess Astraea, "Star Maiden," or the
"Starry One," who weighed the claims of opposing parties in disputes.
The emblem of her office was the scales of Libra, which are next to
Virgo in the sky. It was said Astraea was the last of the immortals to
remain on earth, but she finally left when humans descended into
violence and hatred. She ascended to the sky to hold the scales of
justice that are now part of Libra. Hesiod describes *daimones* that are
invisible spirits who watch over humanity, and Astraea was the
daimone whose province is justice.

Scorpio is identified with the scorpion that stung and killed Orion the
hunter. Some stories say Gaia, the Goddess of the Earth, sent the
scorpion; others say it was Artemis, Goddess of the Hunt, because he
had dared to hunt all the animals under her protection. Others say
Orion had attempted to force himself on Artemis so she sent the
Scorpion after him. Orion was subsequently resurrected by Asclepius,
God of Healing, who appears in the sky as Ophiuchus, the Serpent
Bearer. Asclepius himself was later killed by one of Zeus's
thunderbolts because he brought too many back to life, depopulating

the Underworld. Each year as Orion rises the Scorpion sets, crushed by the heel of Ophiuchus, thus avoiding further conflict.

The myth of Sagittarius refers to Krotus, a satyr who lived on Mount Helicon with the Muses. Satyrs are described as having human heads and torsos with two goat legs. Depending on the source, satyrs can have a horse's tail. Krotus was the son of the goat god Pan and Eupheme, nurse to the Muses, and like the wise centaur Chiron, was a talented musician and devoted to the Muses and their arts. He was also a skilled hunter and credited with the invention of the bow, something not ordinarily used by centaurs. Centaurs and satyrs were wild creatures with no respect for authority or decorum, but Krotus and Chiron were exceptions—both were knowledgeable and kind to humans. Krotus was so well loved by the Muses that they asked Zeus to place him among the stars. Krotus became Sagittarius and Chiron became Centaurus.

Capricorn has been represented with the head and body of a goat and the tail of a fish or a dolphin from ancient times. Pricus was an immortal sea goat who was favored by the Greek gods and could manipulate time. Sea goats were intelligent and honorable creatures. Pricus had many children who lived near the seashore, but when they found themselves on dry land they turned into ordinary goats and lost their special ability to think and speak. Pricus repeatedly turned back time to prevent his children from finding their way to land, but eventually resigned himself to loneliness and misery, letting the little sea goats leave. He did not want to be the only one of his race, so he asked Chronos to let him die. Because he was immortal he must instead spend eternity in the sky as Capricorn. Predating Greek mythology, the powerful Babylonian God Ea watched over the land by day but returned to live in the ocean every night. He also had the head and body of a goat and the tail of a fish.

The water carrier represented by Aquarius is Ganymede, Cupbearer to the Olympian gods. He was a beautiful Phrygian youth whom Zeus watched as Ganymede tended his father's flocks on Mount Ida. The king of gods became enamored of the boy and flew down in the form of a large bird, whisking Ganymede away to the heavens. Since then, the boy was cupbearer to the gods, serving ambrosia, which gave them immortality.

The Pisces story occurs during the same attack on Mount Olympus mentioned in Cancer when the monster Typhon startled the gods into taking different forms to escape. Jupiter transformed himself into a ram, Mercury became an ibis, Apollo took the shape of a crow, and Diana disguised herself as a cat. Venus and her son Cupid were bathing on the banks of the Euphrates River and took the shape of a pair of fish to escape danger. Minerva later immortalized the event by placing the figures of the two fish among the stars. Pisces represents the two fish, tied together with a cord.

How did these individual myths become grafted onto what later became the astrological signs and their sequential significance and interpretation? The mythological source out of which astrology has developed and grown is a rich ore of knowledge that is waiting to be mined at deeper levels. Joseph Campbell lamented that modern culture has no myths that give meaning in a present day context. It seems we look through an ancient lens that no longer has a basis in a technological society. It may be that the millennial old frame of astrology needs to be reconstructed with myths that speak to modern people. But the magic is, astrology still works and peoples' lives follow these chart patterns and are informed by these mythic stories even as our window to the Universe opens wider and more mythic beings are discovered and named, even in our own Solar System.

Atlantis Rising #110 February 2015

CHAPTER 22

ASTROLOGY'S MYTHIC CODE

"nd God said, let there be lights in the firmament of heaven to divide the day from the night; and let them be for signs, and for seasons, and for days and years."

Genesis 1:14 (King James version of the Bible)

Earth, Moon & Sun (1450362 SnappyGoat.com)

The zodiac is a belt of sky within about eight degrees on either side of the ecliptic, the apparent path of the Sun, and the orbital path of the Moon and planets. This belt contains the zodiac constellations: Aries, Taurus, Gemini, Cancer, Leo, Virgo, Libra, Scorpio, Sagittarius, Capricorn, Aquarius, and Pisces. Although the Chaldeans are generally credited with inventing astrology, we don't actually know where and when the zodiac originated. Some scholars have argued convincingly for an ancient Egyptian origin. The Romans inherited the zodiac from the Greeks, and astronomy and astrology still use this "circle of animals."

The oldest description of the constellations as we know them comes from a poem titled *Phaenomena*, written in about 270 BCE by the Greek poet Aratus. After the *Iliad* and *Odyssey*, the *Phaenomena* was the most widely read poem in the ancient world. It was translated into Latin by Ovid and Cicero, quoted by St. Paul in the New Testament, and was one of the few Greek poems translated into Arabic.

Although some cultures still have their own versions of the zodiac and other star groups, some reaching far back in time, since 1930 astronomers worldwide have agreed on eighty-eight constellations. Constellations are divisions of space like states or countries on a terrestrial map. Every star and deep space object within these divisions is plotted on the grid of the Celestial Sphere, which projects Earth's latitude and longitude into space. The Celestial Sphere is an imaginary "globe" of gigantic proportions with Earth conceptually located at its center. The poles of the Celestial Sphere are aligned with the poles of the Earth. The Celestial Equator lies along the Celestial Sphere in the same plane that includes the Earth's equator.

As Earth travels around the Sun each year, the canvas of the night sky changes. For convenience of recognition, and aid in memory, humans have connected bright stars to make pictures. For thousands of years, these star pictures have been created and stories have been told to give meaning to the constantly changing panorama of the night sky. We still tell these stories, using many of the ancient myths, as a powerful way to give meaning to the Cosmos. Most constellation names came from the ancient Middle Eastern, Greek, and Roman cultures who identified clusters of stars as gods, goddesses, animals, and other objects. Many star names are Arabic, stemming from the time when Islamic scholars kept the light of wisdom burning while Europe was engulfed in a dark age.

Myth is sacred narrative, generally cultural in nature, regarding gods and heroes, the origin of the world, or of a people. Joseph Campbell was probably the world's greatest scholar of myth. In his master work, *The Hero with a Thousand Faces*, Campbell says, "It would not be too much to say that myth is the secret opening through which the inexhaustible energies of the Cosmos pour into human cultural manifestation."

Myth uses metaphor and symbol to teach or transmit important truths. For example, in Greek myth the sun god Apollo carries the Sun across the sky in his chariot. We can visualize this, and we are charmed by the idea of the fiery Sun being carried across the sky each day by a powerful god. Myth is a poetic and more memorable way to transmit a teaching than a dry fact. The Mesopotamian *Epic of Gilgamesh* was a way of explaining how the world and humanity were created. The

Maya *Popol Vuh* is another example of a creation myth, as is Genesis. Joseph Campbell has also remarked that myth is what we call other peoples' religions. Myth is a potent way of teaching and transmitting timeless truths.

Because of the phenomenon called Precession of the Equinoxes, which causes Earth's position relative to the stars to shift slowly over time, the star groups that were once seasonal markers have drifted backward. Therefore, the zodiac constellations, and the astrological signs that bear their names, are no longer in synch with the seasons. In the Tropical Astrology of the West, the astrological signs are a function of the seasons, and every year at Spring Equinox the sign of Aries begins. Every subsequent sign is a thirty-degree division of the circle of the year. On Summer Solstice the sign of Cancer begins. Autumn Equinox is the beginning of the sign of Libra, and Winter Solstice is the beginning of the sign of Capricorn.

The alphabet of astrology is written in glyphs and symbols, but the interpretive mechanism is built on myth. The frame of the signs is mythological. Every sign of the zodiac has a mythological origin and a story that explains the origin and significance. The signs are seen by the Tibetan master Djwhal Khul, through the writings of Alice Bailey, to be like great gates, or portals, through which the reincarnating soul enters the earth plane to have a cycle of experience. The myth of the *Twelve Labors of Hercules* recounts his labors as the hero, representing the Sun, journeying through the year and the ages. At a deeper level Hercules represents the incarnating soul, journeying through the experiences of twelve cycles of experience. His labors are symbolic of victory over the spiritual tests we must each face over many lifetimes in each of the signs.

Aries has been seen as a ram since Babylonian times 4,000 years ago. In later Greek myth Aries became associated with the golden ram that rescued Phrixos and Helle. Taurus the Bull is a very ancient constellation whose identity may appear in the Caves of Lascaux, France, dating to 17,000 years ago. In Greek myth the story of Taurus began with an enormous wandering bull known as Cerus that trampled everything in his path. The goddess Persephone taught the bull patience and how to use his strength wisely. Leo is one of the oldest constellations, as far as we know, and was seen as lion by Sumerians and Mesopotamians 5,000 years ago. The symbolism of the signs embodies qualities and characteristics, strengths and challenges on the ever-turning wheels of the seasons and the ages. If we are wise, we study and learn, facing our lessons and recognizing our tests. In this way, the unfolding and developing of our soul is a more guided process.

The Greeks named the visible planets after Olympian gods. Although we have inherited the Roman names for the planets, the identities of the planetary personalities are much older.

We don't know if the gods came first, or the need to name the planets after them, since the Greeks borrowed much from the Egyptians. The way astrologers understand the nature of planetary energies is through the mythic lens of Greek and Roman gods and goddesses. Venus (Aphrodite) was the goddess of love and beauty. She shines brightest of the planets, and is the brightest object in the sky next to the Moon. Mars (Ares) the red planet, was the god of war. Jupiter (Zeus) was king of the gods, who ruled from his throne on Mount Olympus. Mercury, who compared with the other planets, speeds around the Sun, was identified with the Greek Hermes, the fleet footed messenger of Greek myth.

As the planetary deities, which meant "wanderers" in Greek, traveled across the sky they interacted with each other, which created drama in heaven, and also influenced life on Earth. Astrological interpretation is based on these mythical personalities, and in ancient times the gods had faults and blind spots along with their divine powers. They didn't always behave in a noble fashion.

Much later, long after the Greeks and Romans, when Uranus was discovered the planet was named after the father of Saturn, who was Jupiter's father. Blue Neptune became the god of the sea. Because Pluto is now a dwarf planet we can choose to eliminate him from the interpretive mix, or my preference, add Ceres, now a lovely dwarf planet in the asteroid belt. How the ancients arrived at these ideas before telescopes is unknown, but we still use these qualities in our interpretation even though modern astrologers have a more psychological approach to chart interpretation. It wasn't until the Greeks that charts were cast for individuals.

Astrological interpretation uses the metaphor that planets are gods with unique characteristics that are played out on a cosmic stage, that in turn affects human lives. Stories of Mount Olympus and the dramas of the gods are metaphorical and allegorical, attributing personalities and characteristics to the planets. A well-known metaphor comes from Shakespeare's *As You Like It*, "All the world's a stage." The quote expresses a metaphor because the world is not literally a stage, but Shakespeare used points of comparison between the world and a stage to convey an idea about the mechanics of human experience and the behavior of people. We understand his meaning without a long dissertation of specific examples of human drama. Our minds fill in details from our own experience, making the point more effectively. We realize that we are all playing roles according to our natures.

As the planets travel on their orbits around the Sun, they journey through the environment of different zodiac signs that can be like visiting foreign countries. Some signs seem to speak the same "language" and are more energetically compatible and familiar, while others may be difficult to understand, or even hostile. Interactions with other planets along the way can be friendly encounters or clashes of personalities. The combinations of planetary energies and signs, along with the interactions of the planets themselves, creates a constantly shifting and changing mix of energies.

Some writers believe that astrology is universal in nature and is a revealed discipline--a body of vastly ancient knowledge that was taught by some advanced soul in ages past. There are similarities between facets of astrology and the Hindu Vedic system of healing and alchemy. Perhaps the very nature of reality is somehow encoded in the mechanism and the symbolism. But for now, how it works is still a mystery. We can wonder if astrology would work in a similar way on other worlds that orbit other stars. Might beings on those worlds still use the harmony of twelve to measure the apparent course of their star if their "year" was more or less than 360 days? Might they have ten signs rather than twelve? Perhaps their planets have different personalities?

Astrology is a fabulous legacy, which the ancients bequeathed to us in a way to understand the dynamics of the drama of our Solar System. Whatever the origin of this interpretive narrative, and how the stories have grown with the telling, the mechanism has stood the test of time. Astrology continues to serve as a potent device to decode the influences of the signs and planets. In our time of more advanced scientific discoveries and psychological language, perhaps some mythically-inclined astrologer will also find for a way to update the characters and stories for a modern audience.

Atlantis Rising #126 October 2017

CHAPTER 23

MYTHIC THEMES AROUND
THE GREAT WHEEL

"The wheel goes round and round, some are up and some are on the down, and still the wheel goes round."

Josephine Pollard

Historical Timepiece of the Zodiac (745988 Snappygoat.com)

With the sky as a perennial reference point Earth rotates daily and orbits the sun yearly. Another of Earth's cycles causes an imaginary circle to be traced in the sky by the poles. Called the Great Year, and composed of twelve cosmic months which are the astrological ages, this cycle lasts roughly 26,000 years. As the orientation of the north pole shifts relative to the circumpolar stars, a different North Star moves into position.

Another effect of this motion causes a different part of the sky to rise before the sun at spring equinox dawn. The points of reference for this backward motion, called Precession of the Equinoxes, are the zodiac constellations which reside on the ecliptic, the sun's apparent path. This shift occurs at the rate of roughly one degree of arc every seventy-two years, a span of time which conveniently equates with a human life.

The mythical earth is conceived as a flat plane intersected by the frame of the equinoxes and solstices, the cardinal points of the year. The conceptual image might be likened to a platter surrounded by two wire hoops, intersecting the platter at ninety degree angles. This is why the earth is often said to be quadrangular. In this way time can be seen as a circular motion and its frame as a sphere where the seasons intersect the circle of the year. This frame is one of time and is not to be confused with the physical globe which is the planet.

The four zodiacal constellations rising before the sun at the equinoxes and solstices form parts of the frame and determine the archetypal theme, for that age. Every world age has its own "mythic earth." It is for this reason that "ends of the world" are said to occur. A new "earth" then arises when another set of zodiacal constellations brought in by Precession determines the year's points. We are moving out of the mythic earth of Pisces and into that of Aquarius. Metaphorically the world is ending and the sky is falling.

Another metaphor, that of Hamlet's Mill (see also Chapter 9, AR #121) is conceived like a giant water wheel, slowly churning out the ages. This image describes the polar axis, piercing the center of the Earth, and pointing toward the northern and southern axes of the sky. The axis of the mill also pierces the center of the frame of time, and the persistence of this image provides a cosmic timepiece. Numerous myths have a churning mill as their central theme. Great care was taken, and the assistance of gods, goddesses and tremendous forces of nature were sought, to assure that the mill of heaven ground smoothly and without incident. The shifting of cogs in the great mill, which heralded the beginning of a new age, was seen as fraught with peril.

As mortals know, the ways of the gods are capricious, and sometimes disaster struck. Disaster is literally "disorder in the stars," from the French word for star, "aster." Catastrophe has the same root meaning. The ancients probed the night skies, searching for unexpected alterations in the predictable patterns which might portend disaster. Occasionally things in the sky changed, and the alarm was raised.

Astrologically the duration of an age is characterized and defined by the archetypal energies of the constellation whose stars rise before the sun at spring equinox dawn. Each phase of the Great Year is like a month, possessing a distinct and overarching quality of experience. The ages are like spokes of the cosmic wheel, presenting a phase shift of archetypal energy designed to provide an evolutionary schoolroom for developing humanity. Since the great cycle of the ages is a repeating pattern, perhaps we can learn about our present and future from a better understanding of the past.

As the zodiac presents an annual circle of archetypal experience so too does the Great Year. The changing of ages have longs cusps, or transitional periods, and there are no precise demarcations of the circle where one influence stops and a new one begins. We can only look back in time to sense approximately which archetype held sway and what experience humanity drew from to unfold our emerging pattern.

(Note: The dates given can only be approximations, and the decidedly arbitrary lengths of the ages are arrived at by dividing the Great Year by twelve.)

Age of Leo - 10,600 BCE - 8440 BCE - The age of Leo may have been the mythical golden age referred to in legends. The date generally accepted as the final destruction of Atlantis correlates with the time frame for the age of Leo. According to certain occult traditions Atlantean civilization reached its zenith during this age of kings and also failed whatever tests were presented. Symbolically, humanity's task during this age was finding the light within, learning self-rule rather than being subject to external authority. All the legends of Atlantis point to the fact that this lesson was not fully learned or integrated.

Age of Cancer - 8440 BCE - 6280 BCE - Symbolically the oceans of Cancer swallowed up the external evidence of ancient cultures, but new discoveries in Turkey and India, dating to 10,000 years ago, are pushing back the generally accepted dates and ideas about the sophistication of civilizations that existed at this time. The evolutionary lesson for the age of Cancer related to new ideas about home and tribe. After the destruction of Atlantis humanity's relationship with technology was stripped away and the simple values of the hearth, heart, and home became the central focus.

Age of Gemini - 6280 BCE - 4120 BCE - Scholars believe this period was characterized by widespread migrations, which is a very Gemini theme. From a post-flood simplicity cultures expanded and spread out, perhaps in many cases as hunter-gatherers. Shadowy origins of pre-dynastic Egypt puzzle researches as a brilliant and complex civilization seems to have sprung full blown from the sands of the desert. Historically the links have been missing, but ongoing discoveries are filling in the blanks. The lessons of the age of Gemini involved making new connections and reintroducing the rational mind into the repertoire of skills.

Age of Taurus - 4120 BCE - 1960 BCE - During the age of Taurus, the Bull, Minotaurs, Apis bulls, and the Bull of Heaven dominated myth and iconography. Conventional wisdom declares this to be a time of primarily agricultural societies where the domestication of cattle and the mastery of the element of earth is displayed through an emphasis on fertility. Farming and centralized settlements reemerged. In what seems to be a stunning contradiction this period saw the Dynastic period in Egypt where monumental temples and tombs were built. The lessons of the age of Taurus involved humanity's relationship with the physical world and possessions. Greed versus generosity were themes.

Age of Aries - 1960 BCE - 200 CE - Next the march of ages brought the ram-headed god Khnum of Egypt to the stellar throne. This period might be described as an age of heroes as the "lamb" was ritually slain and the mythic focus turned to conquest and a glorification of war. In this period sons became more important than daughters and inheritance through the male line replaced matrilineal succession. By 330 BCE Alexander's conquests had established Greece as a major power and the force that seemed to provide the mindset for "modern" civilization. The lessons of the age of Aries included such positive characteristics as valor and such negative qualities as brutality and mindless exploitation.

Age of Pisces - 200 CE - 2400 CE - The age of Pisces has seen the emergence of hierarchy in organized religion and the growth of monastic orders, following the pattern of the ill-named "Holy Roman Empire." After the destruction of the Jerusalem temple in 70 CE what became Christianity began to emerge. By 200 CE this thrust was well entrenched and we have seen increasing industrialization of parts of the world with the centralization of wealth. The archetype of suffering has hopefully provided a schoolroom for humanity to become more compassionate. If Aries is the first sign in the forward motion of the zodiac, then moving in the reverse direction of Precession it would complete a cycle. Therefore, the age of Pisces the twelfth sign, would have commenced a whole new cycle of precession. That we started counting time again might be seen as confirmation of this.

Age of Aquarius - 2400 CE - 4560 CE - From the disappearance of Atlantis nearly 13,000 years ago we have moved half way around the precessional wheel. This opposition of signs may well bring the ascension of sunken Atlantis. If not literally, then our understanding of how far back our history goes will be ascertained. As we approach the much-heralded age of Aquarius, the stars of the Water Bearer will replace those of the Fishes. At some point a new archetype or symbol for the Aquarian age will emerge. The diversity of this expression can already be witnessed in young people around the world. At the least we can expect a greater degree of scientific detachment. The already exponential growth of technology will continue, and early examples of this are electricity, space travel, and the Internet. The lessons of this age are similar to that of Atlantis. Will the enlightened use of technology be used in service of the collective, or will unleashed forces destroy us again? If we learn our lessons in the new age we will travel to the stars and other worlds.

Key points in the enormous cycle of Precession seem to move in concert with the fixed signs, and key epochs from the distant past have been transmitted to us. The fixed sign Leo was the anchor for the time frame of 12,500 years ago. The fixed sign Taurus was the seasonal anchor during the epoch of 6,000 years ago as well as the pyramid age of Egypt. The fixed sign Aquarius has moved to define the present age, and as this huge clock keeps ticking, the fixed sign Scorpio will be the spring seasonal anchor in another six thousand years. If a message is encoded within a giant time keeping mechanism, anchored to seasonal signposts and ages, what deeper lessons can we learn as we probe the relationship between astronomy and myth?

What drives the mechanism of astrology is a mystery. Many have speculated that astrology is a revealed body of knowledge and partakes of the nature of Reality itself. The zodiac is a description of sequential and repeating experience on multiple levels of simultaneous expression, and we travel this wheel as individuals with brief spans as souls through time. But humanity also moves around this wheel as a collective consciousness, evolving and unfolding according to a pattern. We are on the brink of the changing of an age, the ending of an old world, and everywhere the evidence of the next leap in human consciousness is evident for those who face toward the future.

Atlantis Rising #62 February 2007

CHAPTER 24

THE ZODIAC & THE TWELVE LABORS OF HERCULES

"By mastery of the binding comes radiance."

#40 The Yoga Sutras Of Patangali

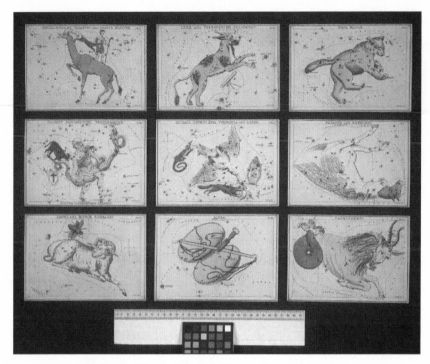

Bodleian Libraries Image of the Heavens (SnappyGoat.com)

The Zodiac of constellations is a circular band of sky eight degrees above and below the ecliptic that contains the familiar constellations from the Ram to the Fishes. Earth's annual orbit causes the Sun to appear to move through these constellations, and each day the Sun rises and sets in a slightly different place along the eastern and western horizons. The zodiac of astrological signs is a seasonal division of time that is based on our motion relative to the Sun.

Different cultures have given their own names to star "pictures," crafting stories to show how the stars move over the year. Others created their own versions of the Zodiac. For example, in about 700 CE, the Venerable Bede saw them as the Twelve Apostles. In 1700 CE Sir William Drummond reformed the zodiac into Biblical Patriarchs, while the classical scholar Reverend G. Townsend transformed them into Twelve Caesars.

Behind its outer meaning, Greek religion often veiled an inner mystical tradition, and so the Twelve Labors of Hercules have been interpreted as a symbol for the spiritual path. In this view, Hercules represents the soul and its journey through the long path of discipleship. Through repeating cycles of experience in the different signs, gradually passing tests and trials, the developing soul ultimately reaches enlightenment.

Hercules is the Roman name for the semi-divine Greek hero *Heracles*, who was the son of Zeus (Roman Jupiter) and the mortal woman Alcmene. Hesiod described Alcmene as the "tallest, most beautiful woman with wisdom surpassed by no person born of mortal parents." While her husband Amphitryon was at war, Zeus disguised himself as her spouse. He slept with Alcmene, who was his great-granddaughter, and she conceived Heracles.

Heracles was famous for his strength and numerous adventures, which took him to the far reaches of the Greco-Roman world. He was multifaceted with contradictory characteristics. The Twelve Labors were a series of penances that took place as a continuous story. The myths sometimes say that the goddess Hera drove Hercules mad in vengeance over Zeus's unfaithfulness. While out of his mind, Heracles killed his wife and children. When he came to his senses he visited the Oracle at Delphi to find out how to atone.

Heracles original name was *Alkeides*, from *Alkeidai* "the strong ones," which was changed to *Heracles* "glory of Hera," by a proclamation of the Oracle Priestess of Delphi. She said "Henceforth you shall perform great deeds and twelve mighty labors." The labors were accomplished over twelve years in the service of his uncle, King Eurystheus. The labors can be seen in three ways: the twelve year orbit of Jupiter (Zeus) around the Sun; the Sun's annual apparent journey through the twelve constellations and signs; and the mystical interpretation of the soul's journey on the Path of Discipleship.

The Twelve Labors are perhaps the most familiar of the ancient myths and at the same time remain the most enigmatic. The sequence varies and may have been forced to fit later authors' desire to match the geography of Greece rather than the symbolism of the stories. The most traditional order is listed in the *Bibliotheca,* which is an ancient Greek compendium of myths and heroic legends arranged in three books, generally dated to the first or second centuries CE.

Other writers matched the Labors to the Sun's journey through the year, and the soul's passage through the stages of discipleship, and assign the Mares of Diomedes to Aries and begin the labors there. Alice Bailey, under the guidance of The Tibetan, Djhwal Khul, used this sequence. Although the alignment is still somewhat unclear, the resulting astrological alignment seems to fit.

1. Aries – The Mares of Diomedes were magnificent, wild, and uncontrollable horses that belonged to the giant Diomedes. Their madness was attributed to an unnatural diet of human flesh, and some versions say that they expelled fire when they breathed. Eating made the horses calmer, so Heracles fed them and bound their mouths shut, easily capturing them. Astrologically the Sun is said to be exalted in Aries. This means that the fire of consciousness must be brought to the "head" to illuminate thought, choice, and action. The lesson for Aires is taming the mind, and the uncontrollable "war horses" of thought and controlling the actions as a result.

2. Taurus – Return the Bull of Crete to the holy place. Heracles sailed to Crete where King Minos permitted him to take the Cretan Bull as it had been wreaking havoc, uprooting crops and leveling orchard walls. Heracles snuck up behind the bull and overpowered it, and then shipped it to his uncle. The Cretan bull was not slaughtered but ridden and guided, thereby giving its power to Heracles. Symbolically, to ride an animal is to master it, so Heracles then controlled the power of the bull. The lesson of Taurus is to learn to move consciously from a position of "holding the ground" in strength and becoming too fixed.

3. Gemini –The Golden Apples of Hesperides grew on a sacred tree under the care of three maidens and were guarded by a dragon. On his way to the Garden of the Hesperides, Heracles offered to hold up the burden of the heavens for a time so Atlas could rest. Atlas was then able to get the apples as he was the father or otherwise related to the Hesperides. The stories vary but Heracles gained the apples as a result of his service to Atlas and the world. Apples are the domain of the goddess and represent knowledge being transformed into wisdom through experience. In Gemini we realize our dual nature of spirit and matter and in this sign instinct is finally overcome by intuition.

4. Cancer – The Golden Hind was an enormous deer sacred to Artemis, goddess of the hunt, and protector of animals. The giant deer had golden antlers and hooves of bronze or brass, and it was said that she could outrun an arrow in flight. Hind comes from old Gothic, meaning "that which must be seized." The golden deer represents the gentleness and innocence that must be recognized and incorporated into our fluid emotional natures. Cancer's lesson is control of the emotions and increasing dominion over the instinctual parts of our psyche that otherwise drive us unconsciously.

5. Leo – The Nemean Lion was a vicious monster that lived at Nemea in Greece that could not be killed with mortal weapons because its golden fur was impervious to attack. Its claws were sharper than swords and could pierce any armor. The Nemean Lion is usually considered to have been the offspring of Typhon and Echidna or to have fallen from the moon as the offspring of Zeus and the moon goddess Selene. The lesson of Leo requires us to track the lion to the inner cave of our undeveloped nature and overcome the personality that is running wild and destructive. The beasts of ego and pride must be "killed" in order that the soul can advance on the journey.

6. Virgo – The Girdle of Hippolyta. Hippolyta was the Amazon queen who possessed a magical girdle, or belt, given to her by her father Ares (Mars) the god of war. The girdle was a waist belt that signified her authority as queen of the Amazons. Most versions of the story say that Hippolyta was so impressed with Heracles that she gave him the girdle without argument, perhaps while visiting him on his ship. However, through the hero's unfortunate choices, Heracles fought with her and the queen died. The lesson of Virgo is to understand the true nature of service, inner worth, and beauty. Even for a hero not everything is about battle.

7. Libra –The stories say that Heracles was given a new bow with which to kill the Erymanthian Boar, but before he departed he became drunk and distracted. This resulted in the death of two friends. After the difficulty in the previous labor that resulted in the death of Hippolyta, he left the bow behind and set out to capture the boar with only his club. He set a trap and captured the animal and then forced it down the mountains on its two front legs while he held the back two legs and balanced the beast. So this labor was performed with a blend of courage, compassion, and humor. This labor shows the extremes of Libra and the balanced and sound judgment that must be attained in the experience of this sign.

8. Scorpio – In both Greek and Roman myth the Lernaean Hydra was an ancient serpentine water monster with reptilian traits. Its lair was the lake of Lerna, which was reputed to be a portal to the Underworld, and the Hydra served as a threshold guardian. Archaeology has established it as a sacred site older than Mycenaean Argos. According to Hesiod, the Hydra was the offspring of Typhon and Echidna. It possessed many heads ("more than the vase-painters could paint") and each time one was lost it was replaced by two more. It had poisonous breath and blood so virulent that even its scent was deadly. This labor represents the lesson of Scorpio that power without love is a corrupting force and the inner battle to overcome the Dweller at the Threshold that must be met on the spiritual path.

9. Sagittarius - The Stymphalian Birds were flesh-eating birds with bronze beaks, sharp metallic feathers they could throw at their victims, and poisonous dung. They were pets of Ares (Mars) the god of war. They bred quickly and swarmed over the countryside, destroying crops, fruit trees, and townspeople. Hercules could not go into the marsh to reach their nests, as the ground would not support his weight. Athena gave Hercules a rattle that Hephaestus had made for the occasion. Heracles shook the rattle and frightened the birds into the air. He shot many of them with arrows tipped with poisonous blood from the Hydra. The rest flew far away, never to plague Arcadia again. The lessons of Sagittarius include restraint of speech through control of thought. We must take careful aim with the arrows of thought to ultimately realize our spiritual goal.

10. Capricorn – Capture Cerberus, Gatekeeper to the Underworld. Heracles went to Eleusis to be initiated in the Mysteries and learn how to enter and exit the underworld. Athena and Hermes helped him traverse the entrance in each direction. He passed Charon with Hestia's assistance. Heracles asked Hades permission to bring Cerberus to the surface. Hades agreed if Heracles could overpower the beast without using weapons. Heracles succeeded and slung the beast over his back, dragging it out through a cavern entrance in the Peloponnese. Capricorn is said to be the sign of the initiate, the place in the great wheel where the focus turns inward toward the Path and away from achievement. The lesson of Capricorn is learning how to open the gate to the inner world, face our inner demons, and climb the mountain of spiritual attainment.

11. Aquarius – The Greeks called the constellation of Capricorn the *Augean Stables*, because the Sun's brightness, the meaning of the a*ugeas*, appears to rest, or "stable" during winter solstice. They thought the darkness was caused by the buildup of sin during the year, and the sins were symbolically washed away as the Sun rose in the next sign of Aquarius, the Water Bearer. The stables had not been cleaned for thirty years, and more than a thousand cattle were housed there. Heracles succeeded in his task by rerouting the Alpheus and Peneus rivers— symbols of the waters of life and the waters of love. The lesson of Aquarius is breaking down mental barriers and structures of limitation, making way for inclusivity.

12. Pisces – Cattle of Geryon. Geryon was a fearsome giant who lived on an island in the mythic Hesperides in the far west of the Mediterranean. He was described as a monster with three human faces. Heracles was given a golden chalice before he began this labor and by virtue of this gift he sailed across the sea to the island. Geryon carried three shields, three spears, and wore three helmets but fell victim to an arrow that Heracles dipped in the venomous blood of the

Lernaean Hydra. It took a year to gather the cattle and herd them back. For Pisces the chalice is the vessel that contains the waters of consciousness. The lesson of Pisces is to transform sensitivity and suffering into compassion and enlightened service.

Atlantis Rising #115 October 2015

CHAPTER 25

TRANS-GENDERING THE SKY:
ARE SATURN AND NEPTUNE
ACTUALLY FEMININE
ARCHETYPES?

"The history of men's opposition to women's emancipation is more interesting perhaps than the story of that emancipation itself."

Virginia Woolf, *A Room of One's Own*

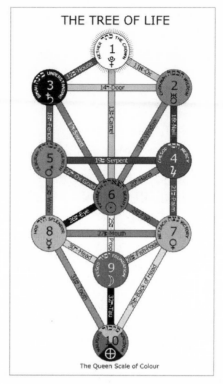

Tree of Life - Queen's Colors (SnappyGoat.com)

Half of the world is female, and in astrology the zodiac signs are six male and six female--or projective and receptive polarities--that alternate polarity as they progress from the first sign Aries to the twelfth sign Pisces. But that gender balance does not extend to the planets. Of the planets used in traditional astrology, Venus is the only goddess, and the remaining all are symbolized by male gods. Although Earth and Moon are considered feminine, goddesses do not symbolize them. Earth's name stems from words that mean "ground" or "soil," and the same linguistic root yields the planet's name in many different languages. The Moon does not have a proper name, although there are many lunar deities in mythology, and Artemis or Diana would have been good choices. A preponderance of god archetypes for the planets creates an imbalance that I believe distorts analysis and interpretation.

In Alchemy the same four "elements" used in astrology are seen to have gender: fire and air are masculine, while earth and water are feminine. Ideally, the planetary rulers of the signs would be gods or goddesses that correspond to the polarity of the sign and element. The larger issue, of course, is a revisioning of the rulerships, or relationships, between the twelve zodiac signs and the planets with which they align.

Prior to the Greeks the Titan gods ruled. They were the powerful children of Gaia (Earth) and Uranus (Sky). The original Titans were six gods and six goddesses. Greek mythology followed where the twelve Olympian deities, also six male and six female, comprised the Greek pantheon, residing on celestial Mount Olympus. The Olympians gained supremacy in a war of gods in which Zeus led his siblings to victory over the elder Titans. Scholars view this as representing the shift from Golden Age to Silver Age in the Greek system of time.

The canonical twelve Olympians, usually portrayed in art and poetry, were Zeus (Jupiter), Hera (Juno), Poseidon (Neptune), Demeter (Ceres), Athena (Minerva), Hestia (Vesta), Apollo (Sun), Artemis (Diana), Aphrodite (Venus), Ares (Mars), Hermes (Mercury), and Hephaestus (Vulcan). Hades, known in the Eleusinian tradition as Pluto, was usually not included among the Olympians because his realm was the underworld and he was confined there.

The concept of "Twelve Gods" is older than any extant Greek or Roman sources, and the idea of twelve divine principles appears in diverse belief systems. Astrology inherited the planetary archetypes largely from the Romans, who in turn, borrowed their gods and goddesses from the earlier Greeks. As the ages changed, about 4,000 years ago, the patriarchy rose in influence and gods usurped the power of ancient goddesses. Earlier goddesses were diminished, or even demonized, and the myths and stories changed to reflect this.

When the first asteroids were discovered, more than 200 years ago, they were named after Roman goddesses: Ceres, Pallas Athena, Juno and Vesta, and they were planets for fifty years. When Astraea, number five, was identified, they were demoted to a new class of objects called asteroids, meaning "star-like." Some astrologers use the first four asteroids in their practice in an attempt to incorporate the influence of Olympian goddesses.

Restoring balance to the planetary rulers of the zodiac requires a close examination of the natures of planets that may in fact express more feminine energy, or archetypal nature, that has been recognized for some time. I would submit that Saturn and Neptune should be renamed to reinstate the status of the Titan goddesses who actually had the roles that were taken over by gods.

Saturn's astrological influence is the embodiment of form, and the dramatic rings that surround the physical planet represent the idea of limitation. The ringed planet gives form to our life experiences and also provides our lessons. Saturn provides the structure of matter as well as the organization in our lives. In Qabalah, Saturn corresponds to the Sephirah (sphere), Binah on the Tree of Life. Binah is called the Great Mother, the matrix of form, and the template of the manifested universe, whose limitation and form-giving power are the womb of creation. Saturn represents gravity and is the cohesive force that binds. The word matter comes from the same root as the words matrix and mother.

I believe that Saturn should be considered as the higher octave of the Moon in a similar way that Uranus is described as the higher octave of Mercury; Neptune the higher octave of Venus, and Pluto the higher octave of Mars. These are relationships of harmonic energy resonance, or "tone," similar to successive octaves in musical scales. The Moon's orbit around Earth is roughly 29 days while Saturn's orbit of the Sun takes about 29 years. Additionally, the Moon's cycle of progression is 29 years. There is a mirroring in these cycles between the two planets that have to do with form.

Isabelle Hickey, author of *Astrology: A Cosmic Science*, describes Saturn as both the "Dweller on the Threshold and the Angel of the Presence, the testing and teaching agency by which we learn and master our life lessons." She describes Saturn as a feminine archetype and penned a poem about her, saying that freedom is only found through Saturn's discipline. Bruno Huber was a Swiss astrologer who, with his wife, Louise Huber, founded the Huber School of Astrology in 1962. The Huber school claims that the Moon is gender-neutral rather than feminine, pertaining to emotional and contact needs, with Saturn representing the mother principle. In this view Saturn governs physical security, survival, protection, boundaries and attachment. Huber believed that Saturn is most comfortable near the bottom of the astrological chart. This is the Moon's domain, but Huber thought Saturn could grow roots and provide stability and assurance to the chart's native. In the midst of crisis, he claimed that it is this strong mother we seek, not the mother figure suggested by the Moon.

In myth, Rhea was the Titan Mother of the Gods and Queen of Heaven. She was a goddess of female fertility, motherhood, and generation. Her name means "flow" and "ease." As the wife of Kronos, also her brother, who became the Roman Saturn, she represented the eternal flow of time and generations. Rhea was also closely identified with the Anatolian mother-goddess Kybele, the Great Mother, *Meter Megale*. In this case, the "flow" was menstrual blood, birth waters, and milk. They were both depicted as beautiful and matronly, usually wearing a turreted crown, and attended by lions, which is a clue to their antiquity. Time and measure is more often feminine because of the natural relationship between the lunar cycle and women's cycles. Rhea was also a goddess of comfort, a blessing reflected in the common Homeric phrase "the gods who live at their ease (*rhea*)." Half of the twelve Olympians were her children: Demeter, Hades, Hera, Hestia, Poseidon, and Zeus.

Rhea, as *Rhea Kronia*, is equated with the Hindu Kali, Mother of Time, who alternatively gives birth and consumes what she has birthed. This may be the origin of the "crone," the third phase of the Triple Goddess: Maiden, Mother, Crone. Kali also has three aspects that were later overlaid on the three main Hindu gods. She was the first creator, sustainer and destroyer. This same archetype became the Celtic Rhiannon. Robert Graves, author of *The White Goddess*, says it was originally Mother Time who wielded the castrating moon-sickle, or scythe, which was later appropriated by Cronus/Saturn. Rhea was the original Grim Reaper. When Rhea wielded the scythe the sky father was cyclically "reaped" as the stars changed in the night sky and heaven fertilized the Earth. Seasonal rebirth was understood as regeneration that naturally followed dissolution of forms in winter and was not seen as a final death. This archetype is called the Dark Goddess, the aspect of creative power that eternally recycles energy by consuming her "children" in her earthen body so they can be born again in higher forms.

Astrologically, Neptune is considered to be the planet of inspiration, dreams and psychic receptivity. Neptune can represent nebulous depths of confusion and illusion, or the loftiest heights of mystical rapture. Neptune is related to the subtle states of dreams, visions, trances, hypnosis, and telepathy. Neptune dissolves material forms and connects us with intangible influences. In fact, Neptune may itself represent the veil between the seen and the unseen. Neptune is also related to the idea of glamour, which creates illusion, and with this planetary energy things are never quite what they seem.

Amphitrite was the ancient Queen of the Sea, usually the daughter of the Titans Oceanus and Tethys. Although Amphitrite does not figure in Greek cults, at an archaic stage she was of outstanding importance. In the Homeric Hymn to Delian Apollo, she appears at the birthing of Apollo among "all the chief goddesses: Dione, Rhea, Ichnaea, Themis and loud-moaning Amphitrite." Poseidon (Roman Neptune), was an Olympian and therefore a later god. He wanted her as his bride so he could become god of the sea. She declined his proposal and hid in the Atlantic Ocean. Amphitrite ultimately married Poseidon (Neptune), and he claimed her throne. Robert Graves says the myth represented the encroachment of male priesthoods into the former feminine control of fishing.

Amphitrite is decorated with the attributes of a queen, her waving hair covered with a net, and sometimes the pincers of a crab are attached to her temples. The Romans referred to her as Salacia, goddess of salt water. Under the continued influence of the Olympian pantheon, she became merely the consort of Poseidon, and was further diminished by poets to a symbolic representation of the sea. Scholar Barbara Walker translates Amphitrite's name as "all-encircling Triad," and says she is the pre-Hellenic Triple Goddess who was transformed into a mere sea nymph by Greek writers. Jane Ellen Harrison recognized an authentic echo of Amphitrite's early importance in the poetic treatment. She says, "It would have been much simpler for Poseidon to recognize his own son . . . the myth belongs to that early stratum of mythology when Poseidon was not yet god of the sea, or supreme there—Amphitrite and the Nereids ruled with their servants the Tritons. Even so late as the Iliad Amphitrite is not yet Neptune's wife."

If we consider that the planets might be represented more equally as male and female archetypes, and begin with Saturn and Neptune, what is the implication for astrological interpretation? How might the meanings change if Saturn and Neptune became goddesses?

Saturn constructs, deconstructs and reconstructs. When we deal with Saturn we deal with authority, both our own capacity to wield authority and our ability to be led by and learn from others. Our first experience of authority is usually our mothers, or a mother figure. Our life flows or not based on how we come to terms with this. Capricorn, the sign ruled by Saturn, is of feminine polarity and better matched with a goddess as ruler. The cycles represented by Mother Time bring all things to harvest. If we embrace Saturn as Rhea, an elder goddess who wields the scythe and rules the cycles, we can more gracefully surrender to her the forms whose time has come. A wise teacher once said, "All pain is caused by holding on."

Water is seen as symbolically feminine in every culture, and in myth the ocean has always been understood as the source of life. Water's fluid nature is shaped by its container, and it represents the emotions and consciousness. It seems that a better interpretative understanding of Neptune's influence can be gained by seeing this ethereal blue sphere as the goddess Amphitrite. The astrological sign of Pisces, ruled by Neptune, is also feminine in polarity and seems better matched to a planet of the same gender. Neptune's energy has been described as veiled strength, and this also seems to be a feminine expression. Going with the flow is a theme for both of these goddesses. Instead of resistance and denial, fighting the inevitable and railing against our fate, surrender and trust in the process are the keys to success.

Atlantis Rising #98 February 2013

CHAPTER 26

ASTROLOGY AND THE ASTEROIDS: WHAT CAN THESE ROCKY OBJECTS TELL US ABOUT THE SACRED FEMININE?

"Life begins when you get out of the grandstand into the game."

P. L. Debevoise

Dwarf Planet Ceres image from Dawn Spacecraft (author Justin Cowart By CC 2.0)

The first asteroid was discovered on January 1, 1801 by Giuseppe Piazzi in Italy. He thought he saw a new comet. Piazzi named the object Ceres, after the Roman goddess of agriculture. Over the next few years three similar "goddesses" were located, which were named Pallas, Vesta, and Juno. By the close of the 19th century several hundred of these small bodies had been identified.

They are called asteroids, which means "star like," but that is really a misnomer. The term planetoid, "planet-like" is more appropriate as they are rocky and metallic objects without atmospheres that orbit the Sun. In August 2006 the IAU (International Astronomers Union), introduced the term "Small Solar System Bodies," or SSSBs. At the same time the term Dwarf Planet was coined to describe the largest minor planets. Pluto is also now considered a Dwarf Planet.

Tens of thousands of asteroids congregate in the so-called main Asteroid Belt. The main belt is a vast, doughnut-shaped ring located between the orbits of Mars and Jupiter but closer to Mars. Asteroids are not visible to the naked eye but many can be seen with binoculars or small telescopes. Some asteroids even have moons, while others orbit in binary pairs.

The strong gravitational force of Jupiter shepherds the asteroid belt, pulling the asteroids away from the Sun, and keeping them from careening into the inner planets. Most asteroids orbit from between 186 million to 370 million miles from the Sun and have slightly elliptical orbits, varying from about three to six earth years. Asteroids range in size from Ceres, which has a diameter of 938 km (578 miles), roughly the size of Texas, down to pebble-size bits of rock. Sixteen asteroids have a diameter of 240 km or greater. Ceres is now considered to be a Dwarf Planet, which in her case is a promotion.

Astronomers theorize that the two moons of Mars, Phobos and Deimos, are actually captured asteroids. Hundreds of thousands have been discovered, with the present rate of discovery at around five thousand per month. So many have been identified that the numbering system had to be expanded. We didn't get our first close-up glimpse of an asteroid until 1991 when Galileo photographed 951 Gaspra while *en route* to Jupiter. NASA's current Dawn Mission hopes to orbit Ceres and Vesta from 2011-2015.

Astronomers believe asteroids are composed of proto-planetary material which was prevented from accreting into a planet-sized body by Jupiter's strong gravity when the Solar System formed 4.6 billion years ago. Author Zechariah Sitchin believed the asteroid belt was once a planet that was shattered by another body entering the Solar System. Either way it is estimated that if the total mass of all the asteroids now present in the Main Asteroid Belt were combined the result would comprise a body approximately 930 miles in diameter (1,500 kilometers), less than half the size of the Moon.

Asteroids are categorized by their composition and their position in the Solar System: Main Belt, Near-Earth Asteroids (NEAs), and Trojans. Trojan asteroids orbit in gravitationally stable Lagrange points within a planet's orbit, either trailing or preceding their planet. Lagrange points are where the gravitational attraction of the Sun and the planet balance each other; about sixty degrees of arc in either direction. Jupiter has the most Trojan asteroids, but Mars also has some. Perhaps they are the rest of the unformed planetary material or shattered material from the Asteroid Belt.

Trojan asteroids have been named after heroes on both sides of the Trojan War. Achilles was the first Trojan asteroid found. The asteroids preceding Jupiter in its orbit were named for heroes on the Greek side, those following Jupiter in its orbit were named for the heroes who fought for Troy. A few asteroids have a dual comet/asteroid nature and are called Centaurs, like Chiron, which was discussed in Atlantis Rising #64 (Chapter 39 in Volume Two).

The first asteroids to be discovered were named for goddesses in Greco-Roman myths, but over time, as hundreds more were identified, the naming process became both random and creative, including famous people, characters from literature, and relatives of the discoverers. The practice of using feminine names lasted until asteroid number 334 which was dubbed Chicago. As the number of asteroids escalated the naming tendencies deteriorated. One asteroid is actually named after a family cat. Even so the trend has been toward predominantly feminine names. It's interesting to speculate if the main asteroid belt had coalesced into a planet would it have been named after a female Olympian?

In terms of the planetary names in our Solar System, and from an astrological perspective, we are decidedly skewed toward the masculine. Of the ten "planets" used in western astrology only Venus and the Moon are feminine, and the Moon doesn't even have a proper name. Some astrologers have suggested calling her Luna. In a more egalitarian approach, and comparable to the twelve zodiac signs, the Greeks had twelve primary Olympians, six male and six female.

Four of the largest asteroids, Ceres, Pallas Athena, Juno and Vesta, were named after Greek and Roman goddesses who correspond to the remaining Greek Olympian goddesses. These four have now become part of astrological interpretation. Astrologers who have incorporated these goddesses into their interpretative toolkit tend to follow the myths as they are told in the Greek stories and their symbolic interpretation is seen through the lens of Greek myth. I believe this approach is incomplete as the archetypes actually stem from much older goddesses whose power had already been diluted, and even negated, by the time of the so-called age of heroes.

Also intriguing is how Zeus/Jupiter's influence parallels that of myth. His introduction by invading groups diminished the role of the goddess over time and the myths demonstrate a gradual decline in the role of the goddesses and their archetypal significance. Today we are witnessing a renaissance of the sacred feminine and perhaps these ancient archetypes will regain their original status and significance.

The asteroid belt itself is a collective with some notable members because of their size relative to others. The belt acts like a dividing line between "terrestrial" planets and the gas giants beyond, representing perhaps a turning from more ordinary concerns to an outer focus. The asteroid goddesses can be seen collectively as four aspects or facets of women's lives. Ceres is the role of mother, Athena was always seen as an independent "virgin," Juno is queen and partner, and Vesta is the priestess archetype. They can also be understood to possess qualities like the four cardinal points of the year revealing stages or phases in women's lives.

Ceres - Renewal - Ceres was the Roman goddess of grain and agriculture. Our word cereal comes from her name. Demeter was her Greek equivalent. Ceres represents the cycle of the year and the waxing and waning of the seasons. Together with her daughter Proserpina, like the Greek Persephone, her story recounts the annual cycle of fertility and the apparent wasteland of winter where life is trapped underground, just like the mythical daughters who were abducted to the underworld. When the daughter is gone the world withers, but when mother and daughter are reunited all life blooms. Ceres's archetypal power lies in understanding that everything in the universe is cyclical, not linear. All forms die and all life is constantly renewed. While we can't alter the annual ebb and flow of light and dark, even though we try with artificial light, we can learn to move in resonance with the cycles and use them to our advantage. Mastery involves moving in synch with the ebb and flow of the cycles of life. Her location in a horoscope can reveal where we need to go with the flow.

Pallas Athena - Wisdom — Although the Greeks saw her as a goddess of both war and wisdom, her earlier archetype embodied the abstract idea of truth, which is similar to the Egyptian Ma'at. Her true essence embodies right relationship to all things; the absolute truth which lies at the heart. Minerva was her Roman counterpart, as was the Gnostic Greek Sophia, and in these goddesses the wisdom aspect was uppermost. Athena was both warrior and peacetime general to the Greeks as well as spinner and weaver, which also gave her domain over fate. Mythically Zeus swallowed his first wife Metis (Justice) so his firstborn child Athena would not be more powerful than he was. Athena sprang from Zeus's head clad in full armor. She even wields the thunderbolt. Increasingly scholars view this as a shift from the Paleolithic orientation to a Great Goddess to a deity who is a solitary sky father capable of giving birth without benefit of a woman. As an archetype Athena shows where courage to face the truth is required and where wisdom concerning our own life battles is needed.

Juno - Sovereignty — Juno, Hera to the Greeks, was the wife of Jupiter (Zeus) and queen of the gods. This once all-powerful goddess of pre-Minoan Crete was reduced over time to a jealous wife. In Greek myth she is cast in a small and spiteful role, seeking vengeance for the numerous amorous exploits of the king of heaven. Perhaps more than any other goddess she is minimized because she was once so powerful. Juno/Hera was literally Queen of Heaven like her Egyptian counterpart Isis. She was Guardian of the Mysteries, including the mysteries of life and death. Juno's deeper message in our horoscopes is learning how we wield and share power and how we express dominion in our own lives.

Vesta - Devotion — Vesta and her Vestal Virgins were keepers of the sacred flame in special temples. This was extended to the flames in the hearth at the center of every home. The cauldron that hangs over the fire is a vastly ancient symbol for the container and metamorphic processes of creation which preceded the Grail by thousands of years. Vesta's domain is a path of devotion and guarding the sacred cauldron and the life-transforming secrets the vessel contains. Curiously, the word for pyramid is Greek and means "fire in the middle," like the hearth fire at the center of every abode. Vesta represents devotion and sacred service and her presence in the chart reveals the area of life where this call to service will be felt.

We all have all of the archetypal patterns whether we are male or female. Some we are aware of and others operate unconsciously. The Swiss psychoanalyst, Carl Jung, described what he called the collective consciousness of humanity, which acts like a vast reservoir of largely unconscious material and is the source and wellspring of archetypes. Jung warned that suppressed or repressed archetypes in the collective psyche of humanity do not disappear. Instead they go underground and emerge in dreams, nightmares, or even dysfunctional or dangerous complexes. Claiming the "missing myths" from the archetypal realms of our psyches can help humanity attain psychological wholeness. Our ability to see the shadow side of unacknowledged archetypes is profoundly healing on an individual and group level.

Although astrology charts can get crowded with all the discoveries that keep popping up in the Solar System, using discretion and intuition can add a rich pallet of symbolic language that yields a depth of understanding not available with a smaller array of planetary deities.

Atlantis Rising #65 August 2007

PART IV
ZODIACS & SIGNS

CHAPTER 27

BEYOND SUN SIGNS: WHAT DEEPER SYMBOLISM MIGHT THE SUN'S FIERY NATURE REVEAL?

"Some painters transform the Sun into a yellow spot, others transform a yellow spot into the Sun."

Pablo Picasso

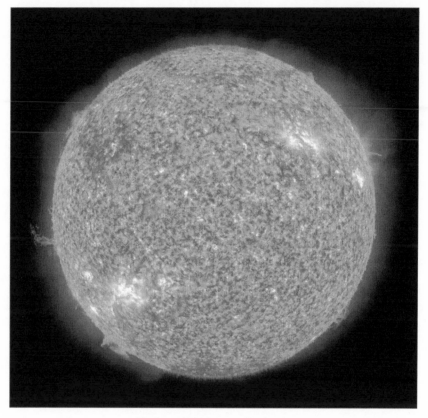

The Sun - NASA image; public domain

Once regarded by astronomers as a small, and relatively insignificant star, our chief luminary is now believed to be brighter than 85%, and in the top 10% by mass, of the hundreds of billions of stars in the Milky Way galaxy. Most other stars in our galaxy are red dwarfs. Our Sun is a main-sequence star, about 4.5 billion years old, and contains more than 99.8% of the total mass of the Solar System, with Jupiter containing most of the remainder.

The Sun generates energy by nuclear fusion of hydrogen nuclei into helium, fusing 430–600 million tons of hydrogen every second. Solar physicists say it takes a million years for the energy created at the Sun's core to make its way to the surface, where it radiates into space. The Sun is about 70% hydrogen and 28% helium by mass, and since its birth, our star has consumed about half of the hydrogen in its heart. It will continue to radiate for another five billion years, and its luminosity is expected to nearly double in that time. At the end of the Sun's life it will expand to become a Red Giant, expelling its outer layers in a dramatic, glowing planetary nebula.

Although the Sun is a huge ball of gas, it appears to have a sharp edge because the energy radiates from the photosphere, a thin layer a couple hundred miles thick, compared with the Sun's overall radius of 432,000 miles (695,000 kilometers). Above this lies the slightly hotter chromosphere, another relatively thin layer that measures between 1,000 and 2,000 miles thick. Above the chromosphere is the corona, a superheated region where temperatures rise to millions of degrees. Because the Sun's gravity isn't strong enough to hold onto such hot gas, the outer atmosphere boils off into space. The corona is invisible in ordinary light, and it is only during a total solar eclipse, when the Moon blocks the much brighter photosphere, that the stunning sight of the corona can be seen.

The Sun is a nearly-perfect sphere that rotates on its axis. But unlike Earth and other solid objects the Sun is a giant ball of gas and plasma, so different parts of the Sun spin at different speeds. We know this by observing sunspots. The region of the Sun near its equator rotates once every 25 days. The rotation rate decreases with increasing latitude, so rotation is slowest near the Sun's poles, which rotate once every 36 days.

Sunlight travels to Earth in about eight minutes and nineteen seconds and supports life by photosynthesis, as well as driving Earth's climate and weather. In addition to heat and light, the Sun's hot corona emits a low density stream of charged particles, mostly electrons and protons, known as the solar wind. The bubble in the interstellar medium formed by the solar wind, called the heliosphere, is the largest continuous structure in the Solar System, extending well beyond Pluto. The solar wind, and the much higher energy particles ejected by solar flares, can have dramatic effects. These range from power line surges to radio interference, the beautiful aurora borealis, pointing the ionized gas tails of comets away from the Sun, and creating measurable effects on spacecraft trajectories.

The most conspicuous features on the Sun are sunspots. Sunspots are the "cool" regions, and their lower relative temperature makes them look dark by comparison. Sunspots are caused by complicated, and not very well understood, interactions within the Sun's magnetic field. They can last anywhere from a few hours to a few months. Sunspots tend to cluster, with some sunspot groups containing a hundred or more individual spots. These large groups possess powerful magnetic fields and often give rise to flares, the largest explosions in the Solar System. A typical flare lasts for five to ten minutes and releases as much energy as a million hydrogen bombs. The biggest flares last for several hours and emit enough energy to power the United States, at its current rate of electric consumption, for 100,000 years.

The Moon circles the Earth, the Earth orbits the Sun, and the Sun in turn orbits the center of the Milky Way galaxy, creating what is called the Cosmic Year. Astronomers have calculated that it takes 225-240 million years for the Sun to orbit the center of the Milky Way, traveling at the astonishing speed of 782,000 km/hour in a circular path. Our Solar System resides in what is called the Orion Arm of the galaxy and is 26,000 light-years from the center. The spiral arms of our great galaxy also twirl through space. The Sun has circled the center of the galaxy about twenty times in its stellar lifetime, and the last time the Sun was in its current position, dinosaurs roamed the Earth. If estimates are accurate, the Sun has roughly thirty more cosmic circuits before it runs out of gas.

The Sun is the largest object in our Solar System and is definitely center stage. Our brilliant day star is the source of light and life on Earth and has been revered from time out of mind. Sunrise probably inspired the first prayers as light returned and dissipated the dark uncertainties of night. Human minds seek meaning through allegory and metaphor, and some of humanity's deepest truths have been transmitted through myth--our sacred stories. Myths about the Sun and Moon are at the heart of beliefs about the possible origins of humanity. In part, these stories grew out of a desire to explain the Sun's apparent motion and daily appearance and disappearance.

The most popular symbolic representation of the Sun is an all-seeing eye. A wheel is the next most common theme with the spokes seen as the Sun's rays. Many cultures saw the Sun being drawn across the sky in a chariot pulled by various magical steeds. Scientists claim we are made of star stuff, and mythically the Sun and Moon are always seen as ancestors, heroes or benefactors, but almost always in a parental role. The ancient Persian's believed that the stars were children of the Sun and Moon. The Greeks called the Sun Helios and the Romans called it Sol.

In western culture we are accustomed to think of the Sun as male and the Moon as female, but the Sun has been seen as a goddess as often as a god. In certain belief systems the Sun's heart is seen as feminine and the fiery outer nature as masculine. In the German language the Sun is feminine and the Moon is masculine, but in Romance languages it is the reverse. In Australia the Moon is male and the Sun female. The Intuit believe that the Sun is the older sister of a male Moon. On the Malay Peninsula, both the Sun and Moon are female.

American Indians most often see the Sun and Moon as brother and sister, but in some tribes they are mates. The Egyptian Sun god, Ra, was seen as a child at dawn, an adult at noon, and an old man at sunset. Ra traveled across the daytime sky in a boat and navigated the treacherous underworld at night. Other Egyptian gods, such as Amun, were combined with Ra to increase their power. It is intriguing that Polynesians also call their sun god Ra.

Some scholars speculate that prevailing climate conditions may have influenced the perception of gender for the Sun and Moon. In climates where the Sun scorched the day, causing people to seek shelter, the cooler dark of night was seen as more nurturing and therefore feminine. However, in places where the warmth of the Sun was a welcome relief after a bitter winter, the Sun was imagined as a nurturing and feminine influence. One example is the great Sun goddess Saule of the Lithuanian and Baltic peoples who live in harsh northern climes.

Important solar festivals have often been held at the solstices, Latin for "sun stands still," when the Sun appears to stop in the sky for three days before changing direction and shifting its apparent annual motion. These two points in the year are the extremes of light and dark. The symbolic rebirth of the Sun king happens at winter solstice in the northern hemisphere when the length of the day increases again. Many European countries celebrate the festival of Yule at winter solstice. The word comes from *yole*, or *yuul*, which means "sun" in several languages. Some linguists suggest it is also the origin of the English word wheel, which is a popular solar symbol representing the turning the year.

In astrology the Sun is seen as the character of the individuality and the main focus of soul lessons and experiences. From a spiritual perspective, we can view the apparent annual journey of the Sun as the soul's sojourn through time and the experiences of the zodiac archetypes. If we view the fire of the Sun as an agent of transformation, we can take a brief alchemical look at the twelve signs.

The first sign Aries embodies the initiating force that emerges out of the collective nature of the twelfth sign Pisces. Aries is irresistible force, and represents the principles of resurrection and individualization, the symbolic point of all beginnings, and the onset of the circle of the seasons. The second sign Taurus embodies the principle of pure substance. Taurus is the matrix that absorbs the impact of the intense energy projected outward by Aries. Energy is action. Matter is reaction. In alchemical symbolism, the matter of Taurus is precipitated from the waters of Pisces, the twelfth sign, by the fire of Aries. The third sign Gemini embodies the principle of motion that is the result of the irresistible force of Aries impinging on the immovable object, Taurus. Spinning motion on an axis is the result. Gemini's expression is to adjust and adapt in an ever-widening collection of data and search for meaning.

The fourth sign Cancer adds the powerful quality of emotion to the mental nature of Gemini. Cancer acts like the womb, and is the universal mother principle, providing the vessel from which all forms are born. The fifth sign Leo brings about the process of individuation through the fire and focus of the individual will. Virgo is the sixth sign and brings the idea of differentiated matter into forms that can become highly specialized. At this phase of the Zodiac, plans can be carried out in detail.

Libra is the seventh sign and embodies balance, and the principle of equilibrium, which results from the interaction of Leo and Virgo, a marriage of spirit and matter. The eighth sign, Scorpio represents the idea of dynamic power. This potent energy of desire can be used in construction or destruction, death or resurrection, and is characterized by great intensity. This is a path of regeneration of the desire nature.

Sagittarius is the ninth sign and embodies the idea of illumination that results from balanced power between Libra and Scorpio. Sagittarius energy is philosophical in nature, seeking wisdom and an understanding of first principles. In the tenth sign Capricorn, matter can now be organized into perfect forms. Capricorn's energy is governing and conserving, focused on achievement, integrity, recognition and responsibility.

Aquarius is the eleventh sign where the unfolding sequence of the zodiac now expresses in group consciousness. At this stage it is possible to be unified by a common ideal. Aquarius looks for truth in all things and desires to unite with others on a universal level. The twelfth sign Pisces can be seen as the universal solvent which both dissolves the boundaries of separation created by all the preceding signs, and creates the fluid environment in which the seeds of a new cycle can germinate. In Pisces the sorrows and joys of others are keenly felt, and this is the sign where compassion is born.

Many spiritual traditions have taught that the fire of the Sun can be used for transmutation. If we are open to the spiritual truth that is not apparent in our science, we can be transformed at a deep level, harnessing the power of the Sun, burning away the imperfections in our personalities, and radiating our own unique light into the word.

CHAPTER 28

HAVE THE ASTROLOGICAL
SIGNS CHANGED?

"I know nothing with certainty, but the sight of the stars makes me dream."

Vincent Van Gogh

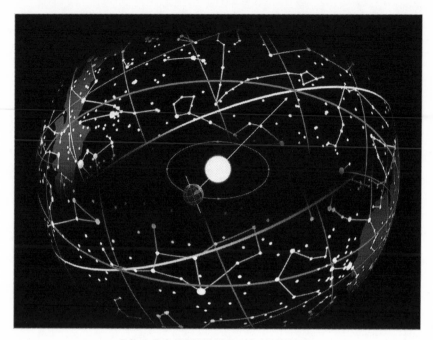

Ecliptic Path (CC BY-SA 3.0; author Tau'olunga)

Controversy arose in January of 2011 after Parke Kunkle, an astronomy professor at Minneapolis Community & Technical College, published a short article in a local paper, announcing that the astrological signs had changed. He also mentioned a thirteenth zodiac constellation, unfamiliar to most readers, which likewise caused a considerable stir. To everyone's surprise, including Kunkle's, the story reverberated like a shot heard round the world. The tale morphed from a simple piece to mangled disinformation like the Repeat Game at a party.

I have received an avalanche of questions and have been called upon to set the record straight. Contrary to the misinformation that spread like a virus, the astrological "signs" have not changed. People can rest easy that their astrological identities are not at risk, but there is a bigger picture to consider. Kunkle's message, while widely misunderstood, does require some technical explanation.

Zodiac comes from a Greek word that means "circle of animals." The zodiac that astrologers use is a celestial coordinate system that takes the ecliptic, the apparent path of the Sun, as the origin of latitude, and the position of the Sun at spring equinox as the origin of longitude. The zodiac of astrological signs is a circle of twelve thirty-degree divisions of Celestial Longitude, which are centered on the ecliptic. The astrological signs are also measures of time that begin each year at spring equinox in the northern hemisphere. Every year, the astrological sign of Aries begins about March 21st when the Sun's apparent motion crosses the celestial equator going north. Unless something alters Earth's orbit, the signs won't change. Of course, a future culture might decide to cast a different set of zodiac characters.

The constellations, on the other hand, are divisions of space, like states, provinces, or countries on a terrestrial map. In the past, different cultures imagined the stars as different "pictures" and had different zodiacs. Over thousands of years the shapes of the constellations have morphed and some stars have changed alliances. For example, the claws of the Scorpion, which still bear the earlier names (Northern and Southern Claws), are now the scales of Libra. Likewise, in times past, Pisces had only one fish. But since 1930 the International Astronomers Union, IAU, has agreed on eighty-eight constellations. The twelve zodiac constellations (not signs), which are essentially Babylonian in origin, have been in use since at least Roman times.

Although the astrological signs do not change, what does shift is Earth's position relative to the stars over a slow passage of time, because of the nature of Earth's rotation. Earth "wobbles" as she spins. This wobble creates the phenomenon called Precession of the Equinoxes, which causes spring equinox sunrise (in the northern hemisphere), to occur due east against a backdrop of stars that slowly shifts. This apparent motion of the sky moves "backward," or clockwise, through the zodiac constellations, instead of the annual counter-clockwise direction in which the Sun appears to move in the sky. This is the slow motion that Kunkle described when he claimed that the astrological signs had changed.

Because this shift occurs on the ecliptic, the slowly moving starry curtain of the twelve zodiacal constellations forms the stellar backdrop. This space contains the familiar star patterns from the Ram to the

Fishes, as well as other stars and deep sky objects. About 4,000 years ago the constellation of Aries, and the sign of Aries, were aligned at spring equinox dawn. Because the sky "moves," the astrological signs are no longer aligned with the constellations that gave them their names, and therein lies the problem. For roughly two thousand years, spring equinox sunrise has occurred against the stars of Pisces, The Fishes, which rise before the Sun in pre-dawn darkness. Soon, the stars of Aquarius will take this position, heralding the Age of Aquarius.

Assuming that this slow motion is constant, the sky seems to move at the rate of roughly one degree of arc in seventy-two years. This creates a long cycle of 25,920 years called the Precession of the Equinoxes, or Great Year. If that number is divided by twelve, the result is 2,160, which is the approximate length of an astrological age. Each constellation (not sign), of the zodiac slowly moves into position to define an age.

The changing of ages has long cusps or transitional periods, and there are no precise demarcations of the circle where one influence stops and a new one begins. We are currently feeling the energies of Pisces diminish as the new wave of Aquarian energy grows in influence. Soon, as the backward march shifts, the "dawning of the Age of Aquarius" will be heralded as this constellation moves to center stage and defines the new world age. Before the stars of Aries provided the backdrop for spring equinox sunrise, the stars of Taurus held that distinction. As the ages changed, bull cults faded and the ram became the sacrificial animal of the new age of Aries. As the shift of the ages transitioned from Aries into Pisces, both Lamb of God and Fisher of Men were sacrificial symbols for the age of Pisces, the Fishes. In our epoch, the fish is a familiar symbol. Aquarius has advanced to the springtime place in the northern hemisphere, and a new symbol for the Aquarian age will emerge. Instead of the sacrificial savior of Pisces, perhaps the symbolic icon of the Age of Aquarius, the Water Bearer, will be a fully-awakened human. Aquarius is sometimes called the "energy bearer," so it could also be a harbinger of new and sustainable forms of energy.

Earth is also inclined on her axis of rotation 23.45 degrees. This tilt creates the seasons and causes the northern hemisphere to lean toward the Sun in summer and away from the Sun in winter, while the reverse is true in the southern hemisphere. As Earth rotates on its axis, the stars appear to rise and set at night in the same way the Sun appears to move across the sky during the day. But the stars near to the north and south poles do not rise and set. Instead, they appear to move in a circle around the poles and are therefore called "circumpolar" stars. Like a slowly spinning top, our planet's north and south axes trace imaginary circles in the heavens as if the Earth's poles draw them. As the axis of the Earth changes slowly over time, the North Pole points to a different spot in the circumpolar stars. A new "north star," or sometimes an empty spot, results.

In our time the pole star is Polaris, Alpha Ursa Minor, but 3,000 years ago it was Thuban, "dragon" in Arabic, the brightest star in the constellation of Draco, the Dragon. In another 4,000 years the pole star will be Errai, "shepherd," the Gamma star in the constellation of Cepheus, the King. The circumpolar stars also change in a similar manner in the southern hemisphere.

The signs of the zodiac are a function of the cycle of the year, while the apparent shifting of the stars relative to the Earth is a measure of an age. The zodiac signs have been compared to stained glass windows that "color" the solar and planetary influences. Symbolically, the zodiac forms a cycle of experience that provides a template of evolution in nested cycles through which Earth receives the influences of the Sun and planets. As the zodiac signs present a yearly circle of archetypal experience, so too does the Great Year. Astrologically, an age is characterized by the archetypal energies of the constellation whose stars rise before the Sun at spring equinox dawn. Each phase of the Great Year is like a cosmic month, possessing a distinct and overarching quality of experience. The ages can be seen like spokes of the cosmic wheel, presenting a phase shift of archetypal energy designed to provide an evolutionary schoolroom for developing humanity.

In his controversial article, Kunkle also introduced the constellation of
Ophiuchus, the Serpent Bearer, to a wider audience. Ophiuchus is a
thirteenth constellation that is also in the zodiac region, but is
ordinarily not part of the traditional circle of twelve. Ophiuchus is an
enormous star group that is actually composed of two constellations,
the Serpent and the Serpent Bearer. I wrote an article about this
constellation in *Atlantis Rising* #44 (Chapter 30 in this Volume). The
foot of the Serpent Bearer is well within the bounds of the ecliptic, the
parameters of the zodiac constellations. Sagittarius the Archer points
his arrow at the foot of Ophiuchus, which in turn, is poised on one
claw of the Scorpion. The tail of the snake is near Aquila, the Eagle,
and the serpent's head nearly touches Corona, the Crown. Rasalhague,
the alpha star of Ophiuchus, means, "head of the snake charmer."
Mythically, Serpent Bearer represents the Egyptian Imhotep and the
Greek Asklepios, famous healers and noteworthy wielders of snake
medicine.

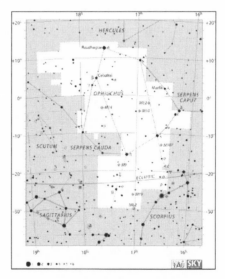

*Ophiuchus Constellation (CC BY 3.0 IAU & Sky & Telescope Magazine;
Roger Sinnott and Rich Flenberg)*

Thirteen is often considered unlucky. I believe this could be a
safeguard, or decoy, to conceal powerful sacred knowledge from the
casual observer. Thirteen appears in interesting groupings: the twelve

tribes of Israel and the Levites; twelve disciples and Jesus, and twelve signs and Ophiuchus, to name a few. Twelve circles around a central thirteenth is a key symbol in sacred geometry, hinting at the mysterious relationship of center versus circumference. The Maya have thirteen "signs" in their cosmology, and there are thirteen lunations each year--new moons or full moons. There is a sense of crossing from the mundane into the mysterious and possible sacred when we move from twelve to thirteen.

The famous Greek physician Hippocrates, originator of the Hippocratic oath of medicine, once said, "A physician without a knowledge of astrology has no right to call himself a physician." I would venture to say that an astronomer who knows nothing of astrology has lost the soul of the discipline he or she has inherited. I think it's unfortunate that professor Kunkle didn't consult a professional astrologer before he published his article, but it has certainly generated a lot of lively discussion.

It's been barely a century since the science of astronomy separated from the ancient discipline of astrology. Whatever the philosophical differences between the disciplines it's still inspiring and empowering to go outside on a clear, dark night and learn to recognize some of the bright stars that occupy the constellations. I believe we should contemplate the majesty of the stars, and the vastness of the Universe of which we are a part, letting the magic infuse our lives with a sense of wonder. Humanity's story is an ancient one, and contrary to apocalyptic notions expressed at the current changing of the ages, the tale is far from finished, although the outcome may be written in the stars.

Atlantis Rising #91 December 2011

CHAPTER 29

SIGN LANGUAGE: THE ENDURING ARCHETYPES OF THE ZODIAC

"Let there be lights in the firmament of heaven to separate the day from the night; and let them be for signs, and for seasons, and for days and for years."

Genesis 1:14

Sunrise on Mattinatella Sea (629571 SnappyGoat.com)

The practice of Astrology dates back thousands of years, and the perceived relationship between what happens in the sky and a resulting resonance on Earth remains perennial. Humanity has long observed the changing and recurring patterns in the sky, correlating these in terms of meaning in the lives of individuals and collectives. Astrological records date back to 1645 BCE in Babylon, and the earliest known horoscope dates to 410 BCE. Astrology's origins can also be traced to several other cultures, including Egypt, which developed sophisticated calendars and skywatching traditions. Astrology was also popular in Greece, where Ptolemy authored influential astrological and astronomical texts, and in Rome, where many learned scholars, including two emperors, wrote laws and counseled citizens based on the stars.

The earliest surviving Babylonian astrology text is the *Enuma Anu Enlil*, which means "When the gods Anu and Enlil ..." This text describes various astronomical omens and their application to national affairs. A segment of the text says, "If in Nisannu the sunrise appears sprinkled with blood, battles will follow." Nisannu is the Babylonian month corresponding to March/April in the Western calendar.

Every year the Earth makes a full circle around the Sun. Earth's orbital motion causes the Sun to appear to move in a path that is called the ecliptic. Astronomically the zodiac is a circular band of sky, eight degrees above and below the ecliptic, which contains the familiar constellations from the Ram to the Fishes. Temporally the Zodiac is a division of time based on our motion relative to the Sun which has the four main divisions of the seasons, the so-called Cardinal Points of year, which are the equinoxes and solstices, as primary anchors.

Symbolically, the Zodiac is a cycle of experience which provides the template of evolution through which Earth receives the influences of the Sun and planets. This circle of the year is separated into twelve equal divisions that represent successive phases of experience. The Zodiac signs have been described like stained glass windows which "color" the solar and planetary influences.

Ancient cultures drew meaning from the stars. Egyptian temple axes, and megalithic monuments around the world, were aligned with bright stars and constellations. Cultures also related to the part of the sky that provided the stellar stage relative to where they lived. People in northern latitudes watched the circumpolar stars overhead. If a civilization lived where an unobstructed view of the horizon was available their orientation was directed toward the ecliptic. Cultures in the southern hemisphere looked to the opposite pole and the different stars that appeared in southern skies. Southern stars offer a different stellar canvas so the myths and star lore tell different stellar stories.

But Earth's relationship to the stars changes slowly over time due to Precession, an apparent backward motion which astronomers believe is caused by a wobble of our planet's axis. So some calendars and prevailing astrological systems have shifted to a solar or seasonal orientation.

What makes Astrology work is difficult to explain as occult tradition holds that this ancient discipline actually operates beyond the third dimension in the realm of the fourth, fifth, and sixth. Our science has not ventured very far into those dimensional realms, although Quantum Physics is blazing new trails. That astrology does work is evidenced by its continued existence for thousands of years. Science really doesn't understand gravity either, but we live with its effects.

From the spiritual perspective of astrology we are eternal souls who move through time and space on the wheel of existence. In this light we first circle around the outer perimeter of the Zodiac where our experiences occur in the mundane realm. To admittedly oversimplify, this boils down to questions of love and money. At some point however, symbolically in the sign of Capricorn, we turn inward. We then move toward the center of the wheel where the energies of the six pairs of opposite signs become balanced and blended. Life's lessons then become more spiritual in nature and our responses yield a synthesis of meaning rather than the antithesis of getting, or not getting, what we desire in the material world.

The twelve signs of astrology are organized into four "elements," or phases of expression, and three ways these elements act: initiating, consolidating or alternating. Ancient Chinese and Hindu systems are organized in the same manner using different vocabulary. Four elements express in three modes to produce twelve signs that are linked in time to the seasons or cardinal points of the year. The first six signs are personal and the second six are collective, and we have all of these components in our horoscopes in varying degrees. According to alchemical sequence the elements are Fire, Earth, Air and Water, and the modes of expression are Cardinal, Fixed and Mutable. The elements form triangles of energy and the modes become squares or crosses of movement. These combine and create the basic energetic signature of the signs.

Esoterically every sign is said to trigger influences in the sign that follows, resulting in effects in the material world. Each sign also reacts to the energies of the one preceding, releasing energy that radiates through the circumference of the zodiac in successive waves.

∼

Zodiac Signs

Aries is a Cardinal Fire sign that begins at spring equinox in the northern hemisphere. The quality of Aries is the outrushing force of spring emerging out of the collective dissolution of the twelfth sign Pisces. Aries is irresistible force and represents the principles of resurrection and individualization and the symbolic point where the wheel begins. Aires is represented by the ram, and its energy tends to be pioneering, initiating, headfirst, impulsive and adventurous. Slowing down to make a prudent choice can be difficult.

Taurus is a Fixed Earth sign and embodies the principle of pure substance. Taurus is the matrix that absorbs the impact of the energy projected outward by Aries. Energy is action. Matter is reaction. Alchemically the matter of Taurus is precipitated from the water of Pisces (the twelfth sign), by the fire of Aries. The nature of Taurus, symbolized by the bull, expresses stability and permanence and the path involves cultivating higher values versus seeking purely material motives. Taurus natives tend to be builders and sustainers and rarely act without reflection.

Gemini is a Mutable Air sign that embodies the principle of motion. The energy of the third sign is the result of the irresistible force impinging on the immovable object. Spinning motion on an axis is the result. Gemini's expression is to adjust and adapt in an ever-wider collection of data and search for meaning. Learning to tame the mind is their quest. Geminis are curious and social, desiring to make connections and form relationships, and they are rarely still.

Cancer is a Cardinal Water sign that marks the summer solstice and adds the powerful quality of emotion to the mental nature of the preceding sign. Cancer acts like the womb and is the Universal Mother principle, providing the vessel from which all forms are born. Cancer energy is highly instinctual, nurturing and protective, making a home and building emotional connections. Learning to stabilize and steady the emotions is the path of Cancer.

Leo is a Fixed Fire sign that adds the element of fire and brings about the process of individuation. Leo energy is creative and proud, loyal, loving and eager to display prowess. Leos see themselves as the creative center of their circle of influence and need to cultivate the quality of personal spiritual dominion, not ruling over others. Leo radiates light and warmth and must learn loving detachment that springs from an understanding heart.

Virgo is Mutable Earth and brings the idea of differentiated matter into forms that become highly specialized. At this phase of the Zodiac matter becomes organized and plans can be carried out in detail. Virgos have a highly developed sense of discrimination and tend to be technical in nature and can be overly critical. Virgo energy is suited to facts and figures but is generally also oriented to service. Virgos often struggle with an impossible quest for perfection that can lead to a sense of inferiority.

Libra is Cardinal Air and holds the place of autumn equinox. Libra embodies balance and the principle of equilibrium that results from the interaction of Leo and Virgo, a marriage of spirit and matter. Libra energy seeks to harmonize and is inclined toward cooperation, compromise and partnership, bringing potential problems from trying to be all things to all people. Libras seek the mirror and lessons of relationship but can have difficulty standing up for themselves as they sometimes try to maintain peace at any price.

Scorpio is a Fixed Water sign that represents the idea of dynamic power. This energy can be used in construction or destruction, death or resurrection, and is characterized by great intensity. In Scorpio we are dealing with issues of power, temptation relating to the use of power, discipline and an urge for emotional control. Scorpios are reserved and more happens internally than what is expressed on the surface. This is a path of regeneration of the desire nature and an orientation toward service releases the coiled energy in a positive manner.

Sagittarius is Mutable Fire and embodies the idea of illumination that results from the joining of balanced power in the two prior signs. Sagittarius energy is philosophical in nature, seeking wisdom and an understanding of first principles. While Gemini tends to gather information Sagittarius looks for wide and varied experiences that will ultimately lead to spiritual understanding. The path of Sagittarius is learning to understand the patterns that lie at the root of our problems and challenges.

Capricorn anchors the winter solstice and combines the principles of Cardinal Earth. In Capricorn matter organizes itself into "perfect" forms. Capricorn represents the crystallization of matter and is the opposite sign to Cancer, the womb of potential. Capricorn's energy is governing and conserving, focused on achievement, integrity, recognition and responsibility. Capricorns are fueled by tremendous ambition and their lessons stem from learning the motive which underlies their drive to climb.

Aquarius is a Fixed Air sign where the unfolding sequence now expresses in group consciousness that is unified by a common ideal. Aquarius looks for truth in all things and desires to unite with others on a universal level. Aquarians are forward thinking and they can be mental pioneers. However this energy is mentally fixed so Aquarians can also rebel at the status quo or object in principle to structures that don't seem to work, or appear to them to be outmoded.

Pisces is a Mutable Water sign and can be seen as the universal solvent, both dissolving the boundaries of separation created by all the preceding signs, and creating the fluid environment in which the seeds of a new cycle can germinate. In Pisces the sorrows and joys of others are keenly felt and this is the sign where compassion is born. More than any other sign Pisces must lose a sense of the personal self in service to something higher. Pisces contains the knowledge of the underlying unity of all things, which is the reality behind the world of manifested forms.

Atlantis Rising #70 June 2008

CHAPTER 30

THIRTEENTH ZODIAC SIGN:
THE MYSTICAL 13TH ELEMENT

"One short sleep past, we wake eternally, and death shall be
no more."

John Donne

Ophiuchus, the Serpent Bearer, 13th Constellation (SnappyGoat.com)

The apparent path of the Sun is called the ecliptic, and the familiar constellations of the zodiac provide the stellar background for the Sun's annual journey. Over thousands of years the shapes of the constellations have morphed and some stars have changed alliances. For example, the claws of the Scorpion, which still bear the earlier names (Northern and Southern Claws), are now the scales of Libra. Likewise, Pisces once had one fish. There is another constellation that occupies this prestigious part of the sky, but for some reason is not included in the circle. Its presence is hinted at symbolically as the path of the Sun has often been described as an undulating serpent.

Ophiuchus is an enormous star group composed of two constellations, the Serpent and the Serpent Bearer. The foot of the Serpent Bearer is well within the bounds of the ecliptic, although he is not counted in the zodiac. Sagittarius the Archer points his arrow at the foot of Ophiuchus, which in turn, is poised on one claw of the Scorpion. The tail of the snake is near Aquila, the Eagle, and the serpent's head nearly touches Corona, the Crown. Rasalhague, the alpha star, means, "head of the snake charmer." Contained within the boundaries of this large constellation is Barnard's star, the stellar body with the largest proper motion. A famous Supernova exploded in Ophiuchus in 1604, called Kepler's Nova, and another in 1987. Serpent Bearer represents the Egyptian Imhotep and Greek Asklepios, famous healers and noteworthy wielders of snake medicine.

The Greek name Asklepios came from the earlier name of Draco, the Great Dragon, and was also associated with the other stellar serpents. Accounts vary but the mythical Asklepios was the child of the sun god Apollo and the human woman Coronis (crow). In the god's continued absence she fell in love with a mere mortal, and in a jealous rage Apollo murdered the pregnant Coronis, mythically destroying the feminine aspect. Then overcome with grief, he snatched the unborn child from her womb as her body burned on a funeral pyre. After his rescue the infant Asklepios was entrusted to the wise centaur, Chiron who taught him medicine. Asklepios became the most renowned of healers, capable of restoring life. Hippocrates, called the father of modern medicine, is the best known descendent of Asklepios.

The famous Caduceus wand, which was later bestowed upon Asklepios, enabled Mercury (Hermes) to travel from the top of Mount Olympus to the depths of the underworld. Two serpents entwined around a central staff with wings at the top is still the symbol of medicine. A similar icon is found on the walls of Egyptian tombs. In fact, the Greeks borrowed Asklepios from the earlier and historical Egyptian architect and healer Imhotep, who is credited with building the step pyramid of Saqqara.

Serpents were the sacred servants of Asklepios. Versions differ, but in one story Athena gave him blood that had flowed in Medusa's veins. Blood from the left side spread a fatal poison, but blood from the right side had healing power. Asklepios knew how to use the wise blood to restore the dead to life. The Oracle at Delphi consisted of a group of priestesses called Pythia (python), who used snake venom to induce a trance state. The women also breathed mind-altering vapors, rising from an underground pit at the shrine. The relationship between serpents, wisdom, and the sacred feminine stretches far back in time.

(In *Atlantis Rising* #43, "Mystery of Malta's long-headed skulls," Adriano Forgione explored similar material).

Myth is a powerful and multi-faceted mechanism, and it is impossible to separate the story of Asklepios, the Healer from that of Orion, the Hunter. The two constellations are never visible in the sky at the same time, and there is an enduring myth to explain this. Orion was a great but boastful hunter, bragging that no game could elude him. This angered Juno, wife of Zeus (Jupiter). One day while Orion slept she had a scorpion sting his heel, proving fatal to the proud hunter. Asklepios came to the rescue, and using his knowledge of the healing qualities of serpents, he brought Orion back to life. In earlier Egyptian myth it is Horus, son of Osiris (Orion), who had trouble with a scorpion, but Horus was healed by the powerful magic of his mother Isis, Queen of Magic.

This in turn angered Hades (Pluto,) god of the underworld. He complained that if human healers had power over death his kingdom would become empty. Zeus intervened and dispatched both Orion and Asklepios, and then immortalized the heroes as constellations. Orion is on one side of the sky, and Asklepios, holding his giant snake, is on the other. As the stars of the Scorpion rise, those of Orion seem to sink defeated in the west. However, when Ophiuchus crushes the Scorpion with his heel, Orion is reborn. In our time frame Orion shines in winter and Scorpio is visible in summer skies. Each year the fabled healer bestows the gift of immortality as the ongoing drama of Hunter and Healer, generation versus regeneration, cyclically unfolds.

Orion is also equated with the Egyptian god/king Osiris in the Pyramid Texts. Osiris was ruler of the mysterious underworld, and his journey through this frightening domain is recorded in the twelve hours of night, painted on the walls of Egyptian tombs in the Valley of the Kings. Osiris, the reincarnation of Egyptian Pharaohs, treads the wheel of rebirth, trying to attain a place among the immortal circumpolar stars. The two opposing figures of King and Healer contrast the secular versus sacred roles of the king.

Diverse cultural myths and symbols of serpent bearers abound. The wise teacher and healer, Quetzlcoatl (Aztec) or Kukulkan (Maya) was depicted as a feathered serpent, like the caduceus, combining serpents and wings. Pakal, lord of Palenque, whose tomb lies at the heart of a great pyramid, is depicted on a stele with "First Mother," doing a snake dance. Hopi snake dancers honor the powerful nature spirit Macibol, who "struggles while dancing with the Great Serpent."

The ancient symbol which appears over doorways of Egyptian temples is a circle with wings, depicting the risen and victorious Horus. Ouroboros, the serpent biting its own tail, is another ancient symbol of eternity. Enigmatic passages appear in the Bible (Numbers 21:9 and 2 Kings 18:4), describing Moses, raising a serpent of bronze in the wilderness. Called *Neshutan*, this bronze serpent on a staff had protective powers for the loyal children of Israel in the desert and became a symbol of worship. Bronze, like copper, is a metal sacred to Venus.

St. George killing the dragon is the medieval representation of Serpent Bearer since the dragon is an ancient symbol of the serpent fire. Christian churches were built on "dragon lines" of serpent power, overlaying previous pagan sites and thus "slaying" or conquering the feminine energies of the Earth. Likewise the last Major Trump of Tarot is the World, sometimes the World Dancer. This symbol of Cosmic Consciousness is holding two spiraling, serpentine currents of energy representing spiritual mastery.

Thirteen is often considered unlucky. I believe this could be a safeguard, a decoy, to conceal powerful sacred knowledge from the casual observer. Thirteen appears in several interesting groupings: Twelve tribes and the Levites, the teachers, make thirteen. Twelve disciples and Christ, and twelve signs and Ophiuchus, equals thirteen. Twelve circles around a central thirteenth is a key symbol in sacred geometry, hinting at the mystery of center versus circumference. The Maya have thirteen "signs" in their cosmology, and there are thirteen lunations each year, New Moons or Full Moons.

Serpent Bearer is a powerful example of how ancient wisdom is transmitted through myth. The story veils a profound truth of spiritual work and immortality that has to do with restoration of the sacred feminine. Serpent Bearer is the secret emblem of the mystical marriage. The work of the Healer is to uncoil and direct the serpent power up through the central pillar of the spine, enlivening the whole chakra system until the body becomes a Caduceus of balanced energies. Kundalini is Sanskrit for "slumbering serpent," the reservoir of coiled power at the base of the spine, and she is a feminine goddess in Hinduism.

Instead of just "holding" the serpent, the real work is joining the two halves of the snake, or the two solar and lunar currents of the serpent power of Kundalini, Ida and Pingali. The severed pieces of the serpentine energy are reconciled into harmonious energy currents, oscillating up and down the spine as this fiery energy activates the higher chakras--spinning wheels of energy. In Hebrew the word is *merkabah*, translated as "wheel" or "chariot." A Caduceus suggests a fully functioning chakra system, which is why the serpent wand symbolizes healing. The placement of Ophiuchus between Scorpio, the life force, and Sagittarius, aspiration toward higher wisdom, is significant. Mercury, the androgynous god, was able to travel safely from the depths of the underworld (root chakra) to the heights of Mount Olympus (crown chakra) by virtue of this serpent staff. The scorpion is symbolic of the root chakra, and the wings of an eagle (falcon in Egypt), are the soaring flight of spiritual attainment. In the Western Mysteries this is called the Great Work, thus the Serpent Bearer and his Caduceus are a perfect emblem of adeptship.

I believe that unveiling the mystery of thirteen contains the mystical knowledge of reclaiming the sacred feminine. The knowledge has been hidden for some time, going slowly underground along with paleolithic goddess culture, while humanity developed the rational aspect of the mind. Ophiuchus may have been removed from the zodiac because of the serpent's dubious role in the Garden of Eden. In the Biblical story there were two trees in the garden; The Tree of the Knowledge of Good and Evil, from which Adam and Eve ate the fruit, and the Tree of Life, guarded by the flaming Cherubim. The serpent "tempted" Eve, hinting at the role of the feminine in ultimate redemption, not damnation. Metaphorically, once we've lost our innocence, and have been exiled from the "garden," the long-term work of walking the Path of Return begins.

Getting off the wheel of rebirth requires engaging the Serpent Bearer. This entails reclaiming the mystical thirteenth element, including the crown above the head of the serpent, which is the emblem of mastery. After we have eaten the fruit of the Tree of Knowledge of Good and Evil we must eventually learn the serpent's secrets of transforming fire and climb the Tree of Eternal Life.

Atlantis Rising #44 February 2004

CHAPTER 31

PHYSICS & METAPHYSICS: DO WE KNOW HOW ASTROLOGY WORKS?

"ny scientific model does not describe the Universe but rather describes what our brains are capable of saying at this time."

Robert Anton Wilson, Ph.D

Gears Mechanical Cog Wheel 153964 (snappy goat.com)

Einstein's general relativity theory and quantum theory are the two most significant theories of twentieth century physics. General relativity describes everything larger than a particle, and how energy and mass behave in relation to each other, while quantum physics explains the uncertain behavior and construction of the particles, to the point where we enter the fabric of space-time itself. It's been shown in the quantum world that light behaves like particles or waves, depending on the expectation of the observer. Perhaps, general relativity tries to explain what the world looks like in four-dimensional space-time, while quantum physics tries to explain what space-time is. That may be why discussions of quantum physics appear on philosophy web sites, where physics and metaphysics merge.

According to certain Euclidean geometrical space perceptions, the universe has three dimensions of space and one dimension of time. In physics, space-time is any mathematical model that combines space and time into a single continuum. By combining space and time physicists have significantly simplified a large number of physical theories, as well as described the workings of the universe at both the super-galactic and subatomic levels more uniformly.

However, scientists are unable to reconcile relativity theory with quantum mechanics, and still don't understand the nature of the space-time continuum. At the level of the smallest elements of reality there is tremendous dynamism, and Heisenberg's Uncertainty Principle attempts to address this. Scientists agree that modern physics and mathematics need models that will work in multidimensional space, and the quest for a Unified Theory, a term coined by Einstein, that allows all of the fundamental forces between elementary particles to be written in terms of a single field, is the Holy Grail of physics.

Astrology is a body of knowledge based on correlation of the sky with alignment to terrestrial events. Linking the rhythm of the natural world, and the repeating cycles of the sky, is as perennial as humanity. In ancient times, there was no difference between astronomy and astrology. Opinions differ on whether astrology is a revealed discipline, originating from some higher source of wisdom, or is the result of accumulated knowledge based on observation over time. Today, Astrology has three main branches: Western, or Tropical astrology, Vedic, or Indian astrology, and Chinese or East Asian astrology.

The earliest known astrological records date back to Babylon, 1645 BCE, and the earliest known horoscope to the fifth century BCE. Astrology's origins can also be traced to Egypt, Greece and Rome, where sophisticated timekeeping and calendar sciences were developed. The Magi of the Bible were astronomer priests. Astrology was further developed by the Arabs from the 7th to the 13th century, and European court astrologers held tremendous power in 14th and 15th centuries. The Maya and Aztecs of Central America, and indigenous peoples of Africa, developed their own zodiacs. During the Renaissance, almanacs published astrological information for ordinary people. Galileo and Copernicus were both practicing astrologers. By the time of Francis Bacon and the scientific revolution, emerging scientific disciplines were based upon experimental observations, and the disciplines of astrology and astronomy began to diverge. Astronomy became one of the central sciences, while astrology was increasingly viewed as superstition by scientists.

Astrology attempts to provide meaning for the individual in relationship to the patterns in the sky and the continual cycles of stars and planets, while astronomy measures the heavens. In Genesis, Creation begins with a series of divisions: heaven and earth, light and darkness, above and below, good and evil. Astrology organizes the divisions and polarities in life and creates a language of symbols to understand how they interact, anchoring consciousness in the dependable cycles of the vault of heaven. Since the time of Ptolemy, the domain of most astrologers has been the realm of the ecliptic, the narrow band of sky in which sun, moon and planets trace their paths against the background of constellations. The viewpoint is relative, and at the most fundamental level astrology is the interpretation, or application of principles, of recurring cycles and planetary patterns.

Like relativity theory, astrology uses three dimensions of space--signs, houses and place of birth--and one dimension of time, the moment of birth, to fix the reference points for a natal chart. Based on the time, date, and place of birth, a snapshot of the heavens, as viewed from the earthly vantage of the moment of birth, is captured. Astrology's frame of reference is defined by the tropical or sidereal zodiac of twelve signs on one hand, and by the local horizon, the ascendant-descendant axis, and midheaven, *imum coeli* axis, on the other. This frame is typically further divided into the twelve astrological houses. Astrological aspects are used to determine the geometric/angular relationships between the various celestial bodies and angles in the horoscope. The ascendant is a point of personal orientation, which essentially is the place of intersection of the horizon at one's birthplace and the zodiac.

Reality is like a set of nested spheres of immense vastness and infinitesimally minute scale. This is stated in the words of an ancient Hermetic axiom, "As above, so below; as within, so without." This line of thought can be compared to fractal mathematics and holographic photography. Astrologically, the individual becomes the symbolic center of the Universe, and the person's inner world is related to the outer world of planetary cycles through the principle of correspondence. The experience of the Microcosm, the individual, is a reflection of the Macrocosm, the Solar System.

Another axiom upon which the Hermetic principles of astrology are based comes from *The Kybalion*. This is the Law of Vibration that says, "Nothing rests; everything moves; everything vibrates." Hermetic teachings state that not only is all matter vibrating, but our emotions are a manifestation of vibration. Therefore thoughts, emotions, and desires are accompanied by vibratory rates, which may be lowered or raised at will by adepts.

Ernst Chladni was a German physicist and musician. Chladni's technique, first published in 1787 in his book, *Discoveries in the Theory of Sound*, consisted of drawing a bow over a piece of metal whose surface was lightly covered with sand. The plate was bowed until it reached resonance, and the sand formed a pattern showing the nodal regions. The results became known as Chladni Figures.

Two centuries later, Hans Jenny, a Swiss doctor, artist, and researcher, published the bilingual book, *The Structure and Dynamics of Waves and Vibrations*. Jenny, like Chladni, showed what happens when materials like sand, spores, iron filings, water, and viscous substances are placed on vibrating metal plates and membranes. Shapes and patterns appear that vary from nearly perfectly ordered and stationary to those that are turbulent, organic, and in constant motion. Jenny called this new area of research Cymatics, from the Greek *kyma*, which means "wave." It seems that the mystery of solid matter is contained in sound.

Musica universalis, universal music, or the music of the spheres, is an ancient philosophical concept that regards proportions in the movements the sun, moon, and planets as a form of *musica,* the Medieval Latin word for music. This music is not audible to the human ear, but is a harmonic/mathematical function. Greek mathematician and astronomer Pythagoras is usually credited with the concept. The discovery of the relationship of geometry and mathematics to music within the Classical Period is also attributed to Pythagoras. Pythagoreans believed this gave music powers of healing, as it could "harmonize" the out-of-balance body.

A modern composer, Greg Fox, created *Carmen of the Spheres,* a composition where he tried to literally hear the planets as they orbit the sun. His approach was to halve the planetary orbital period until he found the "pitch" of a planet orbiting the sun. He created his music by raising that pitch 36 to 40 octaves. Johannes Kepler also believed in the geometric underpinnings of the cosmos and perceived a connection between geometry, sacred geometry, cosmology, and astrology. Kepler explored the significance of ratios of the planetary orbits.

Dr. Percy Seymour is a respected authority in the field of cosmic magnetism. Holding doctorates in astronomy and astrophysics, Seymour's expertise is in the study of the magnetic fields that thread our galaxy. His book, *Cosmic Magnetism,* won him academic acclaim. Seymour formulated a theory of astral influences that describes the Solar System as an intricate web of planetary fields and resonances. According to Seymour, "magnetism is omnipresent throughout the universe and is known to affect the biological cycles of numerous creatures here on Earth, including humans." Seymour's multilink theory proposes that the planets raise tides in the gases of the sun, creating sunspots and their particle emissions, which then travel across interplanetary space to strike Earth's magnetosphere, ringing it like a bell. That could explain the cyclical nature of sunspots as a function of planetary orbital cycles.

Dr. Seymour believes that the resonance between the tidal tug, due to gravity, of the very hot gases trapped in the magnetic field of the sun and earth, and resonance between the resulting fluctuations of the

Earth's magnetic field and the electrical activity of the neural network in the brain, are what link celestial to terrestrial. His research seems to confirm the theory of harmonics put forward by John Addey in 1975 that astrological effects can be understood in terms of the harmonics of cosmic periods. If the Solar System vibrates as a unit, each element or planet is in resonance with the whole.

Astrological researcher Ken McRitchie (TheoryOfAstrology.com) rather than attempting to explain how astrology works, has developed what he terms a Theory of Astrology. This seems to be a wise approach that I liken to Relativity or Quantum theories, which also remain unproved. In McRitchie's view, there are three problems that astrological theory needs to answer:

1. What is the physical correspondence between the individual and the celestial environment that surrounds the individual?

2. What are the essential operations of the signs, houses, aspects, and planets when reduced to definitive meanings?

3. What is the psychological mechanism of astrological interpretation? That should keep astrologers busy for some time.

At our present stage of scientific understanding we might say that the large things in the universe are perhaps mostly matter and can be measured, while the tiniest things are still mostly energy and are fraught with uncertainty and glorious potential. The repeating cycles of large objects, the planets, provides some predictability, which has been observed over thousands of years, while the uncertainties of the small scale of the quantum world allows for the exercise of choice and free will. This is the realm of metaphysics and has been the domain of ancient wisdom teachings for millennia.

Although we still can't provide a mechanism to explain astrology, quantum theory and general relativity have also yet to be reconciled with a unified theory. So it seems premature to say that the mechanism that explains Astrology will never be discovered, and to dismiss this ancient discipline as mere superstition. There is still a great deal about the nature of reality that remains a grand and compelling mystery.

I will give the last word to Dr. Percy Seymour, "The claims made by many scientists that astrology is opposed to the basic principles of western science comes from a total misunderstanding of serious astrology, and an appalling lapse in their understanding of the methodology, philosophy, and history of science itself."

Atlantis Rising #78 October 2009

CHAPTER 32

THE AGE OF AQUARIUS

 "When the Moon is in the seventh house, and Jupiter aligns with Mars, then peace will guide the planets, and love will steer the stars."

Aquarius, from *Hair*, the musical

zodiac and stars 832478 (snappygoat.com)

Aquarius is the eleventh zodiacal sign, and this ancient constellation has retained a consistent mythical theme through various cultural transformations. The Babylonians saw the water jar as an overflowing urn, and associated Aquarius with their eleventh month, equivalent to our January-February, translating to "curse of rain." Aquarius is the first constellation in both the Chinese and Indian calendars and is associated with water in both. The Egyptians saw the figure representing Hapi, god of the Nile, who distributed the waters of life.

In the seventies the Broadway musical *Hair* lyrically informed us of the dawning of the "Age of Aquarius." We sang along, most of us blissfully unaware what defined an age. Before modern clocks and calendars the sun, moon and stars were the way we measured the passage of time. The sun's apparent movement across the sky became the day. The moon's phases around the earth gave us the month. Earth's longer passage around the Sun gave us the year. As ancient sky watchers pondered the heavens over millennia thousands of larger divisions of time were called ages.

Astronomically an age is defined by the constellation that provides the backdrop for spring equinox sunrise in the northern hemisphere. Earth wobbles on her axis of rotation, causing spring equinox sunrise to inch backward through the solar sequence of constellations. There are twelve ages, one for each zodiacal constellation, that "precess" from Pisces to Aries at the rate of one degree in seventy-two years, delineating the passage of a Great Year of 25,920 years. Dividing by twelve, each age lasts roughly 2,160 years.

Astrologically an age is characterized by the archetypal energies of the constellation. At present the equinox sunrise straddles the modern boundaries of Pisces and Aquarius, and the stellar backdrop is the omega star in the constellation of Pisces. As the backward march shifts, the dawning of the Age of Aquarius will be heralded as this constellation moves to center stage and defines the new world age.

But when will the aeonian changing of the guards occur? According to *The Cambridge Guide to the Constellations*, the Age of Aquarius is eight hundred years in the future. Audubon's *Field Guide to the Night Sky* gives a figure of six hundred years. Astrologers differ on when the momentous dawning will occur, and some sources believe the new age has already begun.

If the duration of an age is 2,160 years, and we know the starting point, then the answer is simple arithmetic. However, we don't know for certain when the age of Pisces began, and there are conflicting opinions. Is the duration of an age uniform like an astrological sign, or is the length based on the breadth of the constellation and the positions of the stars it contains? Constellations are not uniform in size, and the constellations of Pisces and Aquarius overlap like the terrestrial states of Texas and Oklahoma. It is also conceivable that over a nearly 26,000-year period the rate of movement might not be constant.

The ages are defined by heliacal (before the sun) risings of certain fixed stars. There may also be some subtle mechanism, working as temporal cogs in the Great Wheel, which we have forgotten over time. If we accept the assumption that the ancients delineated the boundaries of the ages by solar alignments with certain stars, we are still left with the puzzle that the constellations as we configure them today may have altered and shifted over time. Where do we look for ancient benchmarks?

Using the *Skyglobe* astronomy program as a window into the past, and certain fixed stars and points in time as probable markers, a pattern seems to emerge. Tracking the spring equinox sunrise along the ecliptic (apparent path of the sun) shows the sun's relationship to certain bright stars which would have risen before the sun at past points in time.

Toward the end of the age of Taurus, 4,300 years ago, the Pleiades, in the constellation of Taurus, rose before the sun at spring equinox. The bright star Alcyone, shining before dawn, would have aligned with spring sunrise. Some two thousand years later, during the age of Aries, Hamal, alpha Aries, would have risen before the sun. Today, as we contemplate the closing of the age of Pisces, the omega star of Pisces holds the place of spring equinox sunrise.

2000? Some researchers believe the current age of Pisces may have begun before the accepted birth of Christ around 111 BCE. The equinox sun was then aligned with the star Al Rescha, "The Knot," which is now the alpha star of Pisces. If that conjunction signaled the beginning of the Piscean age, adding 2,160 years places us close to the Aquarian age.

2,160? If we accept the time frame of historical zero as the beginning of the last age, then simple arithmetic places the onset of the age of Aquarius as 2,160 CE. In 0 CE, Xi Pisces, an unnamed star, rose before the sun. In 2,160 the sun will rise after the Iota star in Pisces, also unnamed.

2,500? Researchers Robert Bauval and Graham Hancock provided compelling evidence that 12,500 years ago was significant to the ancient Egyptians. The authors demonstrated a convincing sky-ground relationship at Giza, memorializing that time. The bright star Denebola, beta Leo, rose then, marking the Lion's tail, and ushering in the age of Leo. Perhaps the Egyptians recognized that the heights of civilization reached during Zep Tepi, the First Time, would not return for another twelve thousand years.

2,813? Using the calculated rate of precession, the vernal sunrise will not move through the constellation of Pisces for another eight hundred years. That seems a long expanse for a single age. The star we now call Beta Pisces, on the westernmost border of the constellation, is usually not connected to the "circlet" of stars forming the southern of the two fishes. Some sources name this star Al Achsasi, the "Fish's Mouth." In Piscean star lore, for a long time there was only one fish. It is probable that in antiquity the stars now forming the "circlet" of the western fish were part of what is now Aquarius.

2907? In the Middle Ages the year 747 CE was honored as the official birth of Christ due to a planetary conjunction of Jupiter and Saturn. Scholars of the time felt that the spectacular conjunction bore uncanny resemblance to Matthew's Biblical account of the star of Bethlehem. However, adding 2,160 to 747 also seems too far removed to be a serious contender.

And the winner is . . . 2,500

I believe the most compelling candidate for the dawn of the new age is the epoch of 2,500, exactly halfway around the Great Year from 10,500 BCE. The unnamed theta star of Pisces marks the dawn, unremarkable from a light show perspective. Even though no bright star will grace the equinox horizon, the ancients may have understood the principle of opposite energies at work in the larger scheme of precession. They may have sent a message across time that we are now approaching a era of new possibilities.

We are in a long-term "watery" phase as the ages move from the Fishes, to the Water Bearer and then into the Sea Goat. Astrologers speak of cusps and orbs, gray areas of combined influence. While the spring equinox sun rose in front of the stars of both Aries and Pisces, Jesus was seen as both Lamb of God and Fisher of Men during the mingled influences of the ages of the Ram and the Fishes. If the orb for an age is six degrees of arc, we will feel the combined influence of Pisces and Aquarius for more than four hundred years. New energies combine with the death throes of the old age as it gives way to a new dispensation.

The age of Pisces has been characterized by both hierarchy and centralization of power. While a wise and far-sighted monarch can give people vision and leadership, a petty tyrant wields a reign of terror. In the higher symbolic aspect we see the sacrificial king, the crucified savior, who takes on the collective sins of the people. A positive legacy of the Piscean age is a profound spiritual renaissance at work on the planet. Many people, including scientists, are recognizing the existence of subtle energies. Quantum theory mystifies physicists, stretching boundaries of what is possible. Everyday people encounter angels, experience miracles, and survive transforming near-death experiences.

Over the course of the next age secrecy and hierarchy will give way to a more egalitarian decentralization of knowledge and power. I believe the age of Aquarius will see distribution of wealth as a result of free energy and a totally altered monetary system. This newfound freedom will bring its own challenges. Power in the hands of the people can draw on the gifts of each regardless of prior class or station, but can also lead to anarchy. In the Aquarian mode the test of responsible use of resources will rest with the individual.

The transmission of energy and the egalitarian availability of information and education will be ushered in by the idealistic and appropriate use of technology. The Internet, the world wide web, is an early harbinger of the age of Aquarius. Ecology and the greening of the earth will be emphasized in the next age, and the quality of water will become paramount. The Age of Aquarius may see change in the way we track time. The stars have always been used for navigation, and if space travel becomes commonplace we may someday reckon by "star dates" as popularized by the Star Trek series.

Ancient wisdom traditions indicate that humanity is moving toward androgyny. We see glimpses of this in "Generation X" where traditional gender boundaries blur. Same sex marriages, transsexuals (now transgender) and transvestites are becoming more open as we move into Aquarian energies.

One icon of the Aquarian age might be the urn as a sacred vessel. Another image is the chalice, or grail, symbolizing both a vessel of spirit and the sacred quest. Pure water, bubbling from fountains into beautiful gardens may be the way we memorialize the Water Bearer. I believe the "official" new age is still some time off, and we have some time to settle into the new energies. Meanwhile we change the world by changing ourselves.

Atlantis Rising #28 April 2001

CHAPTER 33

THE ORIGIN OF THE ZODIAC: IS ASTROLOGY MUCH OLDER THAN WE BELIEVE?

"The universe begins to look more like a great thought than a machine."

Sir James Jeans

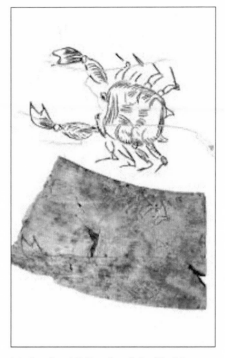

Astrology Board © Staso Forenbaher LiveScience.com

In 2011 a research team published a scientific paper that described the discovery of what they claimed may be the oldest astrologer's board. Staso Forenbaher and Alexander Jones published their paper in the *Journal for the History of Astronomy*. Jones said, "This is probably older than any other known example. It's also older than any of the written horoscopes from the Greco-Roman world." He added, "we have a lot of horoscopes that are documents on papyrus or on walls but none of them are as old as this."

This ivory board was discovered in Croatia, in Nakovana Cave, overlooking the Adriatic Sea. The original board was circular and engraved with zodiac signs. Dating back more than 2,000 years, the surviving portion of the board consists of thirty ivory fragments that are engraved with zodiac signs. The researchers spent years removing the fragments from the dirt inside the cave and reassembling the surviving pieces. Inscribed in a Greco-Roman style, what remains are images of Cancer, Gemini, Pisces, and possibly part of Sagittarius.

While the Croatian artifact is certainly a great find and an impressive artifact, it does not accurately date the antiquity of zodiacs—the story is much older. Human beings have gazed at the stars for many thousands of years, looking up with a sense of wonder. We long to know our place in the universe, and we naturally respond to a universal impulse to seek inspiration and perceive order. Astrology is fundamentally a search for meaning by observing cycles and interpreting correspondences between celestial occurrences, planetary positions, human affairs, and terrestrial events. As the Hermetic Axiom states, "As above, so below."

For most of its history Astrology was considered a scholarly tradition and was a common pursuit in academic circles, often in close relationship with astronomy, alchemy, and medicine. In the "modern" world science views astrology with disdain. However, those who have taken the time to thoroughly research the matter by studying the horoscopes of people they know, or watching correspondences with life events, typically change their minds. Astrology seems to be based on interpreting a resonance with the Solar System and universe that our science has yet to comprehend.

Astrology is seen to have its roots in calendric systems used to predict seasonal shifts and celestial cycles. Among earlier Indo-European people astrology has been dated to the third millennium BCE. From earliest times Chinese, Mesopotamian, Indus Valley, Egyptian, the Maya of Central America, and other cultures have used zodiacs and developed elaborate systems for predicting terrestrial events from celestial observations. The Chaldeans, Phoenicians, Egyptians, Persians, Hindus, and Chinese all had zodiacs. The Central and North American Indians also had an understanding of the zodiac, but patterns and numbers of the signs differed in many details from those in the Eastern Hemisphere. Primitive astronomical observatories have been discovered in many parts of the world. Although the telescope was unknown to ancient sky watchers, these cultures made remarkable calculations with instruments cut from blocks of granite or pounded from sheets of brass and copper.

The historian Herodotus has said, "The naming of almost all the gods has come to Hellas (Greece) from Egypt. The Egyptians had names of all the other gods in their country for all time. The Egyptians knew what god corresponded to each month and each day, and what fortunes someone would meet who was born on any particular day, how he will die, and what kind of a man he would be. These inventions were taken up by those of the Hellenes." Even conventional dating of Egypt stretches back 8,000 years in its pre-dynastic beginnings.

In *Secret Teachings of All Ages* Manly P. Hall states, "It is difficult for this age to estimate correctly the profound effect produced upon the religions, philosophies, and sciences of antiquity by the study of the planets, luminaries, and constellations. Not without adequate reason were the Magi of Persia called the Star Gazers. The Egyptians were honored with a special appellation because of their proficiency in computing the power and motion of the heavenly bodies and their effect upon the destinies of nations and individuals."

The zodiac is an area of the sky that extends approximately eight degrees north and south of the ecliptic, which is the apparent path of the Sun as it seems to move across the celestial sphere during a year. The ecliptic is also the path of the Moon and planets that orbit the Sun within the band of the zodiac. The word zodiac is derived from the Greek *zodiakos*, which means "a circle of animals." The Greeks, and others influenced by their culture, divided the band of the zodiac into twelve sections, each being sixteen degrees in width and thirty degrees in length. Twelve constellations of irregular shape and size occupy the zodiac belt, and some of these shapes have been imagined as figures by connecting bright stars like "dots" to form star pictures like the Scorpion or the Scales of Libra.

In the past, different cultures perceived the stars as different "pictures" and had different zodiacs. Over thousands of years the shapes of the constellations have morphed and some stars have changed alliances. For example, the claws of the Scorpion, which still bear the earlier names of Northern and Southern Claws, are now the scales of Libra. Likewise, in times past, Pisces only had one fish. But since 1930 the

International Astronomers Union has agreed on eighty-eight constellations.

The zodiac astrologers use is a celestial coordinate system that takes the ecliptic, the apparent path of the Sun, as the origin of latitude, and the position of the Sun at spring equinox as the origin of longitude. Astrological signs are related to time and the seasons, using the solstice and equinox points as primary markers. The twelve zodiac signs are thirty-degree divisions of the circle of the year. This same method was used by astronomy until about one hundred years ago. Astronomers now measure the circle of the zodiac from 0-360 degrees, but degrees of Celestial Longitude still define the zodiac.

The constellations are divisions of space like countries on a terrestrial map that contain all the known celestial objects inside those lines of demarcation against the backdrop of the Celestial Sphere. Because of the phenomenon of precession, Earth's seasons relative to the stars shifts very slowly over time. As the zodiac signs present a yearly circle of archetypal experience, the larger cycle of the ages offers a longer dispensation of these energies. Symbolically, the zodiac forms a cycle of experience that provides a template of evolution in nested cycles through which Earth receives the influences of the Sun and planets.

So how old is astrology? Scientists believe that "modern humans" developed about 600,000 years ago. Our ancestors were capable of watching the sky and observing patterns. While no artifacts may have survived, ruling out how they may have used this knowledge seems arrogant and dismissive.

Archeology is undergoing a profound paradigm shift as discovery and recognition of ancient cultures and their amazing achievements forces the awareness that history is not what we supposed. Growing awareness of ancient cultures such as Gobekli Tepe in Turkey keeps moving the timeline backward. In the face of growing evidence archeology and history are challenged to rethink former assumptions about our past.

The famous cave paintings at Lascaux, France have been dated to 17,000 years ago. (I explored their astronomical significance in AR #122

Chapter Three in this Volume). French researcher Dr. Chantal Jegues-Wolkiewiez has worked at Lascaux for a decade. She found orientations to sunset during solstices in more than 120 of the sites. Using modern astronomy software, she believes the famous paintings at Lascaux record the constellations of a prehistoric zodiac, which includes major stars as well as solstice points. She was able to determine that summer solstice sunsets penetrated the caves and illuminated certain paintings. Her work is based on identification of dots and tracings superimposed on the paintings of bulls, horses, and aurochs on the cave walls. These appear to correspond to the constellation of Taurus, the asterism of the Pleiades, and the stars Aldebaran and Antares.

Even more stunning in terms of antiquity is the Gallery of Discs at the *Cueva de El Castillo,* or El Castillo Cave, in the Cantabria region of Spain. The region contains the oldest known cave art in Europe. Researcher and naturalist Bernie Taylor, author of *Before Orion: Finding the Face of the Hero,* believes the image of the red-haired man with a club painted on the wall is a very early depiction of a hero that later became Orion, moving across a stellar landscape. This Orion character appears in Chapter 5 of his book and represents the original hero in what mythologist Joseph Campbell called the "hero journey." He believes the red-haired man is an earlier version of Hercules and his labors.

Taylor has also identified a series of pictorial constellations on the same panel, from Aquila, Pegasus, Pisces, Cetus, Leo, Ursa Major to Cygnus, among others, that the hero encounters and draws strength from on his journey. The naturalist shows that there is a geographic connection for the animals in these constellations, ranging from the Iberian Peninsula to western North Africa, which shows that the earth and sky worlds were once considered as one. He proposes that "certain ancient cave paintings are fundamental pieces in the human journey to self-realization, the foundation of written language, and a record of biological knowledge that irrevocably impacted some of the artistic styles, religious practices, and stories that are still with us."

Ancient sky watchers and astronomer priests did not possess the telescope. Instead, they relied on their eyes to observe the stars and their inner vision to interpret the meaning. It's tempting to imagine how people might have been transformed as they sat in a dark cave 34,000 years ago and gazed at paintings that depicted the sky. How were they changed by the rituals they experienced? Or, how were ancient Egyptians impacted as they stood among immense temple columns and watched bright stars travel over the night sky?

In a real sense, astrology was the beginning of measurement and instrumentation as the ancients used a variety of methods to calibrate cycles. We now live in a time when science has made phenomenal strides. Perhaps the risk of too much instrumentation is losing the faculty of intuition and disconnecting from the mystery of our intimate connection with the Universe. Technology has greatly increased the pallet of interpretation for astrologers, adding outer planets, asteroids, and plutoids. Sadly, most modern astrologers use computers and rarely look at the night sky. They are therefore unable to identify by sight the very planets they interpret or the stars that form the backdrop.

I believe this disconnects us from the deeper impact to the very real energies that these heavenly bodies possess. Perhaps in the not too distant future science will develop instruments capable of measuring subtle energies—maybe even quantify love. Meanwhile, it's worth the effort to go outside on a dark night, looking up at the radiance of the stars and marveling at the wonder of the universe.

Atlantis Rising #131 August 2018

CHAPTER 34

SIGNS OR STARS: WHICH IS THE REAL ZODIAC?

"That which is below is as that which is above, and that which is above is as that which is below, to accomplish the miracle of the One Thing."

The Emerald Tablet, Attributed to Hermes Trismegistus

Imaginative Depiction of the Emerald Tablet from the work of Heinrich Khunrath -
1606 (public domain)

Astronomy and astrology both define the zodiac as a belt in the heavens about eight degrees either side of the ecliptic, the apparent path of the Sun. This space also includes the motions of the Moon and principal planets against a backdrop of stars and deep space objects. Astrologers divide this space, and its sequence of time, into twelve equal divisions called signs that are similar to calendar months but offset by about one week. The twelve signs are: Aries, Taurus, Gemini, Cancer, Leo, Virgo, Libra, Scorpio, Sagittarius, Capricorn, Aquarius, and Pisces. Because most of the constellations in the ecliptic zone represent animals, the ancient Greeks called it *zōdiakos kyklos,* "circle of animals."

Most constellations have Greek and Roman names, but people mapped the sky long before these empires came into being. The Greeks borrowed from the Babylonians and Egyptians, whose origins stemmed from Sumer 3,000 years earlier. Most star names are Arabic as it was Islamic scholars who kept the lamp of wisdom burning during the dark ages in Europe. Scholars are convinced that 17,000 year-old drawings on cave walls at Lascaux in Southern France may depict the Pleiades and Hyades star clusters, making this the first-known star map.

As Earth orbits in its yearly cycle, the Sun appears to pass in front of the zodiac constellations. Much as the Moon appears in a slightly different place in the sky each night, the Sun's position relative to background stars moves one degree of arc in an easterly direction from day to day. This apparent motion is counterclockwise. Our calendar is tied to the seasons--June 21 is summer solstice above the equator and winter solstice below; marking the day the Sun appears at its most northerly point and the North Pole is most tilted towards the Sun. Since our calendar is tied to the solstices and equinoxes, Earth does not actually complete an entire orbit in one year. The seasonal Tropical year is actually twenty minutes less than one full orbit of Earth's Sidereal year where the Earth returns to the same fixed star. These two markers are what distinguish the Tropical and Sidereal zodiacs.

Astronomers explain that the nature of Earth's rotation on its axis (wobble) causes our planet's position relative to the stars to change over a very slow passage of time--more than 26,000 years. This motion, called Precession of the Equinoxes, causes spring equinox sunrise (in the northern hemisphere) to occur due east against a backdrop of stars that slowly shifts. This apparent motion of the sky moves in a clockwise or westward direction, through the zodiac constellations, instead of the annual easterly direction in which the Sun appears to move through the constellations over the year.

The constellations are divisions of space, like countries on a terrestrial map. In the past, different cultures perceived the stars as different "pictures" and had their own zodiacs. China, Babylon, Egypt, Mexico, Peru, and others each saw the sky pictures in their own way. Over thousands of years the shapes of the constellations have morphed and some stars have changed alliances. For example, the claws of the Scorpion, which still bear the earlier names Northern and Southern

Claws, are now the scales of Libra. Likewise in times past, Pisces only had one fish. But since 1930 the International Astronomical Union has agreed on eighty-eight constellations on the Celestial Sphere. Astronomers also have a measurement called Right Ascension that divides the Celestial Sphere into the twenty-four hours of the day. As the Earth rotates each day, a different part of the sky rises, or "ascends." This measurement moves eastward and is the astronomical equivalent of terrestrial longitude.

The classical zodiac was introduced in the neo-Babylonian period, about 700 BCE. Astronomers believe Precession of the Equinoxes had not been discovered, although alternative scholarship indicates otherwise. Classical Greek astrology seems to have developed without consideration of the effects of Precession. The "modern" discovery of Precession is attributed to Hipparchus, a Greek astronomer (circa 130 BCE). Ptolemy, writing some 250 years after Hipparchus, was aware of the effects of Precession but chose to define the Tropical Zodiac of astrology based on the beginning point of spring equinox.

The physical constellations take up varying widths of the ecliptic, so the Sun does not pass through the constellations in the same amount of time. Virgo takes up five times as much ecliptic longitude as Scorpio. To overcome this imbalance, the Tropical zodiac is a circle of twelve thirty-degree equal divisions of celestial longitude, which are centered on the ecliptic. The astrological signs are also measures of time that begin each year at spring equinox, and every year the astrological sign of Aries begins about March 21st.

The Tropical Zodiac is a temporal frame of reference based on the seasons and is the zodiac most western astrologers use. The Sidereal Zodiac is the position of the Sun referenced against the stars. Because of Precession, the two systems do not remain fixed relative to each other, drifting apart about 1.4 degrees every hundred years. With the passage of centuries, the beginning and ending points of the two zodiacs are now out of synch about 24 degrees of arc. The Hindu *Jyotisha* system of astrology opted to define the zodiac based on a sidereal system.

About 4,000 years ago the constellation of Aries and the sign of Aries were aligned at spring equinox. The belief is Aries was a Ram because lambs are born in spring, while Virgo held a sheaf of wheat because the Sun moved through those stars at harvest time. For roughly two thousand years, spring equinox sunrise has occurred against the stars of Pisces, The Fishes, which rise before the Sun in pre-dawn darkness. Soon, the stars of Aquarius will take this position, heralding the Age of Aquarius.

Ophiuchus, the Serpent Bearer, is a constellation that reaches into the ecliptic, but is ordinarily not part of the traditional zodiac circle. Ptolemy noted that Ophiuchus is in contact with the ecliptic, but he evidently preferred the comfortable symmetry of twelve for the 30-degree segments that are the astrological signs. Perhaps this is because thirteen is a prime number, divisible only by one and itself. Ophiuchus is an enormous star group that is actually composed of two constellations, the Serpent and the Serpent Bearer. The foot of the Serpent Bearer is well within the bounds of the ecliptic, the parameters of the zodiac constellations. Sagittarius the Archer points his arrow at the foot of Ophiuchus, which in turn, is poised on one claw of the Scorpion. The tail of the snake is near Aquila, the Eagle, and the serpent's head nearly touches Corona, the Crown. Mythically, Serpent Bearer represents the Egyptian Imhotep and the Greek Asklepios, famous healers and noteworthy wielders of snake medicine.

The zodiac forms a symbolic cycle of experience that provides a template of evolution in nested cycles through which Earth receives the influences of the Sun and planets. As the zodiac signs present a yearly circle of archetypal experience, so too does the Great Year of Precession, also called the Platonic Year. Astrologically, an age is characterized by the archetypal energies of the constellation whose stars rise before the Sun at spring equinox dawn. Each phase of the Great Year can be compared to a cosmic month, possessing a distinct and overarching quality of experience. The ages can be seen like spokes of the cosmic wheel, presenting a phase shift of archetypal energy designed to provide an evolutionary schoolroom for developing humanity. Metaphysically, the ages and the stars provide

JULIE LOAR

an aeons-long framework for the spiritual development of the soul, whereas the short span of human lives and personalities are seen to be more influenced by the cycle of the year.

Stars and planets rotate on their axes and orbit other objects in space. Immense galaxies spiral around each other in vast cycles of millions of years. The heavens are filled with light and motion. On Earth humans and animals alike move with the rhythm of days and seasons and live their lives in response to these shifting patterns of light and dark. As our consciousness evolves we seem to develop a longing to find meaning in these patterns. As far back as we know human beings have watched the skies, carved pictures on rocks and cave walls, and told stories about the shifting characters they perceived in the sky. Over time our ability to measure objects and their motions overtook the way we gave them meaning. Astronomy became a science and astrology became a quaint anachronism to those who merely view and measure the sky through instruments.

Dawn is more than a number on a clock, however. In addition to the quantitative measure that marks the time, there is also a qualitative significance. Dawn heralds sunrise and is the return of light after a period of darkness. We can no longer see the stars and a new cycle of activity begins. At noon the Sun reaches its zenith and expresses its full power, and we too are generally at the peak of daily activity. Sunset brings the close of day and the approaching time of rest. Midnight is the still, silent darkness when the stars move across the sky and we sleep and dream. In astrology, the time of birth shifts the place of the Sun in the horoscope and gives someone a nature that aligns with these cycles of the day. The pattern of light of the month and year also echo this pattern of light and dark in the lunar cycle and the seasons. But in a time of artificial light and 24/7 lifestyles these rhythms are disrupted, and many people no longer move in harmony with the cyclical changes of light and dark.

Every culture has named the stars, created pictures and stories as a way to remember how the sky changes through the year. This adds meaning and significance to the passage of time. Does it really matter which zodiac we use? The Sidereal approach is out of phase with the seasons, and the Tropical method has lost touch with the stars. Both are worthy but also incomplete. A zodiac of thirteen constellations is an odd number and doesn't offer ease of computation. The Maya have thirteen "signs" in their cosmology, and there are thirteen lunations each year--new moons or full moons. There is a sense of crossing from the mundane to the mysterious when we move from twelve to thirteen, but the arithmetic is less comfortable.

It really doesn't matter if our calendar is solar or lunar, or whether we mark time by the stars or the seasons. What does seem important is that we don't lose sight of the Sun, Moon, planets and stars and what connects us to something more vast than our individual lives. Most people never look up to be awed by the stars, or pause in the busyness of their lives to reflect upon the shifting and repeating quality of the seasons--our lives become mechanical like a clock. Human lives are brief in cosmic terms, and we are so consumed with mundane matters that we've forgotten how to be awed and amazed. It seems worthwhile that we should pause to breathe in a deeper scope of existence, remembering that our souls move in eternity as well as in time. We live in a Universe of wonder, and as Joseph Campbell, renowned scholar of myth has rightly said, "We're so engaged in doing things to achieve purposes of outer value that we forget the inner value, the rapture that is associated with being alive. That is what it is all about."

Atlantis Rising #108 October 2014

CHAPTER 35

DRAGONS, TIGERS, AND BOARS

"It is better to light one small candle than to curse the darkness."

Confucius

Dragon - Chinese Zodiac (1165797 - Snappygoat.com)

Anyone who has ever eaten in a Chinese restaurant has probably encountered a superficial introduction to the Chinese Zodiac by way of a place mat. Generally printed in dragon red ink the paper rectangle placemat gives a brief outline of the twelve animals of the Chinese wheel and their characteristics. But like sun sign astrology forecasts, or personality descriptions that appear in newspapers and tabloids, it's premature to judge a complex discipline of thought from simple stereotypes.

The Chinese lunar calendar is actually a chronological device which dates back to 2637 BCE when the Chinese Emperor Huang Ti introduced the first cycle of the zodiac. The Chinese calendar is the longest chronological record that we know of and is composed of the Ten Heavenly Stems and the Twelve Earthly Branches that were created as a means of keeping time. The ten stems each had an archetypal quality, perhaps like the numbers, and the branches took on more mundane characteristics. Twelve signs and ten planets are the archetypes that also combine in astrology and the Qabalah. In the

Chinese calendar this can be seen as two turning wheels, which engage like gears as they turn, similar to the wheel of days and numbers in the Mayan Tzolkin Calendar. Since most people were illiterate the Twelve Branches were also named after animals that would be easy to remember.

Unlike the Western perspective of time, which tends to see the passage of years as linear, the Chinese calendar is cyclical. It's easier to imagine a circular calendar if we think of a clock with twelve numbered hours. Every time the hour hand goes around, or the digital numbers cycle through, we come back to the same place on the clock.

Although the Chinese adopted the western calendar in 1911 for official and business reasons the lunar calendar still defines important festivals such as the major celebration of Chinese New Year. One complete cycle of the Chinese lunar calendar takes sixty years and is made up of five cycles of twelve years each. Although the animals repeat every twelve years, the combination of "stem" and "branch" happens only once in the cycle. Since its inception seventy-seven cycles have completed. The current round began in February of 1984 and will end in February of 2044.

Chinese New Year begins at the second New Moon after the Winter Solstice and is seen as the onset of spring rather than spring equinox. The date of the beginning of the New Year changes each year as the lunar calendar does not move in synch with the solar calendar. This year January 29, 2006 heralds the year of the Dog, and from a western astrological perspective, this is the New Moon of Aquarius.

Each year in a twelve-year cycle of the Lunar Calendar is named after an animal. One legend tells the story that when Lord Buddha was ready to depart the Earth he summoned all the animals. Only twelve came to say goodbye. As reward for their faithfulness he named a year after each of them in the order in which they arrived to say their farewells: Rat, Ox, Tiger, Rabbit, Dragon, Snake, Horse, Goat, Monkey, Rooster, Dog, Boar. Each of the animals gets a turn to head the year in successive twelve-year intervals.

Some versions of the story include elements of betrayal and trickery and involve subplots explaining why certain animals were omitted from the twelve. In one version the gods were asked to decide who would go first in the cycle of years so they devised a contest and twelve candidates were summoned to the bank of a river. Whoever reached the other side first would lead the years. Unknown to the swift swimming Ox the Rat had jumped on its back. As the Ox was about to climb out of the water, thereby winning the place of honor, the Rat leaped ashore. Boar, according to this version of the story, was reputed to be slow moving and somewhat lazy, so he climbed out last. And so the order was decreed even though some might think the Rat cheated. This view seems to hold a degree of philosophical realism for the slings and arrows of fortune.

Western Astrology has twelve Sun Signs divided into four elements: fire, earth, air and water. Chinese astrology contains a fifth element to combine with the twelve lunar signs. The five elements of Chinese astrology are wood, fire, earth, metal and water. As the sixty-year cycle of five elements and twelve signs rotates the animal signs combine with the five elements. The quality of the New Moon half way between Winter Solstice and Spring Equinox therefore is colored by the influence of each branch and stem in turn, adding a unique aspect to the year 's character.

The elements are further divided into two qualitative aspects, Conducive and Controlling. Understanding the interrelationships of these elements can provide a deeper understanding of Oriental philosophy. The Conducive quality shows how one element flows from another and how they are interrelated. For example, Water is said to come from Metal. Metal can form a container to hold Water and Metal is the only other element that changes into a liquid. The Controlling influence is a bit like the childhood game of Scissors, Paper, Rock. In this sense Wood is said to be controlled by Metal as the tallest tree can be chopped down by a metal ax. The idea is that each element is part of the whole and they are interrelated and linked in a cyclical pattern of life.

The astrological or interpretive aspect of the calendar developed later. At first the combined influences described an overall quality to the year cast in the light of the second New Moon after the Winter Solstice. Later the lighthearted and often humorous qualities ascribed to everyone born in the year were layered onto the calendar. In polite Chinese society knowing the animal of someone's birth year is also a nonintrusive way to discern their age without asking. Knowing the animal of the year of their birth, and the place that animal falls in the cycle of years, simple arithmetic reveals their age. This also provides a common ground to open a conversation.

What follows are a few descriptions of the twelve animals and is a bit like a menu in a Chinese restaurant. It's meant to be entertaining, like a Fortune Cookie, which incidentally was an American invention. The next time you're in a Chinese restaurant you can toss out the opening conversational gambit. Remember that the Chinese New Year will always begin sometime after January 21.

Rat - Born in 1912, 1924, 1936, 1948, 1960, 1972, 1984, 2008, — Ambitious, honest, generous with a tendency to be hot tempered and perhaps power hungry.

Ox - Born in 1913, 1925, 1937,. 1949, 1973, 1985, 2009 — Patient, powerful, inspiring to others, easy going but can be stubborn.

Tiger - Born in 1914, 1926. 1938, 1950, 1962, 1974, 1986, 2010 — Unpredictable, charming and sensitive. Can be secretly aggressive.

Rabbit - Born in 1915, 1927, 1939, 1951, 1963, 1975 ,1987, 1999, 2011 — Affectionate, pleasant, desires security and tranquility; dislikes risk.

Dragon - 1916, 1928, 1940, 1952, 1964, 1976, 1988, 2000, 2012 — Passionate and fiery, enthusiastic, artistic and dramatic; softhearted but can be bossy.

Snake - Born in 1917, 1929, 1941, 1953, 1965, 1977, 1989, 2001, 2013 — Wise and clever, often beautiful and romantic. Can be too intense and sometimes vain.

Horse - Born in 1918, 1930, 1942, 1954, 1966, 1978, 1990, 2002, 2014 —
Hardworking, cheerful, outgoing and full of adventure; tendency to
feel superior.

Sheep - Born in 1919, 1931, 1943, 1955, 1967, 1979, 1991, 2003, 2015 —
Creative, artistic, honest and warmhearted. Can be disorganized and
worry too much.

Monkey - Born in 1920, 1932, 1944, 1956, 1968, 190, 1992, 2004 — Clever
and entertaining, magnetic personality but apt to become discouraged.
Opportunistic at times.

Rooster - Born in 1921, 1933, 1945, 1957, 1969, 1981, 1993, 2005 —
Pioneering and thirsty for knowledge, devoted to work and good with
details. Can be eccentric and selfish.

Dog - 1922, 1934, 1946, 1958, 1970, 1982, 1994, 2006 — Honest, loyal
and faithful. Sharp tongue (or bark), is hurtful to others.

Boar (Pig) - 1923, 1935, 1947, 1959 ,1971, 1983, 1995, 2007 — Reliable
and self-sacrificing. Noble spirit and chivalrous. Shy and sincere.
Tendency to be naive brings pain in relationships.

Year of the Dog

If the character of a certain lunar year can be seen to take on the quality
of the animal then 2006 might be seen to emphasize issues of loyalty
and team work. The positive and negative traits of the dog as a symbol
might give us a hint of the year ahead or areas that might require more
attention. We might consider emulating the positive qualities of our
canine friends such as loyalty and group consciousness. In a humorous
vein, should we therefore be careful not to bark up the wrong tree?
Perhaps we'll be lucky and someone will "throw us a bone?"

On a more serious note, it is said that the Chinese believe that the
animal that rules the year of birth has profound influence on your life
remarking, "This is the animal that hides in your heart." A much
deeper understanding of these principles would be required to reflect
on that. I can report, however, that 2006 will be once-in-sixty-year

combination called Bing Xu, bringing together the Third Heavenly Stem, Bing, and the Eleventh Earthly Branch, Xu, Dog. I really can't speculate what profound significance this might have without a great deal more study, but I am able to wish you, *"Gung Hay Fat Choy!"* Happy New Year!

Atlantis Rising #56 February 2006

CHAPTER 36

TIME AFTER TIME

"To everything there is a season, and a time for every purpose under the Sun."

Ecclesiastes 3:1

Four Seasons of a Tree (158601 - SnappyGoat.com)

Before modern clocks and electricity we could see the night sky, and the cyclical motions of the sun, moon and stars were the way we "told time." In the middle ages the Universe was seen as a static, clock-like mechanism, ticking out ages and dispensations. But the ways of the "gods" are capricious. The shifting of cogs in the great mill, which heralded the beginning of a new age, was seen as fraught with peril.

The ancients probed the night skies, searching for unexpected alterations within predictable patterns. Occasionally the sky changed, the alarm was raised, and disaster struck. Disaster and catastrophe meant literally disturbed order in the sky, ill-fated crises in the stars, or "asters," from the French for star. Power grew from predicting the influences of the cycles.

To the Maya of Central America time was seen as circular. Mayan cosmogony depicted humankind as a walker around the wheel of existence, a pilgrim, seeking home through continuous life experiences. Modern Western thought conceives time in a more linear fashion, flowing in a continuous line from the past into the future. Even so our measures of time are increments or intervals that repeat, such as hour, day, month and year.

The sun's apparent rising and setting (Earth's rotation), became day, divided into four corners: dawn, noon, dusk and midnight. The moon's major phases, defined by the cyclical journey around the Earth, gave us the month, which is divided into eight lunar phases. Earth's longer movement around the sky (Earth's orbit), gives the illusion that the Sun moves around us. The Sun's apparent passage through the sky gave us the year, delineating the annual journey of the mythical Solar King. The year is quartered by thirteen-week seasons, marked by equinoxes and solstices.

As ancients watched the skies over millennia, larger divisions of time such as ages developed. The passage of an age lasted more than two thousand years and was replicated in Egypt in statues of bulls in the age of Taurus, and rams in the age of Aries, gracing temples built during those epochs. Once we identify the pattern or interval, we can predict when it will repeat. We observe the cycles and name the intervals. The Hindus observed the small interval of a breath or a heartbeat.

The annual frame of time can be viewed as a sphere where the seasons intersect the circle of the year. Astronomically these intersection points are called *colures*. In the northern hemisphere as summer begins, and the moment of summer solstice reigns supreme, the shifting yearly pendulum "stands still," then moves once again toward darkness. Six months later winter begins, announcing the return of light. The cycle is a balanced dance of polarity, as is the symbol of infinity, mirroring above and below.

The four cardinal points, or beginning of the seasons, in the northern hemisphere are denoted in Astrology by: Aries, Spring Equinox; Cancer, Summer Solstice; Libra, Autumn Equinox; and Capricorn, Winter Solstice.

The passage of the seasons are like the phases of the Moon, ebbing and flowing through periods of maximum light, equal light and darkness, and complete darkness; this fluctuating rhythm seeks equilibrium. Visually, from the vantage point of Earth, the Sun and Moon appear to be the same size. This perspective causes one or the other to be "eclipsed" during the perfect alignment of a total solar or lunar eclipse.

Each season has its special characteristics. Spring is characterized by emergence, or resurrection of new life. Tentative at first, breaking through newly thawed Earth, this young life is courageous and powerful. Summer is a celebration of life in flower, beauty in radiant multiplicity. Autumn is the harvest of life, the fruits of the cycle, and the seed gathering for the next cycle. Winter is the quiescent period of gestation.

The Julian calendar, based on solar cycles, was named for Julius Caesar. This calendar was the system of time measurement widely used between 46 BCE and 1582 CE. The year was divided into twelve alternating thirty and thirty-one day months, with February having twenty-nine days. The Julian year was eleven minutes and fourteen seconds longer than the actual annual solar cycle, resulting in a discrepancy of ten days by the year 1562. Pope Gregory XIII corrected the problem and brought the so-called Gregorian calendar, which we still use, into synchronization with the solar year.

In Eastern traditions the Moon is the more important celestial body since she courses through the "lunar mansions" against the backdrop of stars. The lunar mansions are divisions of the sky that house perils and promises, depending on which stars are engaged in passing. Vedic Astrology focuses on the opportunities presented to everyone by these monthly passages.

Jewish, Islamic, and Hindu calendars are lunar, based on the cycles of the Moon rather than the Sun. Many ancient cultures used multiple calendars, separating the sacred from the mundane aspects of time and cycles. Easter, which echoes Passover, is the only Christian holiday still based on the lunar calendar. Easter Sunday is the first Sunday following the first full moon after spring equinox in the northern hemisphere.

Earlier cultures honored the seasons more consciously. We still have holidays that mark the passage of the year. In the pre-Christian era the halfway points between the equinoxes and solstices were known as "fire festivals." Sometimes marked by a full moon, these festivals divided the year into eight stages. The eight "phases" of the sun are reflected in eight monthly lunar phases. The four fire festivals alternated with the shifting balance of light and dark created by the equinoxes and solstices.

At that time, the year began around October 31st, on Halloween, or All Hallows Eve. Many spiritual traditions believe the veil between the seen and unseen worlds is most thin at that time and rites and prayers for the dead, honoring the continuity of life, are common.

- Samhain (pronounced sow-en), October 31 st (Now Halloween)
- Yule, Dec 21, Winter Solstice (now Christmas)
- Imbolc, February 1 (now Ground Hog Day)
- Ostara, March 21, Spring Equinox
- Beltane, May 1 (now May Day)
- Litha, June 21, Summer Solstice
- Lughnassadh, Aug 1, Mid-summer
- Mabon, Sep 21, Autumn Equinox

Kindling of *Tein Eigin*, "forced fire," was carried into every house and was sustained as the hearth fire throughout the year. These cycles marked the yearly passage of the Sun King as he traversed the sky. As the cyclical march of the seasons, and the annual fluctuation between light and dark continues, we still celebrate the annual rites of passage with other names. Our attempt to Christianize the calendar doesn't alter the seasonal cycles.

Father Christmas, Santa Claus, or Saint Nicholas is a mythical representation of the end of the yearly cycle. The Baby New Year is the birth, or rebirth, of the Solar King at the Winter Solstice that signals the

return of the light. Mithras, who developed from the much older
Indian deity Mithra, was born on Dec 25. Placing the symbolic birth of
Christ on this day overlays a Christian holiday on an ancient myth,
claiming the inherent power of the cycle, and retaining the potency of
ancient belief.

We celebrate January first, rather than winter solstice, as the beginning
of the year. January is named for Janus, the two-headed Roman god
who looked both forward and backward simultaneously. Ground Hog
day replaced Candlemas, the midway point between winter solstice
and spring equinox. If the Ground Hog sees his shadow there will be
six more weeks of winter; if not, spring is said to be imminent.

May Day masquerades as the earlier Beltane rites of spring, between
spring equinox and summer solstice. No modern festival honors the
onset of Summer, although weddings traditionally occur at this time.
Perhaps we are reluctant to acknowledge the annual turn toward
darkness. Instead, in America, we have a festival of lights on July
fourth to celebrate the nation's birth, and we memorialize our war
dead at the end of May. Midsummer, which is Lughnassadh, is the
halfway point between planting and harvest. All Hallows Eve touches
the unseen world of ghosts and goblins. Thanksgiving honors the
harvest. Christmas and Hanukkah celebrate the return of light.

Many have said that we live in perilous times that have been noted by
prophetic traditions for centuries, perhaps millennia. Many have
viewed this as portending the end of the world as we know it. The
Maya saw this as the close of one cycle, a single cog in a vast wheel of
interlocking cycles.

In our modern world mechanical clocks and printed calendars have
replaced the sky as the way we track time and navigate our way
through the cycles of our lives. We have artificial light and 24/7
convenience stores and telemarketing. We no longer move in balance
with natural cycles. This lack of balance with the Earth and sky has
brought us to a dangerous place.

An ancient maxim states, "Equilibration is the secret of the Great
Work." Perhaps by taking a larger view and accepting responsibility

for some of our far-reaching behavior, we can make a difference. Since the great cycle of the ages is also a repeating pattern, perhaps we can learn about our present and future from a better understanding of the past. As George Santayana famously said, "Those who cannot remember the past are condemned to repeat it." Our lesson may be learning to walk in harmony with the ebbing and flowing cycles.

Atlantis Rising #32 February 2002

CHAPTER 37

THE RISING SIGN

e are what we pretend to be, so we must be careful what we pretend."

Kurt Vonnegut

Carved Wooden Masks (140580 - SnappyGoat.com)

The body of knowledge we call astrology has accrued over millennia, correlating countless observations of "as above, so below." This ancient discipline seems to operate in a quantum mechanics fashion, using the language of archetypes to describe the nature of energy that expresses in the three dimensions of space and the fourth dimension of time. In today's world astronomy is seen as science, and measures the domain of the sky, while astrology is often seen as superstition because this discipline seeks to gain meaning from the same data.

Earth's globe is delineated by terrestrial latitude and longitude, imaginary lines drawn on maps to provide a frame of reference for locating intersections on a grid. Similarly, astronomers place Earth at the center of an imaginary globe called the Celestial Sphere. Using Earth's equator and poles as fundamental reference points, terrestrial longitude and latitude are projected into space, and vertical and horizontal lines are etched onto this imaginary sphere. The Celestial Sphere might be likened to cosmic graph paper.

Components of the Celestial Sphere allow astronomers to identify the location and track the apparent movement of objects in the night sky relative to Earth at any point in time or any place on our planet. The celestial equivalents of terrestrial longitude and latitude are termed Right Ascension and Declination respectively. Right Ascension is measured in hours, and declination, like latitude, is measured in degrees above or below the Celestial Equator. Because of Earth's rotational motion these "grid lines" only match up once in twenty-four hours.

The section of this imaginary sphere in which Earth and the other planets orbit the Sun is called the ecliptic. Technically, the ecliptic tracks the path of the Sun's apparent motion. Astronomers divide the ecliptic into the twenty-four hours of Right Ascension (Celestial Longitude), beginning at the spring equinox point or zero degrees of Aries. Astrologers divide the same area of sky into the 360 degrees of the Zodiac and the twelve familiar 30-degree "signs."

As Earth travels each year in its roughly elliptical orbit the changing relationship with the Sun, Moon and planets is charted astrologically against the background of the twelve zodiac signs. From our vantage point on Earth the Sun appears to pass through the twelve signs in twelve months.

It's important to mention another motion of the Earth. Our planet wobbles as she spins, creating a phenomenon known as Precession, which has two effects from the sky-watching perspective. First, the slow wobble causes the polar axis to shift relative to the night sky and over thousands of years, slowly moves a different "pole star" into the northern sky. Second, precession causes sunrise to move backward (toward the west), against different constellations. This second motion is tracked against the familiar constellations that circle the ecliptic, and what evolved over time we now call the astrological ages.

Although the constellations of the zodiac contain the stars themselves the zodiac "signs," like signposts, are divisions of time and space based on the seasons of the solar year. The signs are fixed reference points. Astrologers call spring equinox the zero point of Aries even though the stars of Aries no longer line up with equinox sunrise. Western Tropical Astrology analyzes the positions of Sun, Moon and planets relative to twelve temporal divisions of the solar year, beginning with spring equinox. The twelve zodiac signs are symbolic stages in the annual and mythic journey of the solar king.

Each day we observe the Sun rise in the east, travel across the sky, and set in the west. We know it's an illusion created by Earth's daily rotation on her axis, but the illusion is compelling. In the same way, as Earth rotates on its axis, each of the twelve zodiac signs rises in the east and sets in the west in turn. In the language of the horoscope the zodiac sign that appears on the eastern horizon at the moment of birth is said to be "rising" or ascending, and every two hours a new sign takes the eastern stage. As the Earth turns daily, different stars and planets also move past that marker.

At dawn the Sun is rising so at that time of day the "Sun Sign" is the same as the "Rising Sign." At noon, the Sun has advanced six hours, one-fourth of the day (roughly three zodiac signs), and has risen to the zenith point overhead. As the day progresses Earth's motion causes the Rising Sign to change every two hours.

Because Earth's annual journey around the Sun changes our reference point relative to the sky, a different part of the sky rises in the east at dawn as the seasons change. In spring, sunrise occurs in the sign of Aries (but the stars of Pisces). The first sign Aries only rises at dawn for one month in spring, the symbolic beginning of the year. In summer the Sun rises in Cancer, in autumn Libra, and so on. When Precession moves the stars of Aquarius to spring equinox sunrise, heralding the Age of Aquarius, it will still be zero degrees of the "sign" of Aries.

Astrologers interpret someone's outer personality expression in part by the nature of the zodiac sign rising on the eastern horizon at the exact moment of birth. This eastern angle of the horoscope can be understood as our personal horizon, representing the symbolic point where day begins and the onset of the life of the individual, beginning with the inhalation of the first independent breath. This point of the chart shapes our perspective based on the astrological lens through which we see life.

Astrologer Isabel Hickey, author of *Spiritual Astrology*, likens the significance of the Rising Sign to a window through which we look out onto the world. Our personal windows are unique in shape and size and therefore color our individual outlook. The Rising Sign reveals the circumstances of birth and early life that influence our perspective and shape our point of view. The Ascendant is also seen to influence our physical appearance, temperament, attitudes, disposition, and personality.

In Eastern thought the sign rising at birth is thought to be occupied by the Moon at moment of conception. In a mystical way this energy forms a matrix, or physical template, that shapes the physical form determined by the Soul's choice of a vehicle through which the personality will navigate life events.

I see the Sun Sign as presenting a major emphasis of lifetime learning, and the Moon Sign as revealing our mental-emotional orientation, conditioned responses and genetics. Both of these are inner and "energetic." The Rising Sign is in a sense more concrete or outer. Seen one way the Sun Sign is like a light source, and the Rising sign is like a lamp shade that colors or alters the light and says something about individual personality.

The Ascendant can also act like a mask or facade that we use to reveal some aspects of ourselves and conceal others, affecting how we allow others to see us, and functioning like a wall that keeps things in or out. Understanding the Rising Sign can provide insight into what's visible for all to see, versus other components of the horoscope that are hidden from view in the depths of our psyche.

What follows is an extremely generalized description of the archetypal characteristics of Rising Signs as they may express through human personality. The variables in an individual horoscope create a rich tapestry of interpretation, and an in-depth analysis is required for real understanding. However, it's possible to gain some insight (and entertainment), from generalizations.

Since one metaphor for the Ascendant is the vehicle we utilize to navigate through life I've included a "vehicle" to correspond with each Rising Sign. This is a light-hearted attempt to show astrology's versatility and have a little fun. Laughter is the best antidote to taking ourselves too seriously.

∾

Rising Signs

Aries, The Ram - High energy and impulsive. Apt to act first and think later. Positive, masculine ,and an assertive trail blazer. Headfirst with quick reflexes. Uses anger as a backup mode. Needs to cultivate tact and diplomacy. He drives a big, red pickup truck, probably a Dodge Ram Charger, and passes everyone on the road.

Taurus, The Bull - Strong, stable and persistent. Actions are deliberate and patient unless backed into a corner. Focused on security and possessions. Watch out when Taurus rising becomes overly charming. She likes feeling safe in a Volvo sedan (or Ford Taurus).

Gemini, The Twins - Friendly, witty, talkative and curious. Sense of duality is strong. Active mental nature. Can be high-strung and temperamental. Changeable. Nonstop talking is a typical defense mechanism. The twins are more comfortable in a convertible.

Cancer, The Crab - Sensitive and will retreat into a "shell" when uncomfortable. Sympathetic, receptive. A home base is a vital concern. Can seem traditional. Prone to emotional meltdown when stressed. She likes to take home with her, so she carries her stuff in a camper or RV.

Leo, The Lion - Extroverted and gregarious. Confident, proud, courageous and loyal. It's important to feel loved. Considerable roaring and tail lashing, but it's mostly show. High melodrama is a typical reaction to stress. He prefers to be chauffeured to gala fund raisers in a stretch limousine.

Virgo, The Virgin - Ingenious with an alert mind. Attention to detail is important. Quiet and unassuming personality. Practical, analytical and thoughtful. A perfectionist. Analysis paralysis can bring Virgo rising to a complete halt when on overload. Ever practical and economical, she drives a Honda Civic.

Libra, The Scales - Artistic and creative. Always seeking balance and harmony, but can be a feisty arguer as justice is the ultimate aim. Fair minded. Can be too eager to please, and a deadly calm of sweetness should be a danger signal. Classy, elegant, and stylish he loves to make a statement in his vintage Mercedes.

Scorpio, The Scorpion - Self-controlled and conceals much. Possesses depth of personality and can struggle mightily to overcome powerful and conflicting passions. Willful. Reserved. Goes for the jugular when backed into a corner. She'll surprise you as she speeds away in her high-powered Ferrari.

Sagittarius, The Archer - Philosophical, outgoing and expansive. Talkative and loves to travel. Restless and eager to be on the go. Direct and to the point. Denial of reality can be a means of coping with problems, hoping it will all go away. You never know when adventure will present itself so he's always ready to explore in his Hummer.

Capricorn, The Sea Goat - Determined, reserved and sensitive. Outer reserve masks a great ambition to achieve. Focus on their duty can make them appear "cold." Lashing out in harsh judgment is a means of coping with perceived failure. Expecting to meet responsibility at every turn, she prefers a multipurpose minivan; it would be a Saturn if they still built them. (There were Saturn vehicles at the time).

Aquarius, The Water Bearer - Intuitive, mental and idealistic. Capable and practical but can also be impulsive and rebellious. Oriented to mental nature and not to feelings. A display of eccentricity is often a shield against vulnerability. The "rebel-without-a-cause" likes his leathers and Harley Davison.

Pisces, The Fishes - Sympathetic, hypersensitive, and highly impressionable. Often carries the emotional weight of the world.

Sentimental and secretive. Can be dreamy and impractical unless galvanized. Will retreat and sink under the ocean waves when threatened. She longs to sail away to Neverland on a Magic Carpet, but an Aston Martin Cygnet will do in a pinch to remain inconspicuous.

Atlantis Rising #51 April 2005

PART V
NEW DISCOVERIES

CHAPTER 38

COMET ISON: A COMET'S TALE

"W hen beggars die there are no comets seen; the heavens themselves blaze forth the death of princes."

Julius Caesar, William Shakespeare

Comet Holmes with Tail (CC BY-SA 3.0 author Ivan Eden)

Russian astronomers Vitali Nevski and Artyom Novichonok discovered comet ISON in September of 2012, and it bears the name of their night-sky survey program: International Scientific Optical Network. ISON is a group of observatories in ten countries organized to track objects in space. An unprecedented eighty ground-based telescopes and sixteen NASA spacecraft will observe the comet's approach toward the inner Solar System, and astronauts on board the International Space Station will also be watching. Some writers have predicted that ISON will be the greatest sky-watching event in a thousand years. More serious writers have maintained a cautious perspective. However, if ISON delivers, NASA hopes every telescope on Earth, and in the Solar System, will be trained on the comet.

Comets are erratic members of the Solar System that are usually of small mass. They travel through space and become visible only when they approach the Sun and heat causes them to glow. Based on their orbits, most short-period comets may come from the Scattered Disk, but long-period comets are believed to originate from the Oort cloud at the outer reaches of the Solar System. Halley's comet, so named as he was first to predict a comet's return, is the most famous short-period comet, clearly visible to the unaided eye. The 75-year return cycle of Halley's comet has been recorded for nearly two thousand years; its last appearance was in 1986. Comets with elongated orbits are periodic and return at fixed intervals. Those with parabolic or hyperbolic orbits are expected to return in cycles of hundreds or thousands of years, or be flung into outer space never to return.

ISON is believed to be an object from the Oort Cloud. Named for Dutch astronomer Jan Oort, the cloud is a hypothesized giant sphere of predominantly icy "planestesimals" that lies nearly a light-year from the Sun. This places the cloud at nearly one-fourth the distance to Proxima Centauri, the closest star to our Sun. Voyager I won't reach the inner edge of the cloud for another 246 years and won't exit the outer Solar System for another 28,000 years. In a sense, the Oort cloud is the spherical container of the Solar System.

The outer Oort cloud is affected by the gravitational pull of passing stars and the Milky Way itself. These forces occasionally dislodge comets from their orbits and send them speeding toward the inner Solar System. Comets are notoriously unpredictable, and while Comet ISON has the potential to be stunning, it may also disappoint. One hazard is the Sun itself as tidal forces and solar radiation are known to destroy comets. A recent example is Comet Elenin, a much smaller comet, which broke apart in 2011 as it approached the Sun. The Hubble telescope measured ISON in April of 2013 and estimated the comet to be three to four miles across; the danger zone size to do potential damage for either a comet or asteroid is about one-third of a mile in diameter.

Astronomers can predict where ISON will be in the sky, and when it should be visible. The last two "great comets" were in the southern hemisphere, but ISON will be observable in the northern hemisphere.

Mars orbiters had a ringside seat at the beginning of October 2013 when ISON had a close flyby of the red planet. That occurred at a key time in the comet's journey when it had just crossed the "frost line," a place outside the orbit of Mars where solar heating begins to vaporize frozen water. Although ISON's rank on the brightness scale was disappointing, it is still headed toward the Sun and will continue to brighten.

On November 28, 2013, Thanksgiving Day in the US, ISON will reach perihelion, its closest approach to the Sun. The icy visitor from the outer Solar System will fly through the Sun's atmosphere about 620,000 miles from the stellar surface, earning the designation "sun grazer." If ISON survives, unlike the mythical Icarus whose wings of wax melted, the comet could emerge glowing as brightly as the Moon and briefly visible near the Sun in daylight. Astronomers are optimistic because of ISON's size. The comet should be visible to the unaided eye at night from early November 2013 to mid-January 2014. The comet's dusty tail could stretch across the sky as the dark nights of winter provide the perfect backdrop. If ISON performs it will pass almost directly over the North Pole, making it a brilliant circumpolar object all night long and visible in the dawn skies leading up to Winter Solstice.

For several days around January 12, 2014, Earth will pass through a stream of fine-grained debris from the comet; this shower will rain down on our planet from two directions simultaneously. Astronomers say this kind of "double hit" would be unprecedented. But comet ISON's most spectacular display could be the nights of December 24-26, 2013, perhaps reminding us of a long ago Christmas Star.

Although telescopes now allow us to detect comets a long way off they are still unexpected visitors. They have been viewed both as unwelcome intruders or stunning messengers heralding change. Their journey into the inner Solar System begins when they are knocked out of orbit and propelled inward toward the Sun. They carry disruptive energy on their journey; the period of disturbance is said to be from first appearance to perihelion when they are closest to the Sun.

The Bayeux tapestry, which depicts the Battle of Hastings in 1066, clearly shows a great comet in the sky. The next great comet occurred in 1577, the year when Sir Francis Drake set sail around the world. The Great Comet of 1680, also called Newton's Comet, has the distinction of being the first comet discovered by a telescope. (John Chamber wrote about this in *The Mathematics of Catastrophe* in AR #101). The ancients said the appearance of a comet was a sign that "God had changed his mind." Greek and Medieval observers thought the influence of comets was evil, rather like divine retribution. That view seemed justified in 1994 as we watched comet Shoemaker-Levy collide with Jupiter.

Comets have been seen to usher in political change and shifts in worldview. Astrologer Jonathan Flanery says "Throughout the history of astrology, the appearance of comets was seen as a sign of upheaval, affecting agriculture and the weather. Comets were also seen as heralding the rise to power of an 'agent,' a military or religious leader, or a reformer." Earlier observers looked at the part of the sky comets traversed, and the bright stars they encountered on their path, to determine the nature of the influence they might exert. Vivian Robson, *Fixed Stars And Constellations In Astrology* (1923), says the effects of comets are influenced "through the constellation in which they appear, and also through the zodiacal sign and degree to which their position corresponds." Comet ISON first appeared through a telescope at 29°25′ Cancer between the constellations Gemini and Cancer. As ISON travels towards the Sun it will pass through the signs of Cancer, Leo, Virgo, Libra, Scorpio, and then station, or appear to stand still, at perihelion on November 28, 2013 in Sagittarius, at 6 Sag 49.

In the typically pessimistic view of the astrology of his time, Robson reported that comets "cause inordinate heat, pestilence, sterility of the earth, wars and changes in kingdoms, winds, earthquakes and floods, and are assigned to the planets according to their colors." Science seems to support this view in part as astronomers say comets are ideal vehicles for transporting microbes, including viruses, from planet to planet and Solar System to Solar System. When these organisms are deposited on a world already thriving with life, genes may be exchanged, new species may evolve, or conversely contagion may be released, and disease and plague may spread.

Comets are seen as fiery and are "ignited" by the Sun, blazing across the sky with tails that can stretch for thousands of miles. Some writers believe they are related to the fire of volcanoes. In certain ancient traditions they are seen as messengers from beyond, fiery lives that distribute energy along their orbital paths, acting as purifying triggers for transforming change. Like planets, cometary energies are impersonal, and their effects are based on the system upon which they impinge. Comets are unexpected and unknown until discovered, giving them an influence that is rather Uranian, and like Uranus's other mythic identity Prometheus, comets can also be seen to bring fire to humanity like a flaming two-edged sword.

Drawing again from ancient wisdom, comets are believed to produce electrical, magnetic and psychic energy, burning, cleaning and adjusting energy in the system. In *Cosmos In Man*, H. Saraydarian said, "The unfolding human soul grows through crisis." In this light, each crisis is seen as an opportunity and a test. As awareness expands, crises grow from individual to global. Saraydarian claims that a comet entering an organized sphere such as a Solar System stimulates an atomic release and has the capacity to transmute energy. The results can include an expansion of consciousness, a deconstruction of things not in line with cosmic harmony, and revelations of new laws and elements. If Saraydarian is right, this influence, combined with the ongoing Uranus-Pluto square, could be a potent stimulus.

November 1 (2014) is the next exact square between Uranus-Pluto, and on November 3rd a rare hybrid annular-total Solar Eclipse occurs, spanning the Atlantic Ocean and Central Africa. Part of the eclipse path will experience totality, while the remainder will see an annular eclipse. During totality, well-placed observers might glimpse ISON near the Sun. The eclipse will further intensify these energies--the current "shut down" of the US government being an early example.

Analyzing the symbolic meaning of comets takes astrology into the arena where the Tropical signs and the Sidereal astrology of the stars combine. Around 100 CE, during Ptolemy's time, as the ages changed and the star pictures shifted, the claws of the Scorpion became the scales of Libra. Even so, the symbolic power of the Scorpion has not diminished. How the star pictures are drawn may shift, but the stars retain their energetic signature, and earlier opinion was based more on the nature of the stars. Although ISON will reach perihelion at 6 Sagittarius 49 of the Tropical Zodiac, it will be in the constellation of Scorpio, and will conjunct the delta star in Scorpio, Dschubba, from the Arabic word *jabhat*, which means "forehead." Dschubba is one of three stars that make up the head of the Scorpion and was part of the "crown of the Scorpion" in ancient times. It was an important star, and one of its early names was "jewel."

Richard Hinkley Allen, *Star Names, Their Lore And Meaning*, says this star was called "the Light of the Hero, or the Tree of the Garden of Light, placed in the midst of the abyss, reminding us of that other tree, the Tree of Life, in the midst of the Garden of Eden." The Hindus believed this star was fortunate, and the earliest commentators associated this star with the nature of Mercury. The comet will appear to stand still in association with Dschubba, and if we think of this star as similar to Mercury, this could indeed signify a "message." The ancients might have interpreted this conjunction as the rise of a powerful and enlightened leader, someone who would wear the "crown" and bring the "light of the hero."

Whether striking terror in the hearts of the superstitious, or being welcomed as harbingers of change, comets have always been seen as portents, telegraphing a dramatic message across the sky. ISON's ultimate message may depend on the comet's fate, so we'll have to wait and see. Regardless of interpretation, the so-called great comets become part of collective consciousness. To witness one is to be filled awe and wonder. Anything that captures the attention of the world is powerful, drawing our eyes to the sky, and briefly reminding us that the Universe is larger than our concerns and celestial events are not in our control. If ISON proves to be spectacular, we might gaze heavenward on Christmas Eve and ponder what needs to change on Earth and in our personal philosophies.

Atlantis Rising #104 February 2014

CHAPTER 39

MOVE OVER PLUTO—PLANET NINE HAS ARRIVED

"Last of the Ages of Men came Iron. In that hard age of baser vein all evil broke out, and honor fled with truth and loyalty, replaced by fraud, deceit, treachery, violence and wicked greed for gain . . . Honor and love lay vanquished, Astraea, virgin divine, last of the immortals, fled away."

Ovid, *Metamorphoses* 1.148

On January 20, 2016, Konstantin Batygin and Michael Brown, at the California Institute of Technology, announced calculation-based evidence of a massive ninth planet in our Solar System. They dubbed the object Planet Nine. Batygin and Brown have postulated the planet's existence through mathematical modeling and computer simulations, but the newest member of the Solar System has not yet been observed directly. Batygin was cautious in interpreting the results saying, "Until Planet Nine is caught on camera it does not count as being real. All we have now is an echo."

But what an echo. Planet Nine would be a super-Earth with an estimated mass of about ten times that of Earth and a diameter two to four times larger. Brown speculates that the predicted planet is most likely similar in composition and size to Uranus and Neptune, with a mixture of rock and ice, and a small envelope of gas. They suggest it may be a primordial giant planet core that was ejected from its original orbit during the nebular epoch of the Solar System's evolution. Planet Nine is hypothesized to follow a highly elliptical orbit around the Sun, about twenty times the distance from Neptune to the Sun, with an orbital period of 10,000–20,000 years. They expect the aphelion, or farthest point from the Sun, would be in the general direction of Orion and Taurus, while the perihelion, or nearest point to the Sun, would be in the general direction of Libra and the southerly areas of Serpens Caput and Ophiuchus, the Serpent Bearer.

"This would be a real ninth planet," said Brown, the Richard and Barbara Rosenberg Professor of Planetary Astronomy. "There have been only two true planets discovered since ancient times, and this would be a third. It's a pretty substantial chunk of our Solar System." Brown is well known for his significant role in the demotion of Pluto. "Those who are mad that Pluto is no longer a planet can be thrilled that there is a real planet still out there to be found," he remarked.

Batygin and Brown described their work in the January 2016 issue of *The Astronomical Journal,* showing how Planet Nine helps to explain a number of mysterious features of the Kuiper Belt, the ring of icy objects and debris beyond Neptune. "Although we were initially quite skeptical, as we continued to investigate its orbit and what it would mean for the outer Solar System, we became increasingly convinced that this planet is out there," said Batygin, who is an assistant professor of planetary science and was on the 2015 Forbes list of thirty scientists under thirty who are changing the world.

In 2014, Chad Trujillo, a former postdoc of Brown's, and his colleague Scott Sheppard, published a paper noting that thirteen of the most distant objects in the Kuiper Belt have similar obscure orbital features. They suggested the presence of a small planet to explain the similarities. At the time, Brown thought the planet solution was unlikely, but he was intrigued. He took the problem down the hall to Batygin, and the two began an eighteen-month collaboration to investigate the distant objects. Batygin and Brown realized that the six most distant objects from Trujillo and Sheppard's original collection all follow elliptical orbits that point in the same direction in physical space. That is surprising because the outermost points of their orbits move around the Solar System, traveling at different rates.

The orbits of the six objects are also all tilted in the same way—pointing about thirty degrees downward in the same direction relative to the plane of the eight known planets. The probability of that occurring is about 0.007 percent. "It shouldn't happen randomly, so we thought something else must be shaping these orbits," Brown said. After eighteen months of work, Batygin and Brown noticed that if they ran their simulations with a massive planet in an orbit where the planet's closest approach to the Sun was 180 degrees across from the perihelion of all the other objects and known planets—the distant Kuiper Belt objects in the simulation assumed the alignment that is actually observed.

The researchers were most amazed that their simulations predicted objects in the Kuiper Belt on orbits inclined perpendicularly to the plane of the planets. Batygin kept finding evidence for these in his simulations and took them to Brown. "Suddenly I realized there are objects like that," recalled Brown. In the last three years, observers have identified four objects tracing orbits roughly along one perpendicular line from Neptune and one object along another. "We plotted the positions of those objects and their orbits, and they matched the simulations exactly," said Brown. "When we found that, my jaw sort of hit the floor."

Batygin explained that this ninth planet, that seems like such an oddball to us at first, would actually make our Solar System similar to other planetary systems that astronomers are finding around many other stars. Most planets around other sun-like stars have no single orbital range—some orbit extremely close to their host stars while others follow exceptionally distant orbits. And, the most common planets around other stars range between one and ten Earth-masses. "One of the most startling discoveries about other planetary systems has been that the most common type of planet has a mass between that of Earth and that of Neptune," Batygin said. "Until now, we've thought that the Solar System was lacking this most common type of planet."

Planet Nine is also Planet X, which is a term used by astronomers to describe an unidentified planet in the outer Solar System. Following the discovery of Neptune in 1846, there was considerable speculation that another planet might exist beyond its orbit. The search began in the mid-19th century and culminated at the start of the 20th with Percival Lowell's quest. Lowell proposed the Planet X hypothesis to explain apparent discrepancies in the orbits of the giant planets, particularly Uranus and Neptune. He speculated that the gravity of a large unseen ninth planet could have perturbed Uranus enough to account for the irregularities. Clyde Tombaugh's discovery of Pluto in 1930 appeared to validate Lowell's hypothesis, and Pluto was officially, although temporarily, named the ninth planet.

I have written about dark matter (AR #116, Chapter 40 in Volume Two), which is a hypothetical kind of matter that can't be seen with telescopes and neither emits nor absorbs light, or any other electromagnetic radiation at any significant level. It doesn't interact with "ordinary" matter and is completely invisible to light. Dark matter has not been detected directly, making it one of the greatest mysteries in modern astrophysics. Like Planet Nine, dark matter's existence and properties have been inferred from its gravitational effects on visible matter, radiation, and on the large-scale structure of the universe.

I also examined the Nemesis, or Tyche, theory (AR #90, Chapter One in Volume Two), a hypothesis proposed by two different teams of astronomers. This theory suggests that our Sun may have a binary companion. Scientists believe this object may be a star--either a Brown Dwarf or a Red Dwarf. The difference between the Planet Nine premise, and the Nemesis or Tyche hypothesis, is the binary star would be in a highly elliptic orbit *with* the Sun, and Planet Nine is orbiting *around* the Sun, but also in a highly-inclined elliptical orbit.

In astrological terms planets are said to "rule" certain signs—a terminology that is confusing and unfortunate. The idea is that a particular planet has more power when placed in a certain astrological sign. For example, Mars is more powerful in Aries, and the Moon is more powerful in Cancer. Before the discovery of Uranus and Neptune, most planets ruled two signs. As these relationships have evolved over time, Venus and Mercury still rule two signs each. Venus is said to rule Taurus and Libra, and Mercury is said to rule Gemini and Virgo.

If there are indeed two more objects with significant astrological roles to play in our Solar System, how might we imagine their relationships with the signs that now share planetary rulers? If Planet Nine and a binary companion are visually sited, astrologers will need to make radical shifts in awareness in terms of the correspondence between planets and signs.

I have argued elsewhere (AR #86 Chapter 31, Volume Two)) that dwarf planet Ceres (Greek Demeter) has a strong mythical connection to the sign of Virgo. I suggested that Ceres, goddess of grain and planting cycles, holds space in a sort of quantum manner, along within the larger Asteroid Belt, and functions as the ruler of Virgo, sign of the harvest. A troubling question remains whether a "dwarf" planet is entitled to "rule." There may be a mechanism, like an energetic frequency resonance that we don't yet understand, that explains the dynamic relationship of planets with certain signs. Clearly, astrology is in need of re-visioning.

That brings us to Pluto, which used to be a planet, but is now a dwarf like Ceres. Pluto orbits with tens of thousands of other bodies in the Kuiper Belt. Could Pluto's dwarf planet status bring its role as ruler of Scorpio into question? Perhaps Pluto is also a placeholder for a larger energy or frequency? If a binary companion to our Sun is eventually confirmed, especially if it turns out to be a Brown Dwarf, there is a compelling symbolic connection between the deep mysteries of Scorpio, sign of generation and regeneration, and a dark star that is a hidden companion to our Sun.

My intuition, albeit speculative, suggests that Planet Nine, with its long orbit that moves through ages, is aptly represented by the myth of the goddess of justice, Astraea. Planet Nine might be the perfect ruler of Libra—the sign symbolized by the scales of justice. It's tempting to hope that Planet Nine will first be spotted in Libra. In myth, Astraea, celestial virgin and ancient goddess of justice, was the last of the immortals to live with humans during the Golden Age. As Ovid lamented in the beginning quote, Astraea abandoned humanity during the evil Iron Age. Fleeing to the stars from humanity's growing wickedness, she ascended to heaven in the region of Virgo and Libra.

Astraea's myth says she will return to Earth when people once again seek her wisdom.

Could the "echo" we are now hearing from Planet Nine herald the mythic return of an ancient goddess, bringing a utopian Golden Age, of which she is ambassador? Her long orbit, which moves through multiple ages, is a fitting corollary to the process of her advent, departure, and cyclical return that appears as the concept of the Hindu Yugas and Greek and Roman ages.

Brown and other colleagues have already begun searching for Planet Nine. Only the planet's rough orbit is known, not the precise location in its elliptical path. If the planet happens to be close to its perihelion, Brown says astronomers should be able to spot it in images captured by previous surveys. If it is in the most distant part of its orbit, the world's largest telescopes—such as the twin 10-meter telescopes at the W. M. Keck Observatory and the Subaru Telescope, all on Mauna Kea in Hawaii—will be needed. If Planet Nine is located anywhere in between, many telescopes might see it.

In our time science is allowing us to detect the presence of objects and energy by their influence rather than direct visible evidence. This is a fundamental revolution in a paradigm where "seeing is believing" has been paramount. Is it really such a stretch to imagine that a similar mechanism of unseen energies that have profound effects may be at work in astrology? It's always wise to keep an open mind.

Atlantis Rising #117 April 2016

CHAPTER 40

SNOW WHITE, THE GOBLIN, AND FAROUT: WHAT WILL THESE DENISZENS OF THE OUTER SOLAR SYSTEM REVEAL?

"Look again at that pale blue dot . . . on it everyone you love, everyone you know, everyone you ever heard of, every human being who ever was, lived out their lives."

Pale Blue Dot: A Vision of Human Future in Space, Carl Sagan, PhD

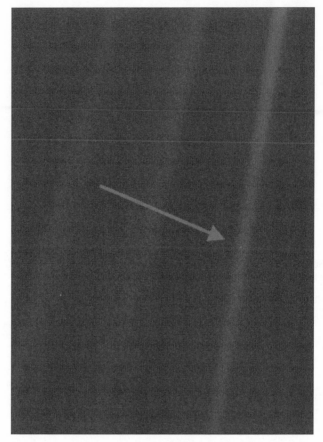

Pale Blue Dot taken by Voyager spacecraft NASA public domain
(look for arrow that points t tiny dot)

Carl Sagan's book *Pale Blue Dot* was inspired by an image, taken at his suggestion, by Voyager 1 on February 14, 1990. As the spacecraft left our planetary neighborhood for the edge of the Solar System and deep space, engineers turned the craft around for one last look at our home planet. Voyager 1 was about 4 billion miles (6.4 billion km) away when it captured a portrait of our world. Caught in the center of scattered rays of light, Earth appeared as a tiny blue point of light, only 0.12 pixel in size. More than four decades after its launch, we know much more about our Solar System and the vast reaches of space beyond, but in some ways the extended mystery only deepens.

The Kuiper Belt is a "disk" in the outer Solar System beyond the orbit of Neptune, believed to contain millions of comets and other small bodies made largely of ice. It extends from the orbit of Neptune (30 AU) to about 50 AU. One AU (Astronomical Unit) is 93 million miles (150 million km) and is the average distance between Earth and the Sun. The Kuiper Belt is similar to the Asteroid Belt but twenty times as wide and potentially two hundred times as massive. While most asteroids are composed of rock and metal, most Kuiper Belt objects are composed of frozen "ices" such as methane, ammonia, and water.

The Kuiper Belt is home to Pluto and several other dwarf planets that have been accepted by the International Astronomical Union (IAU), including Eris, Haumea, and Makemake. Dwarf planet Ceres is in the main Asteroid Belt and is for now the only dwarf planet in the inner Solar System. Dwarf planets are objects that orbit the Sun, are massive enough to be rounded by their own gravity, but unlike planets do not have enough mass to clear the neighborhood of other objects around their orbits. Their paths also sometimes cross those of other similar objects. It's estimated that there may be two hundred dwarf planets in the Kuiper Belt and possibly more than ten thousand in the region beyond. Once named they have a mythic identity, but it's daunting to imagine this growing group as part of ordinary astrological interpretation.

The Scattered Disk is beyond the Kuiper Belt and is sparsely populated by small icy objects that are a subset of the broader family of objects beyond Neptune. Scattered Disk objects such as dwarf planet Eris have extremely eccentric orbits that take them as far as 100 AU from the Sun. The Kuiper Belt is distinct from the theoretical Oort Cloud, which is a thousand times more distant and believed to be mostly spherical, like an immense snow globe encircling the Solar System. Objects within the Kuiper Belt, together with the members of the Scattered Disk, and any potential Hills Cloud (a disk within the Oort Cloud) or Oort Cloud objects, are collectively referred to as Trans Neptunian Objects--TNOs. Most TNOs orbit far enough away from the gas giant planets so they are not affected by their gravity.

However, some TNOs behave as if they are under the influence of a powerful gravitational force in the outer Solar System. "Something" is arranging the orbits of these bodies and bringing them into an alignment. This gravitational effect was first noted by Scott Sheppard and Chad Trujillo in November 2012 when they discovered 2012 CP113, using the Cerro Tololo Inter-American Observatory in Chile. 2012 VP113 is a TNO located in the outermost reaches of the Solar System. 2012 VP113 was abbreviated "VP" and nicknamed "Biden" by the discovery team, after Joe Biden, who was vice-president of the US at the time of discovery.

In 2014 Trujillo and Sheppard published a paper, noting that thirteen of the most distant TNOs in the Kuiper Belt possess similar obscure orbital features. They suggested the presence of a small planet to explain the similarities. Intrigued, Konstantin Batygin and Michael Brown, at the California Institute of Technology, began an eighteen-month study of the objects. Batygin and Brown realized that the six most distant objects from Trujillo and Sheppard's original collection all follow elliptical orbits that point in the same direction in physical space. That is surprising because the outermost points of their orbits move around the Solar System, traveling at different rates. The orbits of the six objects are also all tilted in the same way—pointing about thirty degrees downward in the same direction relative to the plane of the eight known planets. They calculated the probability of that occurring by chance to be about 0.007 percent.

As a result of their research, in January of 2016, Batygin and Brown announced calculation-based evidence of a massive ninth planet in our Solar System and dubbed the object "Planet Nine." They postulated the planet's existence through mathematical modeling and computer simulations. Although astronomers are on the hunt, the newest member of the Solar System has not yet been observed directly. Planet Nine would be a super-Earth with an estimated mass of about ten times that of Earth and a diameter two to four times larger. Planet Nine would most likely be similar in composition and size to Uranus and Neptune, with a mixture of rock and ice, and a small envelope of gas. Planet Nine is hypothesized to follow a highly elliptical orbit around the Sun, about twenty times the distance from Neptune to the Sun, with an orbital period of 10,000–20,000 years.

Although this yet invisible object may seem strange to us, Batygin explained that this ninth planet would actually make our Solar System similar to other planetary systems that astronomers are finding around many other stars. Such seemingly anomalous orbits by some large object show up in most Solar Systems. "One of the most startling discoveries about other planetary systems has been that the most common type of planet has a mass between that of Earth and that of Neptune. Until now, we've thought that our Solar System lacked this most common type of planet," Batygin said. Most planets around other sun-like stars have no single orbital range—some orbit extremely close to their host stars while others follow exceptionally distant orbits.

Three of these objects influenced by Planet Nine are Snow White, The Goblin, and Farout.

Snow White, whose official designation is 2007 OR10, was discovered in 2007 by Mike Brown's team at Cal Tech. Brown nicknamed the object "Snow White" since it would have to be very large or very bright to be detected by their survey. By that time, Brown's team had already discovered "seven dwarves," so Snow White completed the group that included Quaoar in 2002, Sedna in 2003, Haumea, Salacia, and Orcus in 2004, and Makemake and Eris in 2005.

Snow White inhabits the Kuiper Belt and orbits the Sun in 547.5 years, more than twice the duration of Pluto's orbit, but similar to Eris's 558-year solar circuit. Snow White is an icy orb and is actually red like Pluto, rather than white, because of its methane atmosphere. Snow White's 950-mile diameter is considerably larger than originally believed, so for now she is the third largest dwarf planet in the Solar System after Pluto and Eris, and is the largest known object in the Solar System without a name. Snow White also has a moon that is 15% of the size of the dwarf planet at 150 miles across (241 km). Perhaps when Snow White gets a name the dwarf planet will become one of the other figures from the myth of the Trojan War. She might become Helen, who although a human figure, had earlier been a powerful goddess in her own right. Helen's brothers were the famous Gemini twins, Castor and Pollux, and she also had a twin sister.

The Goblin is a dwarf planet that was discovered at its closest approach to the Sun in its enormous elliptical orbit. Scott Sheppard and his colleagues first spotted 2015 TG387 in October 2015, using Japan's 26-foot (8 meters) Subaru telescope at the top of the volcanic peak Mauna Kea in Hawaii. The Goblin never gets closer to the Sun than Neptune, so the timing was fortunate. Although the official designation is 2015 TG387, since it was discovered near Halloween, the letters TG became "The Goblin." It took the team three additional years to identify The Goblin's orbit, which they did with the aid of observations by the Las Campanas Observatory in Chile and the Discovery Channel Telescope in Arizona.

The Goblin adds more evidence to the case for Planet Nine since the orbit of 2015 TG387 shares peculiarities with other extremely distant and far-flung objects that appear to have been shaped by the gravity of a very large object in the icy realm of the Kuiper Belt. "What makes this result really interesting is that Planet Nine seems to affect 2015 TG387 the same way as all the other extremely distant Solar System objects," Chad Trujillo said.

Farout, official designation 2018 VG18, was spotted with the Subaru telescope at Mauna Kea, Hawaii in in December of 2018. Farout is more than eleven billion miles away (eighteen billion km), roughly three and a half times the distance to Pluto. Farout is for now the most distant dwarf planet candidate beyond Neptune in the Solar System at 120 AU, slightly more distant that Voyage 2 is right now, which has been traveling through space since 1977. It is 310 miles in diameter, a bit larger than The Goblin, and pinkish in color, indicating a large amount of ice. Solar System objects like this are found by looking at a series of images of the same spot of sky for any dot that appears to be moving in comparison to the background stars. Reprising John Denver, team member Scott Sheppard said "Far out!" when the team discovered it at the Carnegie Institution for Science in Washington DC. And since it is indeed far out, the nickname stuck.

Planet Nine is being discovered by detecting and interpreting its influences rather than by direct observation. This is a fundamental shift in a scientific paradigm where "seeing is believing" has been paramount. One of the strangest aspects of quantum physics is entanglement—Einstein called it "spooky action at a distance." If one particle of an entangled pair is observed in one place, the other particle of the pair, even possibly long distances apart, will instantaneously change its properties as if the two are mysteriously still connected.

Scientists have observed entanglement in tiny objects such as atoms and electrons. But in two new studies, one in the Netherlands and another in Finland, researchers report observing entanglement that is almost visible to the naked eye. This exciting new evidence suggests that what works at a micro level should also work at macro level—as above, so below. The implications for consciousness are exciting.

The Solar System is gigantic and far more complex than we have imagined. The plethora of new objects, only visible with technology, presents a challenge to traditional astrology that is far greater than the discovery of Uranus and Neptune. What causes something to have influence? We can imagine that unseen energies have profound effects and may also be at work in astrology. How might these objects that have been there all the time, but were invisible to us, blend into an interpretive mix? Stay tuned for more about Planet Nine and its orb of influence.

Atlantis Rising #135 April 2019

ACKNOWLEDGMENTS

A wise teacher once said "the spiritual path is the solitary work we cannot do alone." The same is true of the writing life. I'd like to thank my family for their years of love and support. Thanks to my husband Ted who unselfishly offers both editorial and astrological advice that always improves my efforts. He also provides encouragement when my faith in myself falters. My sister Fran deserves special mention as she gave me the spark that finally ignited this project. My immense gratitude goes to friends, students, and clients for giving life deeper meaning.

Thanks to brilliant artist and graphic designer Sue Lion for the exquisite covers of these volumes and the logo images that appear at the beginning of each section. And a shout out goes to bestselling author Sylvia McDaniel, who introduced me to Vellum software. My heart is full of thanks to all who shared this journey.

Credit for cover photo

Pyramids with Starry Sky; artist: Aliaksei

287795753 Adobe Stock

ABOUT JULIE LOAR

Julie Loar has pursued a lifelong interest in angels, dreams, mythology, space travel and other dimensions through an intensive study of metaphysics, while climbing the corporate ladder in two major companies. Focusing on symbols, mythology, Astrology, Tarot, Qabalah, and dreams, Julie has been a spiritual teacher and counselor since 1975. She has led thirteen sacred journeys to Egypt. She is the author of *Messengers*, co-author of *The Hidden Power Of Everyday Things*, and the award-winning, *Tarot & Dream Interpretation*.

Her latest book, *Goddesses For Every Day: Exploring The Wisdom & Power Of The Divine Feminine Around The World*, has won five national awards. Her books have been translated into several languages. Julie is a frequent speaker, radio guest and workshop leader and is the co-creator of the multiple award-winning board game *Quintangled*. Her popular astrology column appeared for two decades in *Atlantis Rising* magazine, the genesis of this book. She contributes regularly to SatiamaPublishing.com and was also been featured on John Edward's *InfiniteQuest.com*

The second volume in this series will be available soon as well as a compilation of her previously published work on dream interpretation. Visit her at www.JulieLoar.com

OTHER WORKS BY JULIE LOAR

Goddesses for Every Day

Quintangled: A Game of Strategy, Chance & Destiny

The Five Star Series with Ted Denmark PhD

Star Table Trance-Missions

Star Family Excursions

Star World Ascension

Star Time Convergence

Star Light Reflections

Published as Julie Gillentine

Messengers: Among the Stars, Stones & Legends the Ancient Wisdom Dwells

The Hidden Power of Everyday Things

Tarot & Dream Interpretation

Visit Julie's author page on Amazon

Julie Loar author page

www.JulieLoar.com

Made in the USA
Las Vegas, NV
22 September 2021